W9-CDM-292

Criminal Justice
Recent Scholarship

Edited by
Nicholas P. Lovrich

A Series from LFB Scholarly

Forensic Science Evidence
Can the Law Keep up With Science?

Donald E. Shelton

LFB Scholarly Publishing LLC
El Paso 2012

Copyright © 2012 by LFB Scholarly Publishing LLC

All rights reserved.

Library of Congress Cataloging-in-Publication Data

Shelton, Donald E.
  Forensic science evidence : can the law keep up with science? /
Donald E. Shelton.
     p. cm.
  Includes bibliographical references and index.
  ISBN 978-1-59332-517-6 (hardcover : alk. paper)
1. Evidence, Expert--United States. 2. Forensic sciences--United
States.
3. Evidence, Criminal--United States. I. Title.
  KF9674.S535 2012
  345.73'067--dc23
                                            2012012955

ISBN 978-1-59332-517-6

Printed on acid-free 250-year-life paper.

Manufactured in the United States of America.

Table of Contents

Acknowledgements..vii

Chapter 1: Introduction 1

Chapter 2: Historical Development of Forensic Scientific Evidence..... 7

Chapter 3: Admissibility Foundation Questions - The Daubert
Trilogy 13

Chapter 4: Admissibility of Social Science Evidence in Criminal
Cases 27

Chapter 5: Pretrial Forensic Issues.......................................49

Chapter 6: DNA Evidence 63

Chapter 7: Fingerprint Evidence 79

Chapter 8: Handwriting Comparison 99

Chapter 9: Hair Analysis... 111

Chapter 10: Bite Mark Analysis... 117

Chapter 11: Toolmarks, Firearms, and Bullet Lead Comparison....... 125

Chapter 12: Fire, Explosion and Arson Evidence 137

Chapter 13: Bloodstain Pattern Evidence 149

Chapter 14: Human Scent Evidence 157

Chapter 15: Juror Expectations about Scientific Evidence 165

Chapter 16: Summary and Conclusions................................. 187

Chapter 17: Thoughts about the Future of Criminal Forensic
              Science 213

Appendix: Recommendations of the National Research Council of
              the National Academy of Sciences (2009) 219

Bibliography and Table of Cases 227

Index   271

Acknowledgements

Much of the original work for this book was done in 2008 and 2009 with the guidance of Dr. James T. Richardson and I am especially grateful for his counsel and assistance. Since that time the field of forensic science in criminal law has been moving rapidly as courts, legislatures, scientists, police and academics have all been responding to the continuing spate of exonerations in wrongful convictions that were based on forensic science evidence and to the 2009 findings of the congressionally commissioned National Academy of Sciences Report. This book synthesizes the original research with those recent developments and responses.

I am grateful for the invaluable assistance of Ms. Christine Tait and Ms. Kelly Roberts. Personally, I dedicate this work to my wife, Marjorie. and to the four young women who made me break into a smile even when I was so totally engrossed that I was in danger of forgetting what is truly important in life - Elizabeth, Madison, Mackenzie and Makayla.

Chapter 1
Introduction

In criminal cases, jurors are the finders of fact. To determine those facts they are presented with evidence from witness testimony about what the witness observed or heard. It is for the jury to decide whether that testimony proves, either directly or circumstantially, beyond a reasonable doubt that the defendant committed the crime with which he is charged. Additionally, the jury is allowed to hear conclusion or opinion testimony from persons who are regarded as experts. They are not allowed to give opinion testimony as to the ultimate issue of the defendant's guilt or innocence. They may give opinion testimony when those opinions would assist the jury in reaching that ultimate issue. The testimony is limited to areas that are beyond the normal or common experience of jurors and where an expert's special knowledge will help the jury understand the import of the factual evidence it hears.

Testimony from scientific experts is the classic form of such expert testimony. Forensic science evidence is the observation and opinion of a trained person and is designed to aid the jury in understanding the meaning or conclusions that are suggested by the factual evidence. The expert may testify as to whether a particular event occurred, who the person was who caused the event to occur, or how the event occurred. These basic questions of "whether", "who", and "how" are the subjects of the variety of scientific evidence examined in this book. The question of whether an event occurred is one of the primary functions of social science expertise. Who committed an act is the subject of such areas as DNA, fingerprints, handwriting analysis, hair analysis, and bitemark analysis. The question of how an event occurred is often addressed in such areas as toolmarks, firearms and bullet comparisons, fire, explosion and arson testimony, and bloodstain pattern analysis.

1

The rapid development of emerging scientific methods, especially the increased understanding of deoxyribonucleic acid ("DNA"), has had, and will undoubtedly continue to have, an almost stunning impact on our forensic evidence in the justice system, particularly at the trial level. The forensic applications of these new scientific discoveries have been most dramatically seen in the criminal trial court. This book addresses which of these new or old forms of scientific forensic evidence have sufficient validity to be used in a criminal proceeding. It also addresses the "gatekeeping" role assigned to trial judges to answer that question under what has become known as the "*Daubert* trilogy" of cases in which the Supreme Court defined that role and rejected the former "*Frye*" test for admissibility of scientific evidence in federal cases. This includes an examination of the *Daubert* trilogy cases themselves and the subsequent case law that has further defined and refined the standards for evaluating proposed scientific evidence. Since the *Frye* test is still used in some state courts, that standard is also reviewed in the context of the various forms of proffered scientific evidence.

Advanced technology also presents a new variety of pretrial issues in the criminal justice system, especially as they relate to DNA. In a review of existing case law, this book addresses the constitutional questions posed by the development of extremely large DNA databases, including Fourth or Fifth Amendment search or incrimination issues that are presented as a result of the methods used to collect such data. It also addresses the extent to which these databases lead to the adoption or application of new statutes of limitation. Those new statutes are parsed and the meager case law under them is reviewed. It appears that such laws will both proliferate and be upheld in accordance with pre-existing due process principles. This book examines how new technology, particularly DNA, poses significant postconviction issues for the criminal justice system. These issues include whether and which convicts will be allowed access to DNA or other technologies that had not been discovered, or were not available, at the time of their trial. Case law, especially recent pronouncements from the Supreme Court, is reviewed. This part of the book focuses on how the judicial desire for finality weighs against the judicial struggle for truth and certainty.

As the defense responds to new government technology in criminal cases, new forms of pretrial relief have been sought, particularly in the form of pretrial discovery and requests for expert assistance. This book examines how these new forms of scientific evidence may change the nature of pretrial discovery motions and how such requests for expert assistance, particularly for indigent defendants, will impact the criminal justice system. The economic and timeliness consequences of such pretrial changes may well pose significant problems for an already backlogged and underfunded criminal justice system. A significant portion of this work is designed to determine whether various forms of new or old scientific evidence meet the standards set by the Supreme Court in of *Daubert v. Merrell Dow Pharm., Inc.*[1] To do so, the book reviews the history and scientific basis of the most common forms of forensic scientific evidence, and the qualifications of persons who offer expert testimony in each field or discipline. An initial examination is made of common social science evidence, including eyewitness expert testimony and several "abuse syndromes". It then goes on to examine DNA, fingerprints, handwriting analysis, hair comparison, bitemark analysis, toolmarks, firearms and bullet lead comparison, fire, explosion and arson evidence, and bloodstain pattern evidence. In each of these fields, the scientific basis is examined and then compared to the criteria for validity established under *Daubert*. Although several of these forms of scientific evidence may not meet the strict standards of *Daubert*, it turns out that the courts may not strictly apply those standards in the face of traditional legal admissibility rulings and in the face of prosecution demands for admission.

Through the media and through their own life experiences, jurors know about, or at least they think they know about, much of this new technology. This book examines how juror expectations and demands for scientific evidence and the pressure of that so-called *"CSI* effect" may alter criminal trials. The book reviews the nature of juror expectations about scientific evidence as it has been gleaned from the empirical and other research that has so far been performed. The case law that has developed involving judicial efforts to cope with the "*CSI* effect" and juror expectations and demands is reviewed. The variety of issues relating both to attorney conduct and to funding scientific evidence laboratories that are posed by such increased juror expectations and demands are reviewed. It appears that the "*CSI* effect" is not related solely to television watching, but that juror expectations are culturally based phenomena to which the criminal justice system must adapt.

In 2009, the National Academy of Sciences completed a congressionally authorized and funded comprehensive study of the use of forensic science in the criminal justice system. The report to Congress, titled *Strengthening Forensic Science in the United States: A Path Forward*, sent shock waves throughout the various forensic science fields. The report initially addressed the current system for evaluating the admissibility of forensic science evidence[2]:

> The report finds that the existing legal regime - including the rules governing the admissibility of forensic evidence, the applicable standards governing appellate review of trial court decisions, the limitations of the adversary process, and judges and lawyers who often lack the scientific expertise necessary to comprehend and evaluate forensic science - is inadequate to the task of curing the documented ills of the forensic science disciplines.

And the report went on to itemize those "documented ills" in many commonly used forms of scientific evidence. This book reviews the existing case law, the substantive basis for common forms of forensic science evidence, the applicability of *Daubert* tests to that evidence, and an analysis of whether the evidence conforms to *Daubert* criteria, especially in light of the National Academy findings and report.

A number of traditional forms of scientific evidence and expert testimony are not discussed here, such as basic toxicology testing or testimony based on common principles of physics or medicine. There is little or no dispute about such evidence, and these types of evidence do not raise the types of issues that give rise to admissibility questions. Indeed, in many cases the trial court may even take judicial notice of the validity of the science underlying those disciplines pursuant to Federal Rule of Evidence 201 or a state equivalent.

---

[1] *Daubert v. Merrell Dow Pharm., Inc.*, 509 U.S. 579 (1993).

[2] Nat'l Research Council of the Nat'l Acads. , *Strengthening Forensic Science in the United States: A Path Forward* (2009), at 3-1. The National Research Council is the branch of the National Academy of Sciences which produced the report. This report is reported variously as the "National Research

Council Report" (NRC) or the "National Academy Report" (NAS). This book uses "NAS" except when quoting another author.

Chapter 2

Historical Development of Forensic Scientific Evidence

The history of the use of forensic science in criminal cases in the United States is well over a century old.[1] The search for scientific answers to age old human questions that gripped the western world in the 19th and 20th centuries was applied to many aspects of American society, including the criminal justice system. The courts allowed "experts" to give opinions about issues that had previously been left exclusively to the jury, primarily such as identification through fingerprints and details of death or injury through medical testimony. As the use and pursuit of science increased, there were corresponding increases in both areas of claimed expertise and the technological innovations that were used or developed to apply them.

Courts initially exhibited some reluctance to accept some of this claimed expertise as scientific, in handwriting analysis for example. However, courts eventually established a pattern of almost routine acceptance of expert witnesses offered by the prosecution as an aid to the jury in finding guilt. Courts required little or any scientific foundation to be laid by the prosecution for such testimony. In a distinctly non-scientific approach, the case law developed in application of the *Frye* doctrine which required only that such testimony be generally accepted. That standard is almost self perpetuating. As more courts admitted testimony from any particular forensic science field, other courts used those admissibility decisions to bolster the idea that the field became more "generally accepted." There was rarely any defense challenge to the empirical basis, or scientific reliability, of prosecution generated forensic science evidence.

The areas of claimed expertise offered in criminal cases by the government expanded, almost unquestioned by defense counsel or the courts. Prosecutors offered expert testimony based on the conclusions of criminal investigators, many of whom had little or no scientific training. In addition to fingerprints, courts allowed identification testimony (the "who" question) based on the experience and presumed expertise of witnesses in such areas as handwriting comparisons, microscopic hair comparisons, blood comparisons, and bite mark comparisons. The conclusion in such testimony was rarely couched in terms of probability. Not only was such testimony admitted, often these experts were allowed to testify that the claimed crime scene or related item - be it fingerprints, hair, writing, bite marks or whatever other residue investigators found - was a "match" for a similar item from the defendant and even that it was a unique match so that the defendant was the only person who could have generated the crime item.

Experts in other scientific areas were allowed to testify to conclusions about the origin of materials used in the commission of a crime (the "what" question) in order to tie those materials to similar items in the defendant's control. Comparison microscope examination was used as the basis for testimony that scene bullets and test bullets were fired from the same gun, or that a particular screwdriver or other tool was used to make the marks that were left at a scene, or even that the lead from a bullet at the scene came from the same batch of bullets connected to the defendant.

Still other investigators were allowed to give opinion testimony about the origins or mechanism of events at a crime scene (the "how" question). They gave opinions about such things as how a fire started based on pieces of the residue that had not been destroyed in a fire, or reconstruction of the details of how a wound was inflicted based on their observations of blood stain patterns at the scene or on the defendant.

The routine acceptance of forensic expert testimony expanded beyond areas of physical science or physical examination. Social science testimony, as distinct from physical evidence, was created and offered by the prosecutor to bolster the government's claim that an act of alleged sexual abuse had occurred. Psychologists, sociologists, social workers, and even counselors or police officers, were allowed by courts to give their opinion that the testimony, or other conduct, of a complainant were consistent with the testimony and behavior of other persons who had been abused in the manner similar to that described by the complainant. The clear purpose of that testimony, regardless of any instructional limitation given by the judge, was not only that the alleged abuse occurred but that the complainant was telling the truth about how it occurred. On the other end of that spectrum, however, courts were not allowing social scientists proffered by the defense to testify as to the unreliability of eyewitness testimony, either generally or under conditions similar to those that existed at the scene of an alleged crime.

Some forensic science and technology developments were created specifically for use in criminal justice investigation and adjudication. Firearm comparison, hair analysis, and tool mark comparison are good examples. Other forensic evidence originated in scientific and technical fields, particularly medicine, and later found often unexpected applications in the criminal justice arena. Blood typing and DNA are two obvious examples.

Fingerprint comparison was originally developed as a means of identification that was quickly adapted to criminal investigations and has been accepted as evidence in criminal prosecutions for over one hundred years.[2] Early visual analysis gave way to a range of techniques for finding and enhancing prints, and for locating comparison prints from a computerized database. Comparison of handwriting samples is one of the oldest types of forensic evidence. Although it was offered in courts even before the twentieth century, it was not widely accepted as scientific evidence until it became part of the cornerstone of the prosecution case in *State v. Hauptmann*,[3] the Lindbergh kidnapping case.

DNA profiling started as a method of determining paternity. The first use of DNA in a successful United States criminal prosecution was in *Andrews v. State*.[4] In *Andrews*, police matched DNA samples from semen to the defendant's blood in a rape case. The admission of DNA evidence in a criminal case was first approved by a state supreme court in *State v. Woodall*.[5] Subsequently, properly collected and analyzed DNA evidence has been routinely admitted. DNA test results are now admissible in virtually every jurisdiction. DNA matching has almost totally replaced blood typing for identification purposes and is probably the most important forensic science development in the twentieth century. Thirteen states have even adopted statutes authorizing admission of DNA evidence. DNA has become the "gold standard" of forensic scientific evidence and DNA typing is now universally recognized as the standard against which many other forensic individualization techniques are judged.

DNA testing has a remarkable ability, in the right circumstances, to provide conclusive exculpatory evidence after conviction when specimens were not tested at the time of trial. The postconviction power of DNA testing is attributable to the same characteristics of the technology that has made it so valuable during investigation and trial: the durability of DNA permits reliable testing years after the incident, and the polymorphism of DNA sequence systems greatly increases the probability of a conclusive exculpatory result. The highly publicized Innocence Project reports that, as of 2011, there have been 280 postconviction exonerations by DNA testing in the United States.[6]

While the emergence of forensic DNA evidence has proven to be a dramatically positive aspect of new breakthroughs in science and technology, one unanticipated effect is that those same new scientific analyses have cast doubt on some of the more traditional types of forensic scientific evidence that trial judges have long treated as reliable and generally accepted. New scientific methods have caused some to reassess the validity of such things as serology testing, comparative bullet lead analysis, bite mark identification, handwriting analysis, hair and fiber analysis, and tool mark and ballistics testimony. Postconviction DNA testing itself has resulted in proof of wrongful convictions that were based on seemingly reliable non-DNA forensic scientific evidence.[7] For example, twenty-two percent of the first two hundred postconviction DNA exonerations had been based on false hair or fiber comparisons, and almost forty percent had been based on serology evidence.[8] These exonerations are undisputable proof of the "documented ills" of other forms of scientific evidence, including perhaps such traditionally admitted forms of evidence as fingerprints. They have provided some of the impetus for the re-examination of those disciplines by the courts in light of new criteria for the performance of judges' roles as the "gatekeepers" of scientific evidence admissibility.

---

[1] Generally, see William Tilstone, *Forensic Science: An Encyclopedia of History, Methods, and Techniques* (2006).

[2] The landmark case in the United States is *People v. Jennings*, 252 Ill. 534, 96 N.E. 1077 (1911).

[3] *State v. Hauptmann*, 180 A. 809 (N.J. 1935)

[4] *Andrews v. State*, 533 So.2d 841(Fla. Dist. Ct. App. 1988)

[5] *State v. Woodall*, 385 S.E.2d 253 (W. Va. 1989)

[6] The Innocence Project, available online at www.innocenceproject.org (last visited November 26, 2011).

[7] Findley, Keith A., *Innocents at Risk: Adversary Imbalance, Forensic Science, and the Search for Truth*, 38 Seton Hall L. Rev. 893 (2008), available online at http://ssrn.com/abstract=1144886 (last visited December 14, 2011).

[8] Garrett, Brandon L., *Judging Innocence*, 108 Colum. L. Rev. 55, 81-83 (2008).

Chapter 3

Admissibility Foundation Questions - The Daubert Trilogy

The role of the trial judge as the gatekeeper of what scientific forensic evidence is appropriate for consideration by the jury is now firmly entrenched in U.S. law. Although states differ as to the implementation of that role, all have adopted the gatekeeper concept. Some states still use the test established in *Frye v. United States*[1] that proposed that scientific evidence needed to be sufficiently established so that it had gained "general acceptance" in the relevant scientific community.[2] Federal courts and many states, however, use a revised admissibility standard first announced by the Supreme Court of the United States in *Daubert v. Merrell Dow Pharmaceuticals, Inc.*[3] *Daubert* and two subsequent Supreme Court amplifications, *General Electric Co. v. Joiner*[4] and *Kumho Tire Co. v. Carmichael*,[5] are commonly referred to as the *Daubert* trilogy and speak directly to the court's role in the admissibility of scientific evidence as expert testimony.

Rules of Evidence and Tests Applied by States[6]

State	State Rule	Admissibility Test
Alabama	Ala. R. Evid. Rule 702	*Daubert* (eff. 1/1/12)[7]
Alaska	Alaska R. Evid. 702	*Daubert*[8]
Arizona	Ariz. R. Evid. R. 702	*Daubert* (eff. 1/1/12)[9]

Rules of Evidence and Tests Applied by States

State	State Rule	Admissibility Test
Arkansas	A.R.E. 702	*Daubert*[10]
California	Cal. Evid. Code §720	*Kelly/Frye* [11]
Colorado	C.R.E. 702	*Daubert*[12]
Connecticut	Conn. Code Evid. §7-2	*Daubert*[13]
D.C.	N/A	*Frye*[14]
Delaware	Del. Uniform R. Evid. 702	*Daubert*[15]
Florida	Fla. Stat. § 90.702	*Frye*[16]
Georgia	O.C.G.A. § 24-9-67.1	*Daubert*[17]
Hawaii	Haw. Rev. Stat. Ann. § 702	Some *Daubert* factors[18]
Idaho	I.R.E. Rule 702	*Daubert*[19]
Illinois	There is no substantial equivalent to Fed. R. Evid. 702	*Frye*[20]
Indiana	Ind. R. Evid. 702	*Daubert*[21]
Iowa	Iowa R. Evid. 702	*Daubert*[22]
Kansas	K.S.A. § 60-456	*Frye*[23]
Kentucky	Ky. R. Evid. 702	*Daubert*[24]
Louisiana	La. C.E. Art. 702	*Daubert*[25]
Maine	Me. R. Evid. 702	*Some Daubert factors26*

Rules of Evidence and Tests Applied by States

State	State Rule	*Admissibility Test*
Maryland	Md. R. Evid. 5-702	*Frye*[27]
Massachusetts	N/A	*Daubert* mostly[28]
Michigan	Mich. R. Evid. 702	*Daubert*[29]
Minnesota	Minn. R. Evid. 702	*Frye/Mack*[30]
Mississippi	Miss. R. Evid. Rule 702	*Daubert*[31]
Missouri	Mo. Rev. Stat. § 490.065(1)	*Daubert* civil; *Frye* criminal[32]
Montana	Mont. R. Evid. 702	*Daubert*[33]
Nebraska	Neb. Rev. Stat. § 27-702	*Daubert*[34]
Nevada	Nev. Rev. Stat. Ann. §50.275	Some *Daubert* factors[35]
New Hampshire	N.H. R. Evid. 702	*Daubert*[36]
New Jersey	N.J. R. Evid. 702	*Daubert* for toxic tort cases, certain medical causation cases, *Frye* other civil cases; *Frye* for criminal[37]
New Mexico	N.M. R.E. 11-702	*Daubert*[38]
New York	N.Y. C.P.L.R. §4515	*Frye*[39]
North Carolina	N.C. Gen. Stat. § 8C-1	Some *Daubert* factors[40]
North Dakota	N.D. R. Evid. 702	Frye41

Rules of Evidence and Tests Applied by States

State	State Rule	*Admissibility Test*
North Dakota	N.D. R. Evid. 702	*Frye*[42]
Ohio	Ohio R. Evid. 702	*Daubert*[43]
Oklahoma	12 Okl. St. § 2702	*Daubert*[44]
Oregon	Oregon R. Evid. 40.410	*Daubert*[45]
Pennsylvania	Penn. R. Evid. 702	*Frye*[46]
Rhode Island	RI R. Evid. 702	*Daubert*[47]
South Carolina	Rule 702, SCRE	*Daubert* factors[48]
South Dakota	S.D. R. Evid. 702 (SDCL § 19-15-2)	*Daubert*[49]
Tennessee	Tenn. R. Evid. 702	*Daubert* factors[50]
Texas	Tex. Evid. R. 702	Some *Daubert* factors[51]
Utah	Utah R. Evid. Rule 702	Unique Test[52]
Vermont	Vermont R. of Evid. 702	*Daubert*[53]
Virginia	Va. Code Ann. §8.02-401.1	Unique Test[54]
Washington	Wash. R. Evid. 702	*Frye*[55]
West Virginia	W. Va. R. Evid. 702	*Daubert*[56]
Wisconsin	Wis. Stat. Ann. § 907.02	*Daubert*[57]
Wyoming	Wyo. R. Evid. 702	*Daubert*[58]

In *Daubert*, the Supreme Court of the United States held that the newly enacted Federal Rules of Evidence superseded *Frye*'s general acceptance test, and the Court directed the courts to examine the principles and methodology of proffered scientific evidence and not just whether its conclusions were accepted in the scientific community.[59] The Court held that when faced with a proffer of expert scientific testimony under Federal Rule of Evidence 702, the trial judge must make a preliminary assessment of whether the testimony's underlying reasoning or methodology is scientifically valid and can be properly applied to the facts at issue.[60] The Court suggested that the criteria for making that decision included whether the proffered theory has been tested, whether it "has been subjected to peer review," its error rate, the existence of standards controlling its operation, and whether it has acceptance within the relevant scientific community.[61] The Court made it clear that the focus is on the principles and methodology of the scientific proposition and not on the proffered conclusions.[62]

Subsequently, however, Justice Rehnquist seemed to modify the standards announced in *Daubert*. In *Joiner*, the trial judge rejected the testimony of plaintiff's proffered experts that linked his cancer to polychlorinated biphenyls ("PCBs") manufactured by the defendants and granted summary judgment.[63] The plaintiff claimed that the judge had focused on the experts' conclusions, rather than on their methodology, contrary to the clear admonitions of *Daubert*.[64] The Court disagreed and upheld the trial judge's decision:

> Respondent points to *Daubert*'s language that the "focus, of course, must be solely on principles and methodology, not on the conclusions that they generate." . . . He claims that because the District Court's disagreement was with the conclusion that the experts drew from the studies, the District Court committed legal error and was properly reversed by the Court of Appeals. But conclusions and methodology are not entirely distinct from one another. Trained experts commonly extrapolate from existing data. But nothing in either *Daubert* or the Federal Rules of Evidence requires a district court to admit opinion evidence that is connected to existing data only by the *ipse dixit* of the expert. *A court may conclude that there*

is simply too great an analytical gap between the data and the opinion proffered.[65]

Thus, *Joiner* clearly indicates that the trial judge gatekeeper has the discretion to totally reject and disallow an expert's opinion, even if based on an accepted methodology, if the judge finds that the expert's conclusion is not reliably based on that methodology.

In *Kumho*, the Court expanded its *Daubert* ruling and again indicated that significant deference was to be given to trial judges in the exercise of their gatekeeping role. In this defective tire case, the trial court granted summary judgment for defendants after finding that the opinions of plaintiff's expert engineer were not based on a method that the judge found to be "sufficiently reliable."[66] In its opinion, the Court first made it clear that the *Daubert* analysis was to be applied to evidence proffered by all experts, not only by scientists.[67] This distinction was especially important in criminal cases, where much of the expert testimony had been presented by experts based on their experience rather than as scientists. Second, the Court reinforced the *Joiner* holding that trial judges are permitted to examine whether an expert's conclusions are sufficiently reliable, even if based on a proper and accepted methodology.[68] Many States presumably adopted *Daubert* standards by adopting the language of FRE 702 in State rules of evidence.

However, a few State courts have held that the *Daubert* interpretation of FRE 702 does not necessarily mean that the State courts will interpret it in the same way.[69] More pointedly, some State courts have doggedly held that they do not consider *Kumho* to be controlling, or even instructive, precedent in interpreting an evidentiary rule identical to FRE 702. In doing so, they adhere to the prior routine admission of expert testimony if it is not "scientific", but rather based on experience.[70] The Ninth Circuit has used a similar approach to ensure that most police "expert" witnesses can still testify without meeting *Daubert* standards. In *United States v. Hankey*, the court held that a police officer could give "expert" testimony about the "code of silence" and other gang attributes without *Daubert* qualifications stating, "[t]he *Daubert* factors (peer review, publication, potential error rate, etc.) simply are not applicable to this kind of testimony, whose reliability depends heavily on the knowledge and experience of the expert, rather than the methodology or theory behind it."[71] State and some federal courts have readily followed suit for such police testimony, in cases involving expert testimony concerning gangs, drug trafficking, terrorism, and other fields.[72]

These interpretations, and even *Daubert*'s application, or non-application, in criminal cases has raised serious issues about whether the courts apply the standards as rigorously when prosecutors introduce forensic evidence to prove guilt in criminal cases as they do when plaintiffs use it to attempt to prove liability in civil cases. There may be some demonstrable validity to the charge that *Daubert* is not applied fairly in criminal cases.[73] The National Research Council of the National Academy of Sciences recently completed a congressionally authorized study of the use of forensic science in the criminal justice system.[74] After examining the current use of forensic evidence in criminal prosecutions and the *Daubert* reliance on the adversarial process for determining the admissibility of such evidence, the researchers were extremely critical of the current system and stated:

> The report finds that the existing legal regime - including the rules governing the admissibility of forensic evidence, the applicable standards governing appellate review of trial court decisions, the limitations of the adversary process, and judges and lawyers who often lack the scientific expertise necessary to comprehend and evaluate forensic science - is inadequate to the task of curing the documented ills of the forensic science disciplines.[75]

Adequate or not, *Daubert* is nevertheless the process that most criminal court trial judges must use, at least for the time being.

---

[1] *Frye v. United States*, 293 F. 1013 (D.C. Cir 1923). Despite *Frye's* limitations and the subsequent federal cases, it remains the standard by which science is evaluated for courtroom use in several states. See Joseph R. Meaney, *From Frye to Daubert: Is a Pattern Unfolding?*, 35 Jurimetrics J. 191, 193-94 (1995).

[7] *Frye, supra* 293 F. at 1014.

[3] *Daubert v. Merrell Dow Pharm., Inc.*, 509 U.S. 579 (1993). The standards governing expert testimony in the various states are described in Jane Campbell Moriarty, *Psychological and Scientific Evidence in Criminal Trials* (2009). See generally Kenneth R. Foster & Peter W. Huber, *Judging Science: Scientific Knowledge and the Federal Courts* (1999).

[4] *Gen. Elec. Co. v. Joiner*, 522 U.S. 136 (1997).

[5] *Kumho Tire Co. v. Carmichael*, 526 U.S. 137 (1999).

[6] Originally from Flake, Andrew B., Eric R. Harlan, and James A. King, *50 State Survey of the Applicability of Daubert*, American Bar Association Section of Litigation, available online at http://www.abanet.org/litigation/committees/trialevidence/daubert-frye-survey.html (last visited December 14, 2011). The chart has been updated and citations in endnotes have been added November 2011.

[7] Alabama SB 187 (June 9, 2011), available online at http://www.alabamalitigationreview.com/uploads/file/SB187-eng-1.pdf (last visited November 10, 2011), amended § 12-21-160 of the Code of Alabama 1975 to expressly adopt the federal *Daubert* standards. It adopted was part of a lager package of so-called "tort reform" bills that were signed by the Alabama governor. The effective date of the legislative amendment is January 1, 2012.

[8] *State v. Coon*, 974 P.2d 386 (Alaska 1999); *Marron v. Stromstad*, 123 P.3d 992 (Alaska 2005).

[9] After a legislative attempt to change the Arizona practice failed, the Arizona Supreme Court amended the Arizona Rules of Evidence to expressly adopt the *Daubert* standards. *In re Petition to Amend Rules of Evidence and Rule 17.4 (f), Arizona Rules of Criminal Procedure*, Ariz. Sup. Ct. No R-10-35 (Sept. 7, 2001), available online at http://www.azcourts.gov/Portals/21/MinutesCurrent/R100035.pdf (last visited November 10, 2011). The official Comment to the Rule change says, "The amendment recognizes that trial courts should serve as gatekeepers in assuring that proposed expert testimony is reliable and thus helpful to the jury's determination of facts at issue... The trial court's gatekeeping function is not intended to replace the adversary system. Cross-examination, presentation of contrary evidence, and careful instruction on the burden of proof are the traditional and appropriate means of attacking shaky but admissible evidence." The change is effective January 1, 2012.

[10] *Farm Bureau Mut. Ins. Co. of Arkansas, Inc. v. Foote*, 14 S.W.3d 512 (Ark. 2000).

[11] *People v. Kelly*, 549 P.2d 1240 (Cal. 1976); *People v. Nelson*, 43 Cal. 4th 1242 (2008).

[12] *People v. Shreck,* 22 P.3d 68 (Colo. 2001).

[13] In *State v. Porter,* 698 A.2d 739, 746 (Conn. 1997), the Connecticut Supreme Court explicitly adopted the *Daubert* standard but the *Frye* test remains "an important factor in a trial judge's assessment."

[14] *Bahura v. S.E.W. Investors,* 754 A.2d 928 (D.C. 2000); *Roberts v. United States,* 916 A.2d 922 (D.C. 2007).

[15] *Nelson v. State,* 628 A.2d 69 (Del. 1993); *Tolson v. State,* 900 A.2d 639 (Del. Supr. 2006).

[16] *Hadden v. State,* 690 So. 2d 573 (Fla. 1997).

[17] *Moran v. Kia Motors, Inc.,* 622 S.E.2d 439 (Ga. App. 2005).

[18] *Hawaii v. Maelega,* 907 P.2d 758 (1995); *State v. Escobido-Ortiz,* 126 P.3d 402 (Haw. Ct. App. 2005) (although the Hawaii Supreme Court has not adopted the *Daubert* test, in construing Hawaii Rule of Evidence 702 the Court has found the *Daubert* factors "instructive").

[19] *State v. Parkinson,* 909 P.2d 647 (Idaho 1996).

[20] *In re Commitment of Simons,* 821 N.E.2d 1184 (Ill. 2004).

[21] *Steward v. State,* 652 N.E.2d 490 (Ind. 1995); *Kovach v. Alpharma, Inc.,* 890 N.E.2d 55 (Ind. Ct. App. 2008).

[22] *Leaf v. Goodyear Tire & Rubber Co.,* 591 N.W.2d 10 (Iowa 1999) (*Daubert* factors are encouraged, but not required); *State v. Newell,* 710 N.W.2d 6 (Iowa 2006).

[23] *State v. Heath,* 957 P.2d 449 (Kan. 1998).

[24] *Mitchell v. Commonwealth,* 908 S.W.2d 100 (Ky. 1995); *Debruler v. Commonwealth,* 231 S.W.3d 752 (Ky. 2007).

[25] *State v. Foret,* 628 So.2d 1116 (La. 1993).

[26] Maine has not accepted either the *Frye* or the *Daubert* standard in full, but has adopted some of the *Daubert* factors. *State v. MacDonald,* 718 A.2d 195 (Me. 1998).

[27] *Reed v. State,* 283 Md. 374 A.2d 364 (1978); *Wilson v. State,* 370 Md. 191, 803 A.2d 1034 (2002).

[28] In *Commonwealth v. Lanigan,* 641 N.E.2d 1342 (Mass. 1994), the Massachusetts Supreme Court accepted the *Daubert* reasoning but in *Commonwealth. v. Patterson,* 840 N.E.2d 12 (Mass. 2005) stated that "general acceptance in the relevant community of the theory and process on which an expert's testimony is based, on its own, continues to be sufficient to establish the requisite reliability for admission in Massachusetts courts regardless of other *Daubert* factors.".

[29] *Gilbert v. DaimlerChrysler Corp.,* 685 N.W.2d 391 (Mich. 2004).

[30] *State v. Traylor,* 656 N.W.2d 885 (Minn. 2003).

[31] *Miss. Transp. Comm'n v. McLemore*, 863 So.2d 31 (Miss. 2003).

[32] *State Board of Registration for the Healing Arts v. McDonaugh*, 123 S.W.3d 146 (Mo. 20030; *Goddard v. State*, 144 S.W.3d 848 (Mo. Ct. App. 2004); *State v. Keightley*, 147 S.W.3d 179 (Mo. Ct. App. 2004).

[33] *State v. Moore*, 885 P.2d 457 (Mont. 1994), but the Montana Supreme Court has held that *Daubert* applies only to "novel scientific evidence"; *State v. Bowman*, 89 P.3d 986 (Mont. 2004); *State v. Price*, 171 P.3d 293 (Mont. 2007).

[34] *Schafersman v. Agland Coop.*, 631 N.W.2d 862 (Neb. 2001).

[35] In *Hallmark v. Eldridge*, 189 P.3d 646 (Nev. 2008), the Nevada Supreme Court said that *Daubert* and federal court decisions may be "persuasive authority". However, in *Higgs v. State*, 222 P.3d 648 (Nev. 2010), the Court said "We did not, however, and do not today, adopt the Daubert standard as a limitation on the factors that a trial judge in Nevada may consider. We expressly reject the notion that our decision in Hallmark inferentially adopted *Daubert* or signaled an intent by this court to do so." The Court held that the three requirements for admissibility in Nevada are "(1) qualification, (2) assistance, and (3) limited scope requirements" and "[w]hereas the federal rule mandates three additional conditions that trial judges should consider in evaluating expert witness testimony, the Nevada statute mandates no such requirements" , concluding that Nevada admissibility is an "inquiry that is based more in legal, rather than scientific, principles."

[36] *Baker Valley Lumber, Inc. v. Ingersoll-Rand Company*, 813 A.2d 409 (N.H. 2002).

[37] *State v. Harvey*, 699 A.2d 596 (N.J. 1997); *State v. Chun*, 943 A.2d 114 (N.J. 2008).

[38] *State v. Alberico*, 861 P.2d 192 (N.M. 1993).

[39] *People v. LeGrand*, 867 N.E.2d 374 (N.Y. 2007).

[40] *State v. Goode*, 461 S.E. 2d 631 (N.C. 1995).

[41] *State v. Hernandez*, 707 N.W.2d 449 (N.D. 2005).

[42] *State v. Hernandez*, 707 N.W.2d 449 (N.D. 2005).

[43] *Terry v. Caputo*, 875 N.E.2d 72 (Ohio 2007).

[44] *Taylor v. State*, 889 P.2d 319 (Okla. Crim. App. 1995).

[45] *State v. Lyons*, 924 P.2d 802 (Or. 1996).

[46] *Grady v. Frito-Lay, Inc.*, 839 A.2d 1038 (Pa. 2003).

[47] *In Re Mackenzie C.*, 877 A.2d 674 (R.I. 2005).

[48] *State v. Council*, 515 S.E.2d 508 (S.C. 1999).

[49] *State v. Hofer*, 512 N.W.2d 482 (S.D. 1994).

[50] *McDaniel v. CSX Transp., Inc.*, 955 S.W.2d 257 (Tenn. 1997).

[51] *E.I. du Pont Nemours and Co., Inc. v. Robinson*, 923 S.W.2d 549 (Tex. 1995), incorporating *Kelly v. State*, 824 S.W.2d 568 (Tex. Crim. App. 1992).

[52] See *Haupt v. Heaps*, 775 P.2d 388 (Utah App., 2005).

[53] See *985 Associates, Ltd. v. Daewoo Electronics America, Inc.*, 945 A.2d 381 (Vt. 2008).

[54] *John v. Im*, 559 S.E.2d 694 (Va. 2002); *Dagner v. Anderson*, 651 S.E.2d 640 (Va. 2007).

[55] *State v. Copeland*, 922 P.2d 1304 (Wash. 1996).

[56] See *State v. Leep*, 569 S.E.2d 133 (W.Va. 2002).

[57]   2011   Wis.   Act   2,   available   online   at https://docs.legis.wisconsin.gov/2011/related/acts/2 (last visited November 10, 2011) amended Wis. Stat. section 907.02 to expressly adopt *Daubert* standards. The amendment was effective February 1, 2011.

[58] *Bunting v. Jamieson*, 984 P.2d 467 (Wyo. 1999).

[59] *Daubert v. Merrell Dow Pharm., Inc.*, 509 U.S. 579 (1993), at 589-92.

[60] *Id.* at 592-93.

[61] *Id.* at 593-94.

[62] *Id.* at 595.

[63] *Gen. Elec. Co. v. Joiner*, 522 U.S. 136, 140 (1997).

[64] *Id.* at 146.

[65] *Id.* (emphasis added).

[66] *Kumho Tire Co. v. Carmichael*, 526 U.S. 137 (1999).

[67] *Id.* at 141.

[68] *Id.* at 152-53.

[69] For example, in *People v. Rector*, 248 P.3d 1196 (2011) the Supreme Court of Colorado has stated, "Thus, the trial court may, but is not required to, consider a wide range of factors pertinent to the case at bar including the factors mentioned by *Daubert* . . . ". And the Indiana Supreme Court held in *Turner v. State*, ___ N.E.2d ___, 2011 WL 4479926 (Ind. 2011), that "*Daubert* is merely instructive in Indiana, and we do not apply its factors as a litmus test for admitting evidence under *Indiana Evidence Rule 702(b)*. Therefore, it is not dispositive for our purposes whether Putzek's theory or technique can be and has been tested, whether the theory has been subjected to peer review and publication, whether there is a known or potential error rate, and whether the theory has been generally accepted within the relevant

field of study."
[70] *Marron v. Stromstad,* 123 P.3d 992 (Alaska 2005); *Barber v. State,* 952 So.2d 393 (Ala.Crim.App.2005); *Revis v. State,* ___ So.2d ___ , 2011 WL 109641 (Ala.Crim.App. 2011); *State v. Drummond,* 111OhioSt.3d (2006); State v. Humberto, 2011 WL 2518976 (Ohio App. 10 Dist. 2011); State v. Oral H., 125 Conn.App. 276, 7 A.3d 444 (2010); *State v. Torrez,* 146 N.M. 331, 210 P.3d 228 (2009) ; *State v. Segura,* 2011 WL 2027912 (N.M.App. 2011) .
[71] *United States v. Hankey,* 203 F.3d 1160 at 1169 (2000).
[72] See, e.g., *United States v. Mejia,* 545 F.3d 179 (2d Cir. 2008) (gangs); *United States v. Johnson,* 488 F.3d 690 (6th Cir.2007) (drug trafficking); *State v. Humberto,* 2011 WL 2518976 (Ohio App. 10 Dist. 2011) (gangs); *State v. Torrez,* 210 P.3d 228 (N.M. 2009) (admitting police gang expert but refusing to admit defense gang expert as more prejudicial than probative); *State v. Segura,* 2011 WL 2027912 (N.M.App. 2011) (drug trade); *McCloud v. Commonwealth,* 286 S.W.3d 780 (Ky. 2009) (police drug trade expert); *Robbins v. Commonwealth,* 336 S.W.3d 60 (Ky. 2011) (drug trade); *State v. Mosely,* 13 So.3d 705 (La.App. 5 Cir. 2009) (drug trade); and *State v. Smith,* 58 So.3d 964, 2010-830 (La.App. 3 Cir. 2011) (footprint comparison testimony by policeman was lay opinion not requiring *Daubert* analysis); *United States v. Jayyousi,* ___ F.3d ___, 2011 WL 4346322 (C.A.11 Fla. 2011) (interpretation of terrorism "code words" was lay testimony); *United States v. Defreitas,* 2011 WL 317964 (E.D.N.Y. 2011) (terrorism); *United States v. Farhane,* 634 F.3d 127 (2d Cir. 2011) (terrorism); *United States v. Kassir,* 2009 WL 910767 (S.D.N.Y. 2009) (terrorism).
[73] For an overview of how *Daubert* has changed the way judges evaluate expert evidence, see generally Dixon, Lloyd and Brian Gill, *Changes In The Standards For Admitting Expert Evidence In Federal Civil Cases Since The Daubert Decision,* Rand Corp. (2001); Berger, Margaret A., *Expert Testimony in Criminal Proceedings: Questions Daubert Does Not Answer,* 33 Seton Hall L. Rev. 1125 (2003); Findley, Keith A., *Innocents at Risk: Adversary Imbalance, Forensic Science, and the Search for Truth,* 38 Seton Hall L. Rev. 893, 929-950 (2008), available at http://ssrn.com/abstract=1144886 (last visited December 14, 2011); Groscup, Jennifer L. et al., *The Effects of Daubert on the Admissibility of Expert Testimony in State and Federal Criminal Cases,* 8 Psychol. Pub. Pol'y & L. 339 (2002); Neufeld, Peter J., *The (Near) Irrelevance of Daubert to Criminal*

Justice and Some Suggestions for Reform, 95 Am. J. Pub. Health 107 (2005); Risinger, D. Michael, *Navigating Expert Reliability: Are Criminal Standards of Certainty Being Left on the Dock?*, 64 Alb. L. Rev. 99 (2000).

[74] Nat'l Research Council of the Nat'l Acads., Strengthening Forensic Science In The United States: A Path Forward, Executive Summary at S-1 to S-24 (2009).

[75] *Id.* at 3-1.

Chapter 4

Admissibility of Social Science Evidence in Criminal Cases

The Applicability of *Daubert* (or *Frye*) to the Social Sciences

The so-called "soft sciences" have both developed and been called into serious question by modern scientific examination. On the one hand, eyewitness testimony, long considered by jurors to be the most important evidence they hear, is itself being challenged as unreliable and courts are being asked to admit expert testimony as to its fallibility.[1] On the other, scientists are challenging the lack of a scientific foundation for such behavioral science claims of "battered woman syndrome" or "rape trauma syndrome."[2]

There is an underlying question of whether *Daubert*, or even *Frye*, applies to the behavioral sciences at all. It is an interesting conundrum for many behavioral scientists. Many have fought the stigma of the sobriquet "soft" sciences for many years and have insisted that behavioral science is based upon the same demanding standards reflected in the scientific method used by the physical sciences.[3] Now, however, some behavioral scientists are fighting equally hard to escape the gatekeeping standards of *Frye* or *Daubert* by arguing that the same principles of general acceptance or scientific validity and reliability should not apply to them.[4] They insist that behavioral sciences are "different" and should be treated differently by the courts.[5]

After *Daubert*, there was some dispute about whether its gatekeeping requirements applied to what the Court of Appeals for the Eleventh Circuit, for example, characterized as "nonscientific," technical expert testimony.[6] In *Carmichael* v. *Samyang Tire, Inc.*, that court held that *Daubert* should not apply to expert testimony based on experience, as opposed to scientific theory.[7] The Supreme Court of the United States rejected the notion and reversed the Eleventh Circuit in that case in *Kumho Tire Co.* v. *Carmichael*.[8] Similar distinctions used by other federal courts were also presumably invalidated by the broader requirements of *Kumho*.[9]

In *Daubert* states, presumably, there should have been little doubt after *Daubert* and *Joiner* that its prescription applied to social science evidence. In the *Daubert* opinion itself, Justice Blackmun cited with approval, several times, the decision in *United States v. Downing*, where the issue was the admissibility of testimony from a psychologist regarding the reliability of eyewitness testimony.[10] Nevertheless, some social scientists argued that the scientific analysis of *Daubert* should not be applied, or at least not very strictly applied, to the testimony of social science experts.[11] On the other hand, many believe that the issue was already resolved in *Daubert* itself. The Supreme Court was clearly aware of the use and attempted use of social science evidence in criminal courts, when it established precisely the admissibility criteria that some behavioralists claim that they do not utilize. Several social scientists have embraced, or at least accepted the judgment of the Supreme Court and have suggested that the behavioralists need to adapt their processes if they expect them to form the basis of admissible expert testimony, especially when that testimony may be a factor in a criminal case.[12]

As federal cases, neither *Daubert* nor *Kumho* are controlling in the state courts where most criminal cases are tried. Some states that still use the *Frye* type test have held that it simply does not apply to testimony from behavioral science experts. In *People v. Beckley*,[13] the Supreme Court of Michigan held that the Michigan version of *Frye*, known as *Davis/Frye*, simply did not apply to behavioral science testimony. It is unclear whether other *Frye* states will follow the *Beckley* line of reasoning. Michigan more recently became a *Daubert* state[14] and it remains to be seen if the Supreme Court of Michigan will exempt the behavioral sciences from its requirements as well. The state also amended its rules of evidence to correspond with *Daubert*, and it may therefore be more difficult to carve out such an exemption.[15] Nevertheless, one Michigan Court of Appeals panel has subsequently held, in an unpublished opinion, that *Beckley* survives even under *Daubert* and the new Michigan rule and reiterated that, "[a]s the

Beckley Court recognized, human behavior is not a subject matter that lends itself to the type of scientific testing performed in the hard sciences", while admitting the testimony of a counselor as to delayed disclosure of sexual abuse.[16] A different but divided panel of the same Court, in another unpublished opinion, rigorously applied *Daubert* and the new Michigan rule as an appropriate basis for excluding a defense expert on battered woman syndrome.[17]

In Texas, a State which applies some *Daubert* factors, the courts have crafted a special niche for social science testimony, stating that "[w]hen "soft sciences" such as psychology are at issue, the trial court should inquire: (1) whether the field of expertise is legitimate; (2) whether the subject matter of the expert's testimony is within the scope of that field; and (3) whether the expert in his testimony properly relies upon or uses the principles involved in that field."[18]

Predictably, behavioral science experts have not fared as well in state courts that have rigidly applied *Daubert* or even *Frye* to them.[19] Sound scientific theory is testable if its rate of error can be calculated and subjected to peer review and the test of general acceptance. Human behavior, on the other hand, is more difficult to duplicate and is often apparently incapable of providing appropriate testing and review. Several states have applied *Frye* and *Daubert* to behavioral science testimony and found it wanting.[20] More recently, courts which say they are applying both *Daubert* and *Kumho* nevertheless have admitted "experience based" rather than scientifically based social science testimony. In *State v. Perry*, 218 P.3d 95 (Ore. 2009), the Oregon Supreme Court applied *Daubert* and found an M.D. qualified to give scientific testimony about delayed reporting of child abuse stating that the error rate "criterion has limited utility" in this area because "controlled studies are not possible" and the "[l]ack of controlled studies is not, in any event, an absolute bar to the admission of expert testimony by qualified clinicians".[21] In *State v. Rosas* the Ohio Court of Appeals applied *Daubert* and *Kumho* to admit testimony of a psychologist about child sexual abuse syndrome, stating:

> The field of psychology . . . is a complex admixture of science and art. To the extent that they can, psychologists try to apply the principles of scientific methodology. Yet because their object of study is the human mind, science can take them

only so far. This is one of those disciplines, which *Kumho* mentions, that cannot be encompassed entirely by one category of knowledge - "scientific," "technical," or "other specialized."[22]

More recently, several State courts which have adopted the *Daubert* standard have deftly avoided applying *Daubert* analysis to social science testimony by holding that they do not adopt the federal holding in *Kumho* and that much social science testimony is not to be considered scientific. The Alaska Supreme Court has said that it simply will not follow *Kumho* and allows social science experts to testify without applying *Daubert* standards.[23] In *State v. Oral H.,* the Connecticut court held that a *Daubert*-type hearing was not required because the testimony of a clinical psychologist about "the tendency of victims of sexual abuse to delay disclosing such abuse" was not scientific evidence, and bluntly stated that "[n]o appellate court in this state has adopted the approach set forth in *Kumho Tire Co. Ltd.,* and we decline to do so here."[24]

Eyewitness Identification Experts

Unlike much forensic science evidence, eyewitness identification experts are typically proffered by the defense in criminal cases to raise a reasonable doubt about the reliability of a government witness claiming to identify the defendant as a perpetrator. The defense may seek to present expert testimony based on the scientific research that eyewitness testimony in general is not very reliable, and may also want to elicit testimony that the particular conditions present at the particular identification in the case is scientifically suspect. The necessity for such testimony from the defense perspective is strong. Jurors appear to give great weight to the testimony of eyewitnesses, even at the expense of other forensic evidence in the case.[25]

There is a significant body of scientific research to support the defense position. Studies going back over twenty-five years have demonstrated the unreliability of eyewitness testimony generally.[26] These psychological studies have shown that humans are just not very good (some less than 50%) at identifying people they saw briefly during a traumatic incident.[27] They also indicate that identifications of persons of a different race than the witness are especially unreliable.[28]

In the wake of DNA exonerations of persons convicted on the basis of eyewitness testimony, the Department of Justice convened a working group that had studied the issue of eyewitness identifications.[29] The report stated that recent cases in which DNA evidence has been used to exonerate individuals convicted primarily on the basis of eyewitness testimony have shown that eyewitness evidence is not infallible.

In a significant recent photo lineup case, the New Jersey Supreme Court took bold steps to address the problems inherent in eye witness identifications. In *State v. Henderson*[30] the court held that:

> The current legal standard for assessing eyewitness identification evidence must be revised because it does not offer an adequate measure for reliability; does not sufficiently deter inappropriate police conduct; and overstates the jury's ability to evaluate identification evidence. Two modifications to the standard are required. First, when defendants can show some evidence of suggestiveness, all relevant system and estimator variables should be explored at pretrial hearings. Second, the court system must develop enhanced jury charges on eyewitness identification for trial judges to use.

As to the initial admissibility question, the Court now requires that when a defendant can demonstrate some evidence of suggestiveness that could lead to a misidentification, the judge must hold a pretrial hearing. At the hearing, the ultimate burden is on the defendant to prove a very substantial likelihood of irreparable misidentification. If the identification testimony is not suppressed and the case proceeds to trial, then "enhanced instructions [must] be given to guide juries about the various factors that may affect the reliability of an identification in a particular case."[31] In reaching its decision, the Court expressly recognized the substantial literature questioning the reliability of eyewitness identifications:

> Research that has emerged . . . reveals that an array of variables can affect and dilute memory and lead to misidentifications. The variables are divided into two categories: system variables, which are factors like lineup procedures that are within the control of the criminal justice

system; and estimator variables, which are factors related to the witness, the perpetrator, or the event itself - like distance, lighting, or stress - over which the legal system has no control. . . . Regarding some of the estimator variables, the Court finds that the reliability of an identification can be affected by: high levels of stress on the eyewitness; when the interaction is brief, the presence of a visible weapon; cross-racial recognition; and witness interaction with non-State actors like co-witnesses and other sources of information. In addition, the studies reveal generally that people do not intuitively understand all of the relevant scientific findings. As a result, there is a need to promote greater juror understanding of those issues. [32]

Notwithstanding the research recognized by the New Jersey court, some courts have been reluctant to admit expert testimony about eyewitness identification. A few jurisdictions even have adopted a *per se* rule excluding it, most notably the 11th Circuit in *United States v. Holloway*.[33] A few States have also employed a *per se* exclusion.[34] The 11th Circuit revisited its *per se* exclusion after *Daubert* in *United States v. Fred Smith* but did not change its position and relied on the trial judge's finding that such testimony "would not assist the jury,"[35] The 11th appears to be the only federal circuit to have a rule that such testimony is not admissible *per se*.[36]

More generally, however, courts have held that the admissibility of expert testimony about eyewitness identification is to be decided by the same factors used in evaluating other proffered scientific testimony, whether under *Frye*, *Daubert* or general relevancy considerations. Courts have always focused on whether the accuracy of eyewitness identifications is a matter in which jurors need assistance. Even before *Daubert*, trial judges were required to consider many traditional admissibility factors in deciding the admissibility of such testimony, including how it might "fit" the facts of a particular case. Several courts held that, contrary to the 11th Circuit position, the failure to make such an analysis and the blanket exclusion of eyewitness identification expert testimony was error.[37] As one court recently stated in *Benn v. United States*:

The state of social science research with respect to the reliability of eyewitness testimony has developed in recent years to the point where it can credibly be argued by defense counsel that it has reached that critical juncture. Whereas once we could only speculate as to the inaccuracy of an eyewitness identification, now there is published scientific research that questions its accuracy when made under certain conditions and exonerations, based on DNA evidence, that confirm what previously were only suspicions.[38]

The Supreme Court of Utah recently reversed its apparent proscription against eyewitness expert testimony in *State v. Clopten*:

Our previous holdings have created a de facto presumption against the admission of eyewitness expert testimony, despite persuasive research that such testimony is the most effective way to educate juries about the possibility of mistaken identification. . . . We ultimately hold that the testimony of a qualified expert regarding factors that have been shown to contribute to inaccurate eyewitness identifications should be admitted whenever it meets the requirements of rule 702 of the Utah Rules of Evidence. We expect this application of rule 702 will result in the liberal and routine admission of eyewitness expert testimony, particularly in cases where, as here, eyewitnesses are identifying a defendant not well known to them.[39]

Using these parameters many courts, however, still exclude expert testimony about eyewitness identification in particular cases on the grounds that it is not a proper subject because it will not assist the jury. The rationale is that jurors are able to evaluate the credibility of an eyewitness using their common knowledge and experience after hearing competent cross examination, and that expert testimony is simply not useful in making the credibility decision.[40] Others, especially in more recent cases, have rejected this "common knowledge" approach in favor of scientific research casting doubt on such "myths."[41]

While some judges still insist that jurors are fully capable of understanding the dangers of eyewitness identification without the necessity of expert assistance, the trend appears to be in the opposite direction. The spate of recent exonerations after post-conviction DNA testing has some lessons that appear not to be lost on judges when considering whether to admit expert testimony about eyewitness identification. The "Innocence Project" analysis of such cases led them to conclude that "[m]istaken eyewitness identifications contributed to over 75% of the more than 248 wrongful convictions in the United States overturned by post-conviction DNA evidence."[42] When eyewitness identification is a principal part of the government's prosecution in a particular case, courts are increasingly recognizing the need to allow expert testimony about the limitations of human perception and recall and how situational factors affect the accuracy of such identification.

Forensic Abuse Syndromes

Much of the debate about the application of legal standards of admissibility has arisen in the context of proffered expert testimony of psychiatrists and psychologists. Even before *Daubert*, some maintained that testimony from clinical psychologists and psychiatrists could rarely if ever meet the legal standard of reasonable certainty that would aid the trier of fact. Indeed, such clinicians may be no more accurate than laypersons.[43] Nevertheless, over the last twenty years, prosecutors have sought to present expert testimony concerning various "syndromes" of symptoms or characteristics that the government claims are typical of, or at least consistent with, the behavior of victims of certain crimes. Various syndromes have been offered including child sexual abuse accommodation syndrome, battered child syndrome, battered woman syndrome, battering parent syndrome, separation trauma and rape trauma syndrome.[44] The testimony is usually offered to corroborate the testimony of the complainant or to rebut certain claims of the defendant. Some preliminary legal issues that arise in these cases are common to the behavioral concept of a "syndrome." Initially, as noted earlier, some courts have held that the *Frye* or *Daubert* admissibility analysis may not be applicable at all to testimony from experts in the behavioral sciences, and many of those cases arose in the context of proffered "syndrome" testimony.[45] The idea that social and political pressure to redress gender imbalance, and not good science, is the basis for forensic syndrome evidence is not shared by all, but many agree that such social pressures are at least one of the factors leading to the production of such testimonial evidence and even to the willingness of the courts to accept it. As one group of scholars concluded:

> Media attention to social issues (e.g., battering), or specific high profile cases, may facilitate the readiness of a legal culture to adopt evidence that addresses the social issue. Increased media attention to the problem of battering in each country has undoubtedly contributed to the education of the public regarding the prevalence of domestic violence, as well as to demands that domestic violence be taken into account in legal actions related to such evidence.[46]

The syndrome concept has a theoretical basis within the psychiatric parlance. The current American Psychiatric Association Diagnostic & Statistical Manual of Mental Disorders offers a general definition of "syndrome" as "a grouping of signs and symptoms, based on their frequent co-occurrence, that may suggest a common underlying pathogenesis, course, familial pattern, or treatment selection.[47] A "syndrome" is not necessarily a medical diagnosis but rather a collection of related symptoms.[48] A diagnosis depends on whether the pattern of symptoms is the result of an underlying pathological process which is recognized as a "disorder."[49]

The "battered woman syndrome" is a psychological and behavioral phenomenon that describes characteristics of women living in battering relationships.[50] Although expert testimony on the syndrome originated in self-defense cases, it has been proffered by prosecutors for a variety of reasons and by defendants claiming duress short of self defense.[51] The syndrome has been discussed for over thirty years and it is regarded as a subcategory of post-traumatic stress disorder which has four principle elements: (1) the woman believes that the violence was her fault; (2) the woman has an inability to place the responsibility for the violence elsewhere; (3) the woman fears for her life and/or her children's lives; and (4) the woman has an irrational belief that the abuser is omnipresent and omniscient.[52]

Prosecutors often offer evidence of the syndrome in prosecutions of alleged batterers to explain to the jury why the complainant may have changed her testimony to favor the defendant and in general to portray "normal" reactions to domestic abuse.[53] Yet, prosecutorial use of the syndrome raises substantial questions and some courts have held that it constitutes impermissible bad character or "bad acts" evidence.[54]

The battered woman syndrome has received more attention from the legal system, and greater acceptance by the courts, than perhaps any other area of psychological research or testimony.[55] Courts applying *Frye* have admitted it.[56] Nevertheless, its underlying scientific basis has been the subject of criticism that neither the legal nor empirical bases for the syndrome are sound.[57] At least one court has reviewed battered woman syndrome under a *Daubert* type standard and found that it was not based on a valid underlying scientific theory.[58]

"Rape trauma syndrome" is "used to describe common responses to a sexual assault."[59] The term was coined by Burgess and Holmstrom to describe two stages of recovery from rape.[60] Rape trauma syndrome evidence is usually offered to prove lack of consent. Courts are fairly clear about the purposes for which the evidence cannot be used. As with other syndrome evidence, it is not probative that a rape occurred[61] and cannot be used simply to bolster the credibility of the alleged witness that the rape occurred.[62] The most accepted use of rape trauma syndrome is as evidence when the defense is consent and the prosecutor wishes to show that the complainant's behavior is consistent with that of a rape victim.[63] It usually speaks to post rape behavior. It has specifically been allowed to explain post incident behavior of minor victims where the defendant denies any misconduct.[64]

Feminists, activists and others advocated strongly for the introduction of rape trauma syndrome testimony in rape trials. Rape trauma syndrome clearly has primarily social and political origins. Shirley Dobbin and Sophia Gatowski examined those origins and attempted to place the resulting forensic syndrome in evidentiary context:

> After examining the sociopolitical emergence and production of RTS [rape trauma syndrome] testimony and the development of the evidence industry that surrounds that production, the question remains one of whether or not RTS testimony has a place in court. Feminists, activists and others

advocated for the introduction of RTS testimony in rape trials to give voice to women, to empower them and to combat negative myths and stereotypes about women and rape. However, while RTS was introduced into the court with the best of intentions, it has not had the intended consequences. Any perceived benefits of its introduction must be weighed against its negative impact. In deciding what place RTS evidence should have in court, we must recognize its social and political history and the social and political consequences of its use in court. We must question the legitimacy of a type of evidence that medicalizes and pathologizes women, that removes rape from its political and social context and potentially opens the door for the revictimization of women by the legal system.[65]

They urge that social science is "science" and that the application of *Daubert* to rape trauma syndrome evidence is appropriate, at least to the extent of determining if it really is "good science."[66]

"Child sexual abuse syndrome" is the phrase often used to describe the profile of characteristics experienced by children after being sexually abused.[67] Originally, it was described as the "child sexual abuse accommodation syndrome" by Dr. Ronald Summit.[68] His theory described five coping mechanisms commonly observed in sexually abused children: "(1) [s]ecrecy; (2) [h]elplessness; (3) [e]ntrapment and accommodation; (4) [d]elayed, conflicted, and unconvincing disclosure; and (5) [r]etraction."[69]

The shorter phrase "child sexual abuse syndrome" is a broader term than Dr. Sutton's original theory and includes a longer list of observed characteristics.[70] The American Medical Association has many more characteristics on its list, including: overt or subtle and indirect disclosures to a "relative, friend, or teacher;" highly sexualized play; withdrawal and excessive daydreaming; low self esteem, "feelings of shame or guilt;" falling grades; pseudo-mature personality development; sexual promiscuity; poor peer relationships; suicide attempt; positive relations exhibited toward the offender; and frightened or phobic reactions, especially toward adults.[71]

Many courts have admitted expert testimony regarding child sexual abuse syndrome in light of the significant problems associated with the testimony of children in general and especially the testimony of children relating to sexual abuse. There are significant challenges presented by such testimony. In light of these difficulties, expert testimony has been allowed for a variety of purposes.[72] Among the courts that allow child sexual abuse syndrome testimony a typical approach is that (1) an expert may not testify that the sexual abuse occurred, (2) an expert may not vouch for the veracity of a victim, and (3) an expert may not testify whether the defendant is guilty. But an expert may testify regarding typical and relevant symptoms of child sexual abuse for the sole purpose of explaining a victim's specific behavior that might be incorrectly construed by the jury as inconsistent with that of an actual abuse victim, and with regard to the consistencies between the behavior of the particular victim and other victims of child sexual abuse to rebut an attack on the victim's credibility.[73] In many cases the testimony is admitted to offer a government explanation for the complainant's delay in reporting the alleged abuse.[74] On the other hand, a few courts have taken a very rigid stand against any child sexual abuse syndrome testimony and find that it does not meet the scientific requirements of *Frye* or *Daubert*.[75]

Other Social Science Evidence

The post-conviction exoneration of many individuals who had previously confessed has given rise to several attempts by defendants to introduce expert testimony during trial to buttress their recantation of a confession made to police. The concept of a false confession is not something that most jurors understand. As Prof. Brandon Garrett put it:

> False confessions present a puzzle: why do innocent people confess in detail to crimes they did not commit? For decades, commentators doubted that a suspect would falsely confess.
> . . . While we may not know how often false confessions occur, there is new awareness among scholars' legislators, judges, prosecutors, police departments, and the public that innocent people can falsely confess, often due to psychological pressure placed upon them during police interrogations. Studies increasingly examine the psychological techniques that can cause people to falsely confess.[76]

Indeed, there is a now a substantial body of social science research dedicated to the psychological and social factors that may produce false confessions of guilt.[77] Some courts have admitted testimony from sociologists and psychologists to explain why a defendant may have given a false confession.[78] Others however have upheld the exclusion of such defense-proffered testimony, claiming that such testimony would "not assist the trier of fact"[79] and that the reliability of a confession is not "a proposition that was outside the common knowledge of a layperson."[80]

Prosecutors have also recently offered expert testimony about the "characteristics" of people who commit certain crimes, particularly sexual abuse. The concept that testimony about "profiling" is generally inadmissible was initially established in cases involving alleged drug trafficking.[81] However, some courts have now allowed psychologist testimony describing the characteristics of sex offenders, or the *modus operandi* of child molesters, and upheld such testimony against a *Daubert* challenge.[82] Other courts have adhered to the prohibition against profiling and disallowed such evidence as unreliable under *Daubert* analysis.[83]

Conclusion

The development of new forms of scientific evidence and the use of DNA makes us reexamine the types and purposes of evidence which are considered admissible in criminal proceedings. The trial court is firmly established as the gatekeeper for making that examination to ensure that only "good science" and not "junk science" is presented to the jury as reliable. The *Daubert* standards for determining admissibility based on a scientific analysis by judges are well established in the federal courts and in many of the state courts as well. The implementation of those standards in criminal proceedings is not so clear and some courts apply *Daubert* in a manner that appears to be biased in favor of prosecution evidence. Prosecution proffers of social scientists are often routinely admitted in spite of its *Daubert* inadequacies while defense proffers, especially as to eyewitness reliability, are regularly excluded.

The implementation of *Daubert*, or even *Frye*, in the evaluation of proffered social science testimony is at best unpredictable and at least irregular across the many criminal jurisdictions. Some courts have held that neither form of scientific analysis is applicable to the social sciences and the only question is whether the evidence will "aid the jury." Courts that apply a *Daubert* analysis are troubled by the deficiencies of social science evidence, especially in the important *Daubert* criteria of falsifiability and error rates. Two contrasting examples demonstrate these difficulties. There is a demonstrable scientific basis for the testimony of social scientists as to the reliability of eyewitness evidence and yet some courts, before and after *Daubert*, have been reluctant to allow the jury to hear such testimony. On the other hand, expert evidence about forensic abuse syndromes has little demonstrable scientific basis but often continues to be admitted, perhaps because of the social and political origins and impetus for the production and use of such testimony.

---

[1] Garrett, Brandon L., *Judging Innocence,* 108 Colum. L. Rev. 55, at 125 (2008).

[2] Duncan, Krista L., Note, *"Lies, Damned Lies, and Statistics"? Psychological Syndrome Evidence in the Courtroom after Daubert,* 71 Ind. L. J. 753,760-61 (1996).

[3] See Steele, Dara Loren, Note, *Expert Testimony: Seeking an Appropriate Admissibility Standard for Behavioral Science in Child Sexual Abuse Prosecutions,* 48 Duke L. J. 933 (1998).

[4] *Id,.* at 968.

[5] *Id.,* at 968 (citing *Hadden v. State,* 690 So. 2d 573, 579-80 (Fla. 1997).

[6] *Carmichael v. Samyang Tire, Inc.,* 131 F.3d 1433, 1435 (11th Cir. 1997), *cert. granted sub nom. Kumho Tire Co. v. Carmichael,* 526 U.S. 137 (1999).

[7] *Id.*

[8] *Kumho Tire Co. v. Carmichael,* 526 U.S. 137 (1999), at 157-58 (quoting *Gen. Elec. Co. v. Joiner,* 522 U.S. 136, 146 (1997)).

[9] Some of the earlier distinctions were made in *United States v. Bighead,* 128 F.3d 1329 (9th Cir. 1997); *United States v. Cordoba,* 104 F.3d 225 (9th Cir. 1997); and *Berry v. City of Detroit,* 25 F.3d 1342 (6th Cir. 1994).

[10] *United States v. Downing,* 753 F.2d 1224 (3d Cir. 1985).

[11] See, e.g. Faigman, David L., *The Evidentiary Status of Social Science under Daubert: Is It "Scientific," "Technical," or "Other" Knowledge.* 1 Psychol., Pub. Pol'y & L., 960 (1995); Renaker, Teresa, *Evidentiary Legerdemain:*

Deciding When Daubert Should Apply to Social Science Evidence, 84 Cal. L. Rev. 1657 (1996).

[12] See, e.g. Richardson, James and Gerald Ginsberg, *"Brainwashing" Evidence in Light of Daubert*, in *Law and Science: Current Legal Issues* (Helen Reece ed., 1998); Moore, David T., *Scientific Consensus & Expert Testimony: Lessons from the Judas Priest Trial*, 17 Am. Psy. L. News 3 (1997).

[13] *People v. Beckley*, 434 Mich. 691, 456 N.W.2d 391 (1990).

[14] *Gilbert v. DaimlerChrysler Corp.*, 470 Mich. 749, 685 N.W.2d 391(2004).

[15] Mich. R. Evid.702.

[16] *People v. Bailey*, 2009 WL 3323252 (Mich.App. 2009).

[17] *People v. Sandoval-Ceron*, 2010 WL 3021861 (Mich.App. 2010).

[18] *Briones v. State*, 2009 WL 2356626 (Tex.App.-Hous. 2009) at p.4; relying upon *Nenno v. State*, 970 S.W.2d 549 (Tex.Crim.App.1998), *overruled on other grounds, State v. Terrazas*, 4 S.W.3d 720 (Tex.Crim.App.1999). But cf. *Figueroa v. State*, 2009 WL 2183460 (Tex.App.-San Antonio 2009) approving the rejection of favorable psychological testing results as to "sexual interest" when offered by the defendant.

[19] "Not surprisingly, when social science-based testimony is subjected to the *Frye* test or to the *Daubert* factors, that testimony fails either standard." Steele, Dara Loren,Note, *Expert Testimony: Seeking an Appropriate Admissibility Standard for Behavioral Science in Child Sexual Abuse Prosecutions*, 48 Duke L. J. 933 (1998), at 956.

[20] *Newkirk v. Commonwealth*, 937 S.W.2d 690 (Ky. 1996) (holding that child sexual abuse syndrome evidence offered for any use would fail to meet the standards set forth in either *Frye* or *Daubert); State v. Foret*, 628 So.2d 1116 (La. 1993) (holding that child sexual abuse accommodation syndrome fails *Daubert* because it is not scientifically reliable); *Commonwealth v. Dunkle*, 602 A.2d 830 (Pa. 1992) (holding that syndrome evidence does not meet *Frye* standards); *Fowler v. State*, 958 S.W.2d 853 (Tex. App. 1997) (holding that testimony regarding domestic violence might satisfy state equivalent of *Daubert* and therefore be admissible, but that it did not meet the reliability requirements here); *State v. King*, 713 S.E.2d 772 (N.C. 2011) (rejecting evidence of "repressed memory").

[21] *State v. Perry*, 218 P.3d 95 (Ore. 2009).

[22] *State v. Rosas*, 2009 WL 805404 (Ohio App. 2 Dist.) at p. 5.

[23] *Marron v. Stromstad*, 123 P.3d 992, 1006–08 (Alaska 2005); *Neal v. State*, 2011 WL 766546 (Alaska App.)

[24] *State v. Oral H.,* 7 A.3d 444, at 449 (2010).

[25] In an empirical study of the so-called CSI Effect, jurors demonstrated that they had high expectations that the prosecutor would produce scientific evidence *but* that they were nevertheless willing to find a defendant guilty without any scientific evidence if the government had eyewitness testimony. The demand for scientific evidence as a prerequisite for a guilty verdict was prominent only in rape cases, or where the government was relying on circumstantial evidence. Shelton, Donald E., Young S. Kim and Gregg Barak, *A Study of Juror Expectations and Demands for Scientific Evidence: Does the "CSI Effect" Exist?,* 9 Vanderbilt J. Ent. & Tech. L 334 at 363-4 (2006); Shelton, Donald, *The CSI Effect: Does It Exist?,* Nat'l Inst. Just. J., Mar. 2008, at 1, 5 (2008), available online at http://www.ojp.usdoj.gov/nij/journals/259/csi-effect.htm (last visited December 14, 2011); Shelton, Donald E., Young S. Kim & Gregg Barak, *An Indirect-Effects Model of Mediated Adjudication: The CSI Myth, the Tech Effect, and Metropolitan Jurors' Expectations for Scientific Evidence,* 12 Vand. J. Ent. & Tech. L. 1 (2009), available online at http://law.vanderbilt.edu/publications/journal-entertainment-technology-law/archive/index.aspx (last visited December 14, 2011).

[26] See Cutler, Brian L. & Steven D. Penrod, *Mistaken Identification: The Eyewitness, Psychology, And The Law* 6-7 (1995); Neil Brewer, Nathan Weber, and Carolyn Semmler, *Eyewitness Identification* in *Psychology and Law* (Neil Brewer ad Kipling D. Williams, eds. 2005); *Modern Scientific Evidence: The Law and Science of Expert Testimony,* (eds. David L. Faigman, Michael J. Saks, Joseph Sanders, and Edward K. Cheng), 2009-2010 edition, § 16: 1 *et seq.*; Loftus, Elizabeth F., et al., *Eyewitness Testimony: Civil And Criminal* § 4-18, at 112 (4th ed. 2007); Brigham, John C. & Robert K. Bothwell, *The Ability of Prospective Jurors to Estimate the Accuracy of Eyewitness Identifications,* 7 Law & Hum. Behav. 19 (1983).

[27] Cutler, Brian L. & Steven D. Penrod, *Mistaken Identification: The Eyewitness, Psychology, And The Law* (1995) at 8.

[28] Moriarty, Jane Campbell, *Psychological and Scientific Evidence in Criminal Trials,* (2009), §13:54.

[29] Reno, Janet, *Introduction* to Nat'l Inst. of Justice, U.S. Dep't of Justice, *Eyewitness Evidence: A Guide For Law Enforcement,* at iii-iv *(1999),* available online at http://www.ncjrs.gov/pdffiles1/nij/178240.pdf (last visited December 14, 2011).

[30] *State v. Henderson*, 27 A.3d 872 (N.J. 2011).

[31] *Id.*

[32] *Id.*

[33] *United States v. Holloway*, 971 F.2d 675 (11th Cir. 1992).

[34] See *State v. Goldsby*, 650 P.2d 952, 954 (Or. Ct. App. 1982); *Commonwealth v. Simmons*, 662 A.2d 621 (Pa. 1995); *State v. McKinney* 74 S.W.3d 291 (Tenn. 2002), *cert. denied*, 537 U.S. 926 (2002); *State v. Coley*, 32 S.W.3d 831 (Tenn. 2000).

[35] *United States v. Smith*, 122 F.3d 1355 (11th Cir. 1997).

[36] However, at least one District Court in the 11th Circuit has cast doubt on the continuing viability of the *Holloway* decision. In *United States v. Smith*, 621 F.Supp.2d 1207 (M.D. Ala 2009), stated that a *per se* proscription against all eyewitness expert testimony is "irreconcilable" with *Daubert*. The court distinguished the 11th Circuit precedent by finding that those cases only held that it was not an abuse of discretion to refuse to admit eyewitness expert testimony, not that it was an abuse of discretion for a trial judge to allow such testimony.

[37] See, e.g., *United States V. Downing*, 753 F.2d 1224 (3d Cir. 1985); *United States v. Smith*, 736 F.2d 1103 (6th Cir. 1984); *State v. Chapple*, 660 P.2d 1208, (Ariz. 1983) (en banc); *Echavarria v. State*, 839 P.2d 589, (Nev. 1992); *State v. Hill*, 463 N.W.2d 674 (S.D. 1990); *Pierce v. State*, 777 S.W.2d 399 (Tex. Crim. App. 1989) (en banc); *Smither v. Commonwealth*, 2011 WL 1642333 (Ky. 2011).

[38] *Benn v. United States*, 978 A.2d 1257 at 1278-9 (D.C. Ct. App. 2009).

[39] *State v. Clopten*, 223 P.3d 1103 at 1112 (Utah 2009).

[40] See, e.g., *United States v. Martin*, 391 F.3d 949 (8th Cir. 2004); *United States v. Hicks*, 103 F.3d 837 (9th Cir. 1996); *United States v. Kime*, 99 F.3d 870 (8th Cir. 1996); *United States v. Larkin*, 978 F.2d 964 (7th Cir. 1992); *State v. Higgins*, 898 So.2d 1219 (La. 2005); *State v. Manson*, 984 A.2d 1099 (Conn. App. 2009); *United States v. Bunke*, 412 Fed.Appx. 760 (6th Cir. 2011).

[41] *United States v. Moore*, 786 F.2d. 1308 (5th Cir. 1986). See also *United States v. Mathis*, 264 F.3d 321 (3d Cir. 2001) (providing a detailed analysis of whether an expert's testimony should have been admitted), *cert. denied*, 535 U.S. 908 (2002); *United States v. Langan*, 263 F.3d 613 (6th Cir. 2001) (allowing the jury to weigh eyewitness testimony without the aid of any expert); *United States v. Feliciano*, 80 Fed. R. Evid. Serv. 1813 (D. Ariz.

2009); *People v. Lee*, 750 N.E.2d 63 (N.Y. 2001) (holding the inclusion of eyewitness expert testimony was not an abuse of discretion); *People v. Radcliffe*, 764 N.Y.S.2d 773 (Sup. Ct. 2003) (identifying the traditional safeguards of eyewitness testimony); *People v. Abney*, 31 Misc.3d 1231(A), 2011 WL 2026894 (N.Y.Sup. 2011) (finding an abuse of discretion in excluding expert testimony concerning weapon focus, event stress, event duration and cross-racial identification); *State v. Maner*, 2011 WL 3671909 (Conn. Super. 2011)(an excellent description of evolving case law and an application of reliability standards to eyewitness expert testimony).

[42] The Innocence Project, *Eyewitness Identification Reform*, available online at http://www.innocenceproject.org/understand/Eyewitness-Misidentification.php (last visited December 14, 2011). In *Houston v. Commonwealth*, 2011 WL 3962511 (Ky.App. 2011), however, the court held that the trial judge could limit an eyewitness expert testimony to the facts of the particular case and exclude testimony that a Justice Department report concluded that "in 80 percent of cases where there is mistaken conviction, it was eyewitness identification that convicted the defendant".

[43] "Studies show that professional [psychiatry and psychology] clinicians do not in fact make more accurate clinical judgments than laypersons. . . . We began by asking whether expert witnesses achieve reasonable certainty to aid the trier of fact. The scientific evidence clearly suggests that clinicians fail to satisfy either legal standard for expertise." Faust, David and Jay Ziskin, *The Expert Witness in Psychology and Psychiatry*, 241 Science 31 at 32, 34 (July 1, 1988).

[44] See generally Cohen, Andrew, Note, *The Unreliability of Expert Testimony on the Typical Characteristics of Sexual Abuse Victims,* 74 Geo. L. J. 429 (1985) (analyzing the use and admissibility of expert testimony in sexual abuse cases).

[45] See, e.g., *People v. Peterson*, 450 Mich. 349, 537 N.W.2d 857 (1995); *People v. Beckley*, 434 Mich. 691, 456 N.W.2d 391 (1990); *Neal v. State*, 2011 WL 766546 (Alaska App. 2011); *People v. Bailey*, 2009 WL 3323252 (Mich. App. 2011).

[46] Gatowski, Sophia I., et al., *The Globalization of Behavioral Science Evidence about Battered Women: A Theory of Production and Diffusion*, in 15 Behavioral Sciences And The Law 285, 296 (1997).

[47] Am. Psychiatric Ass'n, *Diagnostic and Statistical Manual of Mental Disorders*, app. C at 771 (4th ed. 1994).

[48] Lorenzen, Dirk, *The Admissibility of Expert Psychological Testimony in Cases Involving the Sexual Misuse of a Child*, 42 U. Miami L. Rev. 1033 (1988), at 1046-48 (citing J.P. Chaplin, *Dictionary of Psychology* 529 (1985)).

[49] See *id.* at 1048; and Steele, Dara Loren, Note, *Expert Testimony: Seeking an Appropriate Admissibility Standard for Behavioral Science in Child Sexual Abuse Prosecutions*, 48 Duke L. J. 933 (1998), at 942-46.

[50] Walker, Lenore ED., *The Battered Woman* (1979); Walker, Lenore E., *The Battered Woman Syndrome* (1984).

[51] Nat'l Inst. of Justice, U.S. Dep't Of Justice, NCJ 160972, *The Validity And Use Of Evidence Concerning Battering And Its Effects In Criminal Trials: Report Responding To Section 40507 Of The Violence Against Women Act* 20-22 (1996), available online at http://www.ncjrs.gov/pdffiles/batter.pdf (last visited December 14, 2011).

[52] Walker, Lenore E., *Terrifying Love: Why Battered Women Kill and How Society Responds* (1989), at 48-49; Michael McGrath, *Psychological Aspects of Victimology, in Forensic Victimology: Examining Violent Crime Victims In Investigative And Legal Contexts* 229, 241 (Brent E. Turvey & Wayne Petherick eds., 2009) (indicating that the four general characteristics of battered woman syndrome are often attributed to Walker's *The Battered Woman Syndrome* but that no such characteristics are in fact found in that text); and see Walker, Lenore E., *The Battered Woman Syndrome* (1984), at 95-97.

[53] See *Arcoren v. United States*, 929 F.2d 1235 (8th Cir. 1991); *People v. Brown*, 94 P.3d 574 (Cal. 2004); *Thompson v. State*, 416 S.E.2d 755 (Ga. Ct. App. 1992); *People v. Donastorg*, 83 Fed. R. Evid. Serv. 434 (V.I. Super 2010) (claiming that "numerous courts around the country have found expert testimony on the behavioral and emotional characteristics common to victims that have been battered or subjected to domestic violence, 'to have a scientific basis for admissibility' ")

[54] *Parrish v. State*, 514 S.E.2d 458 (Ga. Ct. App. 1999); People v. Howard, 712 N.E.2d 380, (Ill. Ct. App. 1999); *State v. Pargeon*, 582 N.E.2d 665 (Ohio Ct. App. 1991); *Ryan v. State*, 988 P.2d 46 (Wyo. 1999).

[55] *Modern Scientific Evidence: The Law and Science of Expert Testimony*, (eds. David L. Faigman, Michael J. Saks, Joseph Sanders, and Edward K. Cheng), Thomson/West Pub., 2009-2010 edition, §13:1 *et seq.*

[56] See, e.g., *People v. Christel*, 449 Mich. 578, 537 N.W.2d 194 (1995).

[57] Faigman, David L., Note, *The Battered Woman Syndrome and Self-Defense: A Legal and Empirical Dissent,* 72 Va. L. Rev. 619 (1986).

[58] *Fowler v. State,* 958 S.W.2d 853 (Tex. App. 1997). And more recently see *People v. Sandoval-Ceron,* 2010 WL 3021861 (Mich. App. 2011)

[59] *Modern Scientific Evidence: The Law and Science of Expert Testimony,* (eds. David L. Faigman, Michael J. Saks, Joseph Sanders, and Edward K. Cheng), Thomson/West Pub., 2009-2010 edition, §15:1.

[60] Burgess, Ann and Linda Holmstrom, *Rape Trauma Syndrome,* 131 Am. J. Psychiatry 981 (1974).; and see *People v. Taylor,* 75 N.Y.S.2d 277, 552 N.E. 2d 131 (1990).

[61] *Commonwealth. v. Federico,* 425 Mass 844, 683 N.E. 2d 1035 (1997); *People v. Seaman,* 657 N.Y.S. 2d 242 (1997); *State v. Kinney,* 171 Vt. 239, 762 A. 2d 833 (2000).

[62] *State v. Taylor,* 633 S.W.2d 235 (Mo. 1984); *State v. Chul Yun Kim,* 318 N.C. 614, 350 S.E.2d 347 (1986); *State v. Alberico,* 116 N.M. 156, 861 P.2d 192 (1993).

[63] *United States v. Smith,* No. 96-5385, 1998 WL 136564, at *2 (6th Cir. Mar. 19, 1998); *People v. Burkett,* No. 254996, 2005 WL 2401634, at *4-5 (Mich. Ct. App. Sept. 29, 2005); *People v. Stull,* 127 Mich. App. 14, 338 N.W.2d 403, (1983).

[64] See *State v. Moran,* 728 P.2d 248 (Ariz. 1986); *People v. Bledsoe,* 681 P.2d 291 (Cal. 1984) (en banc); *People v. Fasy,* 829 P.2d 1314 (Colo. 1992) (en banc); *State v. Spigarolo,* 556 A.2d 112 (Conn. 1989); *Townsend v. State,* 734 P.2d 705 (Nev. 1987); *State v. J.Q.,* 617 A.2d 1196 (N.J. 1993); *People v. Thompson,* 699 N.Y.S.2d 770 (App. Div. 1999); *State v. Hall,* 412 S.E.2d 883 (N.C. 1992); *State v. Middleton,* 657 P.2d 1215 (Or. 1983); *State v. Jensen,* 432 N.W.2d 913 (Wis. 1988); and *Chapman v. State,* 18 P.3d 1164 (Wyo. 2001).

[65] Dobbin, Shirley A., and Sophia I. Gatowski, *The Social Production of Rape Trauma Syndrome as Science and as Evidence,* in *Science in Court: Issues in Law and Society* (eds. Michael D. Freeman and Helen Reece, 1998), at 140.

[66]*Id* at 134-135.

[67] Steele, Dara Loren, Note, *Expert Testimony: Seeking an Appropriate Admissibility Standard for Behavioral Science in Child Sexual Abuse Prosecutions,* 48 Duke L. J. 933 (1998), at 944.

[68] Summit, Roland C., *The Child Sexual Abuse Accommodation Syndrome,* 7 Child Abuse & Neglect 177, 181 (1983).

[69] *Id.*

[70] For an excellent description of the history and judicial reactions to the child sexual abuse syndrome, see generally Steele, Dara Loren, Note, *Expert Testimony: Seeking an Appropriate Admissibility Standard for Behavioral Science in Child Sexual Abuse Prosecutions,* 48 Duke L. J. 933 (1998), at 933-73.

[71] Council on Scientific Affairs, *AMA Diagnostic and Treatment Guidelines Concerning Child Abuse and Neglect,* 254 1. Am. Med. Ass'n 796, 798 (1985); see also *People v. Peterson,* 450 Mich. 349, 537 N.W.2d 857 (1995) (citing with approval the behavioral signs in the American Medical Association's guidelines); and *State v. J.Q.,* 617 A.2d 1196 (N.J. 1993), at 1201-02.

[72] For a discussion on the use of expert testimony in child sexual abuse cases, see generally Askowitz, Lisa R. and Michael H. Graham, *The Reliability of Expert Psychological Testimony in Child Sexual Abuse Prosecutions,* 15 Cardozo L. Rev. 2027 (1994); Myers, John E. B., *et al., Expert Testimony in Child Sexual Abuse Litigation,* 68 Neb. L. Rev. 1 (1989); and Serrato, Veronica, Note, *Expert Testimony in Child Sexual Abuse Prosecutions: A Spectrum of Uses,* 68 Boston U. L. Rev. 155 (1988).

[73] *People v. Peterson,* 450 Mich. 349, 537 N.W.2d 857 (1995).

[74] See, e.g., *State v. Perry,* 218 P.3d 95 (Ore. 2009); *People v. Spicola,* 947 N.E.2d 620 (N.Y. 2011); *People v. Bailey,* 2009 WL 3323252 (Mich. App. 2011). Cf. *State v. Vidrine,* 9 So.3d 1095 (La.App. 2009) (while witness was qualified to discuss delayed reporting, it was error for the court not to hold a Daubert hearing as to the scientific basis for her testimony).

[75] *Newkirk v. Commonwealth,* 937 S.W.2d 690 (Ky. 1996) (finding that child sexual abuse syndrome offered for any use would fail to meet the standards set forth in either *Frye* or *Daubert); State v. Foret,* 628 So.2d 1116 (La. 1993) (finding that child sexual abuse accommodation syndrome fails *Daubert* because it is not scientifically reliable); *Commonwealth v. Dunkle,* 602 A.2d 830 (Pa. 1992) (finding that syndrome evidence does not meet *Frye* standards).

[76] Garrett, Brandon L. *Convicting the Innocent,* Harvard Univ. Press: Cambridge, Mass. 2011 at p. 18.

[77] See, e.g., Garrett, Brandon, *The Substance of False Confessions,* 62 Stanford L. Rev. 1051 (2010); Gudjonsson, Gisli H., *The Psychology of Interrogations and Confessions,* John Wiley & Sons, Ltd.: West Sussex,

England 2003; Alschuler, Albert, *Constraint and Confession*, 74 Denver U. L. Rev. 957 (1997); Chojnacki, Danielle, et al, *An Empirical Basis for the Admission of Expert Testimony on False Confessions*, 40 Ariz. St. L. J. 1 (2008); Drizin, Steve and Richard Leo, *The Problem of False Confessions in the Post-DNA World*, 82 N. Car. L. Rev. 891 (2004);.

[78] See *United States v. Hall*, 93 F. 3d 1337 (7th Cir. 1996); *United States v. Shay*, 57 F.3d 126 (1st Cir. 1995).

[79] *United States v. Adams*, 271 F.3d 1236 (10th Cir. 2001).

[80] *People v. Kowalski*, 2010 WL 3389741 (Mich. App. 2011). See also *State v. Craven*, 790 N.W.2d 225 (Neb. App. 2010).

[81] See, e. g., *United State v. Lim*, 984 F.2d 331 (9th Cir. 1993) and *United States v. Beltran-Rios*, 878 F.2d 1208 (9th Cir. 1989) ("'[e]very defendant has a right to be tried based on the evidence against him or her, not on the techniques utilized by law enforcement official in investigating criminal activity").

[82] *United States v. Batton*, 602 F.3d 1191 (10th Cir.2010*); United States v. Hitt*, 473 F.3d 146 (5th Cir. 2006); *United States v. Schneider,* 83 Fed. R. Evid. Serv. 820 (E.D. Pa. 2010).

[83] See *United States v. Raymond*, 700 F.Supp.2d 142 (D. Me. 2010); *State v. Wright*, 2009 WL 3111047 (Del. Super. 2009).

Chapter 5
Pretrial Forensic Issues

DNA Databases

The DNA Identification Act of 1994[1] mandated the creation of the FBI's Combined DNA Index System ("CODIS") forensic DNA database. CODIS is a "computer software program that operates local, state, and national databases of DNA profiles from convicted offenders, unsolved crime scene evidence, and missing persons."[2] All fifty states mandate DNA databases of some sort, although the types of crimes that require inclusion in a DNA database vary from state to state.[3] In 2004, the Justice for All Act[4] significantly increased funding for the use of DNA in the criminal justice system, including an expansion of CODIS to allow state crime laboratories to include even more persons in the database. The Act's DNA backlog grant program authorized $755 million in grants over five years. This created significant expansions of previous police databases, which had primarily focused on fingerprints. CODIS now includes what has been estimated to be over five million DNA samples.[5] CODIS DNA databases are searched for matches based on specimens collected at a crime scene to identify a potential perpetrator. While these searches are often used in serious cases of murder, rape, or robbery, it has been suggested that they should be used to solve multiple minor crimes.[6]

There is a debate about the scope and use of these DNA databases. The debate focuses on which crimes should prompt a DNA sample collection and the stage in the criminal process at which DNA samples should be taken from defendants. On the one hand, some suggest that the largest possible database is an important tool in law enforcement and that a government DNA database should be collected and maintained on the entire population. There is no universal DNA database system but clearly the trend is to expand the breadth of genetic criminal identification databases, from violent felons, to felons, to misdemeanants. Other questions about DNA sampling include: (1) at what stage in the process DNA samples are taken (arrest, indictment, or conviction); and (2) what should happen to DNA samples after acquittal or dismissal?[7] At least twenty-one states have enacted statutes requiring DNA sampling at felony arrests, before any guilt has been established even preliminarily.[8]

A recent report to Congress summarized the legal status of mandating the taking of DNA samples:

> As DNA database programs have widened in scope and grown in numbers, their consistency with the Fourth Amendment's prohibition on unreasonable searches and seizures has increasingly been challenged. In the context of compulsory DNA collection, courts have widely upheld laws mandating the collection of DNA from persons who were convicted and are subject to the penal system's custody or supervision. However, no judicial consensus has emerged regarding the constitutionality of mandating DNA collection from arrestees who have been criminally indicted. Instead, courts have split over the existence and scope of an arrestee's reasonable expectation of privacy and the degree of privacy intrusion caused by DNA sampling. The limited number of court decisions in this area also suggests that there are conflicting opinions about the analogousness of DNA collection and fingerprinting.[9]

For its part, Congress has determined that the DNA of all federal arrestees should be obtained. Amendments to the DNA Act in 2006[10], as implemented recently by Attorney General Regulations,[11] allows the collection of samples from all arrestees. In *United States v. Pool*[12] the Ninth Circuit held that mandating DNA samples from arrestees did not violate the Fourth Amendment, but that Court subsequently granted an en banc rehearing of the issue.[13] The Third Circuit took a definitive stand in *United States v. Mitchell* holding that "under the totality of the circumstances, given arrestees' and pretrial detainees' diminished expectations of privacy in their identities and the Government's legitimate interests in the collection of DNA from these individuals, we conclude that such collection is reasonable and does not violate the Fourth Amendment".[14] The Supreme Court has not yet spoken to the issue.

Many people are concerned about the threat of eugenics posed by continuing to enlarge the scope of DNA databases. Their concern is that genes contain information about the racial and ethnic heritage, disease and mental illness susceptibility, and even behavioral tendencies, of every person in the database. In this respect, they point out that DNA databases are inherently different than the fingerprint databases that law enforcement has maintained for many years and which are useful only for identification purposes.[15]

Recently, such concerns have been heightened by the use of DNA databases to locate potential relatives of an unidentified suspect. An "indirect genetic kinship analysis" uses crime scene DNA to search the convicted offender/arrestee DNA databases to identify not just the perpetrator, but also any biological relatives of the potential suspect.[16] Familial searching of large DNA databases has the potential to develop valuable investigative leads regarding the source of a forensic sample so that police can narrow their investigation to a small range of related suspects. Familial searches are specifically authorized in Colorado[17] and California[18] and its apparently successful use in identifying an alleged serial killer has heightened interest in expanding the process.[19] Congress is apparently favorably considering legislation that would encourage the FBI to expand its use of familial DNA searches, subject to "appropriate protections for the privacy rights of those in the NDIS database". [20] Familial searching does raise compelling policy questions that the legislatures and the courts have yet to definitively answer.[21]

The danger opponents see is that this personal, private health data will be used for a variety of discriminatory and currently unlawful purposes. This debate poses what many see as a conflict between public safety and individual privacy. Some maintain that balancing these conflicting interests is ultimately a political issue and that privacy interests are best protected through regulatory control over the law enforcement agencies that have access to the DNA databases.[22]

Search Issues

DNA database issues may most often present themselves in pretrial motions alleging that they are the result of unlawful searches and seizures in violation of the Fourth Amendment. Generally, such motions have failed. The federal courts have consistently ruled that the federal statute and various state statutes mandating the taking of DNA samples for law enforcement databases are not constitutionally infirm.[23] The physical gathering of a DNA specimen from a suspect for DNA testing is, of course, governed by the same Fourth Amendment constraints that apply to any seizure, and the DNA purpose of that seizure does not change that analysis.

Statutes of Limitations and "John Doe" Warrants

One of the side effects of the use of newly developing DNA techniques and ever- expanding DNA databases in "cold" cases is an often lengthy delay in charging a defendant whose identity is finally revealed by that DNA comparison. Applicable statutes of limitation may well have expired in the interim. In response, federal and state legislatures have begun to revise the statutory limitation periods.[24]

The Justice for All Act of 2004[25] that expanded the CODIS database also extended the federal statute of limitations in cases which DNA testing implicates a perpetrator until the time that the actual identity of the perpetrator is discovered. Several states have similarly extended some periods of limitations, including "Colorado, Florida, Indiana, Michigan, Nevada, New Jersey, and New York."[26] Many states have created special statutory limitation extensions applicable to sexual assault cases.[27] A myriad of additional extensions and modifications of state limitations periods are currently under consideration.[28] The proposals range, for example, from eliminating the limitations period entirely for certain offenses[29] to extending the statute when DNA evidence is recovered at a crime scene but the evidence does not currently match anyone in the DNA database.[30]

Additionally, prosecutors in several states have tried to toll the statute of limitations by filing a criminal complaint and warrant naming "John Doe" as the defendant and identifying him by the DNA profile obtained from a crime scene specimen. Prosecuting attorney organizations and the Justice Department are encouraging the filing of such "John Doe" warrants.[31] These warrants were first originated in Wisconsin in 1999 but are now being used by prosecutors in many other jurisdictions.[32] Federal and some state statutes have specifically authorized the use of such warrants.[33] The legal issue is whether such warrants or indictments sufficiently identify the defendant so as to toll the statute of limitations. The Fourth Amendment requires that warrants particularly describe the person to be seized.[34] The Federal Rules of Criminal Procedure require that an arrest warrant "contain the defendant's name or, if it is unknown, any name or description by which the defendant can be identified with reasonable certainty."[35] Most states have similar requirements.[36]

"John Doe" warrants without further identifying information are clearly constitutionally insufficient,[37] even when they contain some physical description such as race, height, or weight.[38] Prosecutors contend, however, that including the DNA profile not only meets but exceeds the reasonable certainty requirement because the profile can only identify one person. Defense lawyers disagree on the basis that "DNA samples will degrade over time, even under optimal conditions and errors in the collection, handling and storage of DNA samples can result in errors in identification."[39] Defense lawyers assert that nameless DNA warrants do not meet the requirement of reasonable certainty and that allowing such John Doe warrants vitiates their rights under the applicable statute of limitations.

Courts which have reviewed John Doe DNA warrants have generally upheld their validity.[40] As the Supreme Court of Massachusetts recently put it, "[w]here a general John Doe indictment, bereft of any particularity, must fail as generally anonymous, the converse is true of a DNA indictment: it prevails as precisely eponymous".[41]

Defense Discovery and Requests for Assistance

The increase in the use of forensic scientific evidence by the government also heightens the need for the defense in a criminal case both to investigate and respond to the government's evidence and possibly to affirmatively seek forensic evidence of its own.

Preliminarily, this means that the defense will seek to discover the test results obtained by the government as soon as possible. Unfortunately, many government crime laboratories are simply incapable of performing forensic tests within a reasonable period of time.

In 2002, the federal government estimated that state crime laboratories "ended the year with over 500,000 backlogged requests for forensic services—a more than seventy percent increase in the backlog of requests compared to the beginning of the year."[42] They also "estimated that about 1,900 additional FTEs [full time equivalent personnel] would have been needed to achieve a 30-day turnaround for all 2002 requests for forensic services . . . [and the] estimated cost of the additional FTEs exceeds $70.2 million."[43] More recently, the federal government estimates that, just as to DNA, there was a national backlog of 100,628 DNA cases as of January 1, 2009, which grew to 111,647 by the end of the year.[44] The backlogs have also resulted in some very high profile mistakes, delays and even closures at police laboratories.[45] The federal government has recognized the problem and initiated a program designed to assist States in reducing the backlog, at least as it relates to DNA testing[46] but it remains a significant problem.[47]

Often laboratories seem to base the priorities for testing on the proximity of a trial date, and defense attorneys rightly complain that this leaves them with little time to prepare a response or even to responsibly advise their clients about the weight of the evidence against them. In its simplest form, this may come before the trial court as a defense motion to compel or enforce discovery. It may even come up in a motion to reduce bond based on an assertion that the laboratory results may be exculpatory.[48] Ultimately, if the prosecution fails to produce the test results in spite of a court order, the judge may have to hear a request for a variety of sanctions against the prosecution.

Some states have enacted statutes to relieve the pressure on their crime laboratory personnel by specifically allowing the admission of laboratory reports in lieu of the testimony of the persons who performed the testing. Those laws were struck down by the Supreme Court in *Melendez-Diaz v. Massachusetts*.[49] The Court held that laboratory reports are indeed "testimonial" under the Supreme Court's prior holdings in *Crawford v. Washington*[50] and *Davis v. Washington*.[51] Therefore it was a violation of the Sixth Amendment right of confrontation to allow the government to submit a chemical drug test report without the testimony of the scientist. Since *Melendez-Diaz*, the holding has been applied to other forensic evidence reports as well, including DNA testing reports.[52] However, the scope of the close ruling in *Melendez-Diaz* remains a current topic in the courts. In *Bullcoming v. New Mexico*[53] the Supreme Court applied Melendez-Diaz to strike down the admissibility of a blood-alcohol laboratory report, when the accompanying testimony was from a laboratory technician who did not perform the analysis or write the report. In *Williams v. Illinois*[54] the Supreme Court is considering whether the a report from an independent laboratory and accompanying testimony from a state analyst who reviewed the data also violates the confrontation clause. It has been common for experts to testify about DNA matches though they did not actually perform the testing and the court's decision in *Williams* could end that practice.

The Supreme Court, however, has left open a different option which would be constitutional. Justice Scalia, writing for the majority, stated that alternative "notice and demand" laws which require the prosecution to provide notice to the defendant of its intent to use an analyst's report, and give the defendant a period of time in which he may object to the admission of the evidence or forfeit that objection, are permissible. Given the already existing backlog and demands on state crime laboratories,[55] many states are quickly trying to follow up on that suggestion.[56]

Aside from the issue of the admissibility of laboratory reports, a defendant has a constitutional right of confrontation to examine the evidence against him, and that would include the specimens used in laboratory tests as well as the details of the testing performed on those specimens. The discoverable materials at the pretrial stage would certainly include more than just the laboratory report. Pretrial discovery would normally include a right by the defense to obtain, and perform its own testing and analysis on, the specimen. The circumstances of that examination, especially when the evidence is subject to contamination or even consumption, often may be tightly controlled by the terms of a discovery order. Note, however, that the failure of the police to preserve a specimen may not amount to a constitutional violation absent a showing of police bad faith.[57]

Indigent defendants clearly have the same discovery rights. Trial judges often, however, have to address the desire of indigent defendants to retain defense experts for analysis and testimony. In *Ake v. Oklahoma*,[58] the Supreme Court of the United States established that an indigent defendant in a criminal case has a constitutional right to the assistance of publicly funded experts.[59] Some commentators believe that the right granted by the Supreme Court in *Ake* has proven to be illusory in practice.

In determining whether the court must make public funds available for a defense expert witness, the trial judge must consider the probable value of the expert analysis to the defense. Public funding is required when the issue is likely to be significant in the trial. The burden is on the defense to show that the expert is necessary.[60] However, at the least, when the prosecution has conducted a forensic examination of evidence, the defense would clearly seem to be entitled to its own similar expert examination of that evidence.

---

[1] The DNA Identification Act of 1994, Pub. L. 103-322, 108 Stat. 2065 (1994).

[2] Nat'l Inst. of Justice, U.S. Dep't of Justice, *Using DNA To Solve Cold Cases* 9 (2002), available online at http://www.ncjrs.gov/pdffiles1/nij/194197.pdf (last visited December 14, 2011).

[3] *Id.*

[4] 42 U.S.C. § 14135(j) (2006 & Supp. 2007).

[5] Matejik, Laura, *DNA Sampling: Privacy and Police Investigation in a Suspect Society*, 61 Ark. L. Rev 53 (2008).

[6] Nat'l Inst. of Justice, U.S. Dep't of Justice, *DNA in "Minor Cases" Yields Major Benefits in Public Safety*, in *In Short: Toward Criminal Justice Solutions*, Nov. 2004, at 1, 3, available online at http://www.ncjrs.gov/pdffiles1/nij/207203.pdf (last visited December 14, 2011).

[7] For a discussion of some of these issues, see Cole, Simon A., *Fingerprint Identification and the Criminal Justice System: Historical Lessons for the DNA Database,* in *DNA and the Criminal Justice System: the Technology of Justice*, ed. David Lazer, (2004), at 80-84.

[8] DNA Research Report, *Domestic DNA Legislation*, available online at http://www.dnaresource.com/documents/2007DNAExpansionLegislation.pdf (last visited December 14, 2011).

[9] Barbour, Emily C., *DNA Databanking: Selected Fourth Amendment Issues and Analysis*, Congressional Research Service No. 7-5700 (June 6, 2011), available online at http://fulltextreports.com/2011/07/19/crs-dna-databanking-selected-fourth-amendment-issues-and-analysis/ (last visited November 17, 2011).

[10] DNA Fingerprint Act, 42 U.S.C. § 14135a(a)(1)(A).

[11] 28 C.F.R. § 28.12, 73 Fed. Reg. 74932 (eff. Jan. 9, 2009).

[12] *United States v. Pool*, 621 F.3d 1213 (9th Cir. 2010).

[13] *United States v. Pool*, ___ F.3d ___, 2011 WL 2151202, at *1 (9th Cir. June 2, 2011).

[14] United States v. Mitchell, ___ F.3d ___ (3d Cir. No. 09-4718, July 25, 2011).

[15] See Steinhardt, Barry, *Privacy and Forensic DNA Data Banks, in DNA And The Criminal Justice System: The Technology Of Justice*, ed. David Lazer, (2004) at 173; and Preston, Corey, *Faulty Foundations: How the False Analogy to Routine Fingerprinting Undermines the Argument for Arrestee DNA Sampling*, 19 Wm. & Mary Bill Rts. J. 475 (2010).

[16] See Bieber, Frederick R, Charles H. Brenner, and David Lazer, *Finding Criminals Through DNA of Their Relatives*, Science: Vol. 312 no. 5778 pp. 1315-1316, (June 2, 2006) available online at http://www.sciencemag.org/content/312/5778/1315.citation (last visited November 18, 2011); and Ge, Jianye, Ranajit Chakraborry, Arthur Eisenberg and Bruce Budowle, *Comparisons of Familial DNA Database Searching Strategies*, J. Forensic Sci.Vol.56, No. 6 (November 2011).

[17] Colorado Bureau of Investigation, *DNA Familial Search Policy* (October 22, 2009), available online at http://www.denverda.org/DNA/Familial_DNA_Database_Searches.htm (last visited December 14, 2011).

[18] Information Bulletin from Edmund G. Brown, Jr., Attorney General, DNA Partial Match (Crime Scene DNA Profile to Offender) Policy No. 2008-BFS-01 (2008), available online at http://ag.ca.gov/cms_attachments/press/pdfs/n1548_08-bfs-01.pdf (last visited November 19, 2011).

[19] Steinhauer, Jennifer, *'Grim Sleeper' Arrest Fans Debate on DNA Use*, N.Y. Times, July 2, 2010, available online at

http://www.nytimes.com/2010/07/09/us/09sleeper.html   (last   visited
November 19, 2011).

[20] The House and Senate have approved a Conference Report that states "The
Committee encourages the FBI to undertake activities to facilitate familial
DNA searches of the National DNA Index System (NDIS) database of
convicted offenders, and work with the NDIS Procedures Board to consider
the establishment of procedures allowing familial searches only for serious
violent and sexual crimes where other investigative leads have been
exhausted. The procedures should provide appropriate protections for the
privacy rights of those in the NDIS database." *Commerce, Justice, Science
and Related Agencies Appropriations Bill, 2012*, House Report 112- 169,
112th Congress (2011-2012) available online at http://thomas.loc.gov/cgi-
bin/query/z?c112:H.R.2596 (last visited November 26, 2011) . See Schiff,
Adam, *Schiff's Familial DNA Language Passes as Part of Conference
Report*, Press Release (Nov. 21, 2011) available online at
http://schiff.house.gov/index.cfm?sectionid=49&parentid=6&sectiontree=6,4
9&itemid=869 (last visited November 26, 2011).

[21] See Ram, Natalie, *Fortuity and Forensic Familial Identification*, 63 Stan. L.
Rev. 751 (2011); and Murphy, Erin, *Relative Doubt: Familial Searches of
DNA Databases*, 109 Mich. L. Rev. 291 (2010) arguing for the prohibition or
at least restriction of familial database searches.

[22] See Etzioni, Amitai, *A Communitarian Approach: A Viewpoint on the Study
of the Legal, Ethical and Policy Considerations Raised by DNA Tests and
Databases*, 34 J. L. Med. & Ethics 214, 219-20 (2006).

[23] See, e.g., *Jones v. Murray*, 962 F.2d 302, 308 (4th Cir. 1992).

[24] For a general description of statute of limitations issues relating to DNA, see
Imwinkelried, Edward J., *The Relative Priority That Should Be Assigned to
Trial Stage DNA Issues*, in *DNA And The Criminal Justice System: The
Technology Of Justice*, ed. David Lazer, (2004); Diehl, Jonathan W. , Note,
*Drafting a Fair DNA Exception to the Statute of Limitations in Sexual
Assault Cases*, 39 Jurimetrics J. 431 (1999); and Dunn, Amy, Note, *Criminal
Law—Statutes of Limitation on Sexual Assault Crimes: Has the Availability
of DNA Evidence Rendered Them Obsolete?*, 23 U. Ark. Little Rock L. Rev.
839 (2001).

[25] Justice for All Act of 2004, Pub. L. No. 108-405, 118 Stat. 2260 (2004).

[26] Imwinkelried, Edward J., *The Relative Priority That Should Be Assigned to
Trial Stage DNA Issues*, in *DNA and the Criminal Justice System: The*

Technology of Justice, ed. David Lazer, (2004) at 94, 103 n.26.

[27] For a listing of legislative enactments by state, see Nat'l Conference of State Legislatures, *Statute of Limitations for Sexual Assaults* (2007), available online at http://www.ncsl.org/default.aspx?tabid=12723 (last visited December 14, 2011). For a discussion of early statutory limitation changes in response to DNA developments, see Ulmer, Frank B., Note, *Using DNA Profiles to Obtain "John Doe" Arrest Warrants and Indictments*, 58 Wash. & Lee L. Rev. 1585 (2001).

[28] For an updated list of DNA related state statute of limitation proposals, see Gordon Thomas Honeywell Gov't Affairs, *2008 Statute of Limitations DNA Legislation* (2008), available online at http://www.dnaresource.com/documents/2008StatuteofLimitationsLegislatio n.pdf (last visited December 14, 2011).

[29] *Id.*

[30] *Id.*

[31] See Nat'l Inst. of Justice, U.S. Dep't Of Justice, *Using DNA To Solve Cold Cases* 9 (2002), at 22, available online at http://www.ncjrs.gov/pdffiles1/nij/194197.pdf (last visited December 14, 2011).

[32] See Akehurst-Moore, Scott, *An Appropriate Balance?–A Survey and Critique of State and Federal DNA Indictment and Tolling Statutes*, 6 J. High Tech. L. 213, 216 (2006); and Ulmer, Frank B., Note, *Using DNA Profiles to Obtain "John Doe" Arrest Warrants and Indictments*, 58 Wash. & Lee L. Rev. 1585 (2001), at 1586-88.

[33] See, e.g., 18 U.S.C. § 3282 (2006); Ark. Code Ann. §§ 5-1-109(b)(1)(B), (i)-(j) (2006); Del. Code Ann. Tit. 11, § 3107 (2007); Mich. Comp. Laws § 767.24(2) (2008); N.H. Rev. Stat. Ann. § 592-A:7(II) (Supp. 2008).

[34] U. S. Const. amend. IV; Frank B. Ulmer, Note, *Using DNA Profiles to Obtain "John Doe" Arrest Warrants and Indictments*, 58 Wash. & Lee L. Rev. 1585 (2001), at 1600.

[35] Fed. R. Crim. P. 4(b)(1)(A); Frank B. Ulmer, Note, *Using DNA Profiles to Obtain "John Doe" Arrest Warrants and Indictments*, 58 Wash. & Lee L. Rev. 1585 (2001),at 1600-01.

[36] Ulmer, Frank B. , Note, *Using DNA Profiles to Obtain "John Doe" Arrest Warrants and Indictments*, 58 Wash. & Lee L. Rev. 1585 (2001), at 1600-01.

[37] See, e.g., *United States v. Doe*, 703 F.2d 745 (3d Cir. 1983); *United States v. Swanner*, 237 F.Supp. 69 (E.D. Tenn. 1964); *Winters v. Campbell*, 137 S.E.2d 188 (W. Va. 1964).

[38] See, e.g., *People v. Montoya*, 63 Cal. Rptr. 73 (Ct. App. 1967); *McIntyre v. State*, 530 N.Y.S.2d 898 (N.Y. App. Div. 1988).

[39] Nat'l Ass'n of Criminal Def. Lawyers, *Resolution Of The Board Of Directors Regarding John Doe DNA Warrants/Indictments* (2004), available online at http://www.nacdl.org/About.aspx?id=19672 (last visited December 14, 2011).

[40] See *State v. Dabney*, 663 N.W.2d 366 (Wis. Ct. App. 2003); *State v. Davis*, 698 N.W.2d 823 (Wis. Ct. App. 2005); *State v. Belt*, 179 P.3d 443 (Kan. 2008); *People v. Robinson*, 222 P.3d 55 (Cal. 2010); *Commonwealth v. Dixon*, 458 Mass. 446 (Mass. 2010); *State v. Danley*, 138 Ohio Misc.2d 1 (2006); *People v. Martinez*, 855 N.Y.S.2d 522 (2008). For a history of how courts have treated such warrants, see Sucherman, Micah, *People v. Robinson: Developments and Problems in the Use of "John Doe" DNA Arrest Warrants*, 99 Cal. L. Rev. 885 (2011).

[41] *Commonwealth v. Dixon, supra* at 452-453.

[42] Office of Justice Programs, U.S. Dept. of Justice, *Census of Publicly Funded Forensic Crime Laboratories* , Bureau Of Justice Statistics Bull., 2002, Feb. 2005, at 1 (2005), available at http://bjs.ojp.usdoj.gov/content/pub/pdf/cpffcl05.pdf (last visited December 14, 2011).

[43] *Id.*

[44] National Institute of Justice, U.S. Department of Justice, *DNA Evidence Backlogs: Forensic Casework*, 2011, available online at http://www.nij.gov/topics/forensics/lab-operations/evidence-backlogs/forensic-evidence-backlog.htm (last visited November 20, 2011).

[45] See, e.g., Hornbeck, Mark, *Law officials: Closing of Detroit Police Crime Lab a Crisis for State Justice System*, Detroit News (Feb. 18, 2010); Van Derbeken, Jaxon, *DNA Lab Chief Quits as SFPD Considers Outsourcing*, San Francisco Chronicle (June 23, 2010), available online at http://www.sfgate.com/cgi-bin/article/article?f=/c/a/2010/06/22/BALL1E32QP.DTL (last visited November 20, 2011); Lystra, Tony, *Statewide Increase in Cases Delay Crime Lab Results*, The Daily News (Washington Nov. 3, 2011), available online at http://tdn.com/news/local/article_cffa5634-068a-11e1-b26f-

001cc4c03286.html (last visited November 20, 2011); Pinkerton, James, *Backlog at HPD Crime Lab is Causing Trial Delays*, Houston Chronicle (Sept. 28, 2010) available online at http://www.chron.com/news/houston-texas/article/Backlog-at-HPD-crime-lab-is-causing-trial-delays-1717970.php (last visited November 20, 2011).

[46] National Institute of Justice, U.S. Department of Justice, *Forensic DNA Backlog Reduction Program* (2011), available online at http://www.dna.gov/funding/backlog-reduction/ (last visited November 20, 2011).

[47] See Strom, Kevin J. and Matthew J. Hickman, *Unanalyzed Evidence in Law-Enforcement Agencies: A National Examination of Forensic Processing in Police Departments*, 9 Crim. & Pub. Pol'y 381 (May 2010).

[48] Shelton, Donald E. *Twenty-First Century Forensic Science Challenges for Trial Judges in Criminal Cases: Where the "Polybutadiene" Meets the "Bitumen"*, 18 Widener L. J. 309 (2009), at 368.

[49] *Melendez-Diaz v. Massachusetts*, 557 U.S. 1256 (2009).

[50] *Crawford v. Washington*, 541 U.S. 36 (2004).

[51] *Davis v. Washington*, 547 U.S. 813 (2006).

[52] See, e.g., *Cuadros-Fernandez v. State*, 316 S.W.3d 645 (Tex. Ct. App. 2009).

[53] *Bullcoming v. New Mexico*, ___ U.S. ___, 131 S.Ct. 2705 (2011).

[54] *People v. Williams*, 939 N.E.2d 268 (2010), cert. granted *sub nom Williams v. Illinois*, __ U.S. __, 131 S. Ct. 3090 (2011). For ongoing commentary about these issues, see Friedman, Richard D., *The Confrontation Blog*, available online at http://confrontationright.blogspot.com/ (last visited December 14, 2011).

[55] Office of Justice Programs, U.S. Dept. of Justice, *Census of Publicly Funded Forensic Crime Laboratories* , Bureau Of Justice Statistics Bull., 2002, Feb. 2005, at 1 (2005), available at http://bjs.ojp.usdoj.gov/content/pub/pdf/cpffcl05.pdf (last visited December 14, 2011).

[56] See, e.g., Jackman, Tom and Rosalind S. Helderman, *Kaine Calls Session To Amend Laws On Trial Testimony*, The Washington Post, July 23, 2009, (Virginia). For updated information on statutory changes and evolving case law arising out of the *Melendez* case, see Federal Evidence Review, *The Melendez-Diaz Resource Page*, available online at

http://federalevidence.com/evidence-resources/melendez-
diaz.v.massachusetts-overview (last visited November 20, 2011).

[57] See *Arizona v. Youngblood*, 488 U.S. 51, 55-59 (1988).

[58] *Ake v. Oklahoma*, 470 U.S. 68 (1985).

[59] *Id.*, at 74.

[60] Findley, Keith A., *Innocents at Risk: Adversary Imbalance, Forensic Science, and the Search for Truth*, 38 Seton Hall L. Rev. 893 (2008), at 930.

Chapter 6
DNA Evidence

The Basis for DNA Identification Evidence

DNA is the molecular structure in all living things that contains genetic information.[1] DNA evidence is very durable and can be extracted from the smallest of remains many years after a crime.[2] Equally significant is its "polymorphism," meaning that, depending on the method used for its extraction, it is unique among humans and can identify the donor of the specimen with overwhelming accuracy.[3] DNA testing can be extremely precise and can often provide overwhelming evidence regarding the source of the specimen evidence.[4]

DNA profiling, was first described in 1985 by the English geneticist Alec Jeffreys, who discovered that certain regions of DNA contained repeated sequences next to each other and that the number of repeated sections in a sample differed between individuals.[5] He devised a technique to compare the length variations of these DNA repeat sequences, or variable number of tandem repeats (VNTR) and thus created the ability to perform human identity tests. The technique was called restriction fragment length polymorphism (RFLP). Later Dr. Kary Mullis discovered that DNA could be duplicated in the laboratory. This polymerase chain reaction (PCR) uses an enzyme to replicate the DNA regions and by repeating the process, a small amount of DNA is increased enormously. PCR analysis requires only a minute quantity of DNA and therefore allows analysis of tiny and degraded evidence samples. Another form of analysis, short tandem repeat (STR) technology, evaluates specific regions (loci) that are found on nuclear DNA. The nature of the STR regions that are analyzed intensifies the differentiation between one profile and another. The FBI adopted 13 specific STR loci as the standard for CODIS.

Y-chromosome analysis is a form of DNA analysis that can be very valuable when the DNA of two persons is mixed together, as is often the case in sexual assault situations, because the Y-chromosome markers include only the male fraction of a sample. Since the Y chromosome is transmitted directly and only paternally, it can also be used to trace family relationships among males. Mitochondrial DNA (mtDNA) analysis allows identification from samples that may not be sufficient for RFLP or STR analysis. MtDNA technology analyzes DNA found in a different part of the cell than the nucleus, and therefore can be used to examine samples where there is no nuclear DNA, such as hair shafts, bones, or teeth fragments. All maternal relatives have identical mtDNA and thus it can be used to trace family relationships among females.

Admissibility of DNA at Trial

Other than issues of laboratory procedures and safeguards which present themselves in all forensic science cases, the admissibility questions concerning DNA which remain today arise mainly from the development and discovery of new methods of DNA analysis. DNA profiling started in the legal system "as a method of determining paternity."[6] The first use of DNA in a successful U.S. criminal prosecution was in *Andrews v. State*,[7] when police matched DNA samples from semen to the defendant's blood in a rape case.[8] The admission of DNA evidence in a criminal case was first approved by a state supreme court in *State v. Woodall*.[9] Subsequently, properly collected and analyzed DNA evidence has been routinely admitted.[10] DNA test results are now admissible in every U.S. jurisdiction.[11] DNA matching has almost totally replaced blood typing for identification purposes and is probably the most important forensic science development in the twentieth century.[12] Many states have even adopted statutes "authorizing admission of DNA evidence."[13]

While the National Academy of Sciences report was critical of the basis for some other types of forensic evidence, there is no remaining doubt about the reliability of properly performed DNA analysis. The report found that "[a]mong existing forensic methods, only nuclear DNA analysis has been rigorously shown to have the capacity to consistently, and with a high degree of certainty, demonstrate a connection between an evidentiary sample and a specific individual or source." DNA evidence is now universally admitted by courts in the United States because of its reliability and the fact that, absent fraud or an error in labeling or handling, the probabilities of a false positive are miniscule.[14] Moreover, the testimony regarding the miniscule probabilities of another person matching the DNA of the defendant and the crime scene sample are often stated in astoundingly small numbers.[15]

Current opinions are almost unanimous that PCR-based laboratory procedures satisfy standards of admissibility under *Frye* or *Daubert* evaluations.[16] It has reached the point where courts have held that there is no need to conduct a *Daubert* hearing[17] or a *Frye* hearing[18] since there is no disagreement in the scientific community about the reliability of most DNA processes. Courts in more than thirty-five states have specifically admitted evidence based on the PCR method of amplifying DNA.[19] Use of the now common "product rule" for testing the frequency of genotypes in the population in PCR-based tests is widely recognized as both scientifically sound and generally accepted.[20] More than twenty-five states have admitted evidence of accompanying population frequency statistics.[21] The value of DNA evidence goes beyond proving identity. DNA evidence may be used by the prosecutor to prove or corroborate many elements of the charged crime. Prosecutors have been urged to use DNA evidence "just as any other form or type of evidence—to corroborate, validate and/or impeach evidence or testimony."[22] The location of a tested specimen of blood or other evidence may corroborate a complainant's description of where the offense occurred or could be used to refute a defense claim of alibi.[23] The location of DNA tested samples may show single sources or mixed DNA from both the complainant and the defendant and may demonstrate a sequence of events.[24] DNA evidence may even be offered by the prosecutor to show purpose or intent.[25] DNA evidence may also be offered as impeachment of a defendant's testimony or earlier statements or to enhance the credibility of a complainant.[26] Prosecutors have also sought to use DNA at sentencing as evidence of prior uncharged acts.[27]

Recently, issues have arisen in DNA cases where there is not a sufficient sample to allow testimony about probabilities but the prosecutor nevertheless offers testimony that the defendant's DNA is "consistent with" the sample or that the defendant "cannot be excluded" as the source of the crime scene DNA. Courts have allowed such testimony as relevant. For example, in *Commonwealth v. Matei*,[28] 892 N.E.2d 826 (Mass.App.Ct. 2008) the Court approved the admission of testimony that an incomplete sample "could not be excluded as having come from defendant". Other States have reached the similar, but seemingly anomalous, result that testimony of a DNA "match" must be accompanied by a statistical analysis of the probability of a random match but evidence of a non-match is admissible without any statistical support.[29] When a statistical analysis is presented, even when it is far from overwhelming, it is a matter of the weight of the evidence for a jury.[30]

In the same vein, courts have also allowed testimony based on Mitochondrial DNA testing even though by its nature mtDNA can only identify maternal lines and not individuals. In *People v. Humphrey*[31], a California appellate court heard the defendant's challenge to the mtDNA profile evidence introduced at his trial on the basis there is no generally accepted means to calculate population frequencies. The Court explained:

> A match between two mtDNA samples is not definitive. It simply means that the suspect's mtDNA sample cannot be excluded as originating from the same maternal lineage as the source of the mtDNA sample found at the crime scene. Identity cannot be established definitively because all individuals having the same maternal lineage possess identical mtDNA.

Nevertheless, the Court held that testimony "that either defendant or someone maternally related to defendant was the source of the three hairs tested" was admissible.

Although DNA profiling is clearly scientifically superior to other forensic identification evidence, it is not infallible.[32] DNA evidence and its underlying methodology are, of course, subject to human error. False positive DNA results have occurred and will undoubtedly continue to be part of the DNA testing landscape.[33] Proffered evidence may still, as with other forensic science evidence, be the result of mistakes or contamination in its collection, testing, or interpretation.[34]

As the technology and methodology of DNA testing has progressed, it is the human errors that may present the biggest evidentiary challenges for trial judges. DNA evidence has been recently challenged on a variety of factors, including poor laboratory proficiency testing, contamination, lack of proper laboratory protocols or accreditation, improper techniques, lack of quality control, and broken chains of custody.[35] Laboratory temperature variances are a source of challenge because DNA is very sensitive to environmental conditions and can "start to degrade depending on the sample's exposure to extreme temperatures, oxygen, water, sweat, and breath."[36] If the sample evidence is contaminated before PCR amplification, the identity of the donor may be masked by over-amplification.[37] Before and at the laboratory, DNA testing errors result from sample mislabeling, or otherwise switching samples, or from cross-contamination between samples in the same or different cases.[38]

Currently, the immense demand for DNA testing by police and prosecutors may inadvertently pose the most serious threat to its use in criminal trials. The overwhelming demand may be resulting in poor laboratory practices by inexperienced or overworked technicians to the degree that confidence in DNA test results is being affected. For example, the Department of Justice Inspector General officially reported that the FBI laboratory still "was riddled with flawed scientific practices that had potentially tainted dozens of criminal cases, including the bombings of the Federal Building in Oklahoma City and the World Trade Center in New York."[39] Suspected and documented cases of poor practices and false reports by forensic scientists at various state and local crime laboratories have been rampant.[40] As Professor William Thompson concluded:

> Although generally quite reliable (particularly in comparison with other forms of evidence often used in criminal trials), DNA tests are not now and have never been infallible. Errors in DNA testing occur regularly. DNA evidence has caused false incriminations and false convictions, and will continue to do so. Although DNA tests incriminate the correct person in the great majority of cases, the risk of false incrimination is high enough to deserve serious consideration in debates about expansion of DNA databases.[41]

The reality is that there are few accepted standards for the performance and practices of forensic science laboratories, either public or private. The National Academy of Sciences report recommends significant strengthening of the oversight of crime laboratories in light of the fact "that there are no requirements, except in a few states (New York, Oklahoma, and Texas), for forensics laboratories to meet specific standards for quality assurance or for practitioners to be certified according to an agreed set of standards." Trial judges are the primary guardians of the integrity of scientific evidence that is sought to be introduced to prove guilt. When it comes to DNA evidence, the gatekeeper role assigned to trial judges may find its most important function not in an evaluation of the reliability or general acceptance of new scientific theory, but rather in the very traditional functions of insuring that proffered evidence meets basic standards of authenticity, relevance, and reliability in the particular application of a scientific theory.

Deficiencies in a particular application may be found to go more to weight than admissibility. Nevertheless, when it comes to human error, particularly of the types recently reported, the application may indeed be "so altered" as to skew the results beyond the limits of admissibility. It would be a mistake to assume, as the public is wont to do, that all proffered DNA evidence is genuine, reliable, and admissible. As the Gallup poll reported in 2005:

> More than 8 in 10 Americans (85%) think DNA evidence is either completely (27%) or very (58%) reliable. A majority considered it reliable when Gallup first asked the question in 2000; the percentage backing the reliability of DNA has increased since then.[42]

DNA evidence, like other types of forensic evidence, is subject to laboratory and other errors. In performing the gatekeeper role, trial judges will need to demand more than mere testimony of a genetic match and not disregard the apparently distinct possibility of human error.[43]

Postconviction DNA Testing

The availability of DNA testing has given rise to numerous postconviction requests for DNA testing on the basis that it could produce important exculpatory evidence. Many states have responded with legislation addressing the standards for those requests, and courts will continue to deal with such requests for some time.

DNA testing has a remarkable ability, in the right circumstances, to provide conclusive exculpatory evidence after conviction where specimens were not tested at the time of trial.[44] The postconviction power of DNA testing is attributable to the same characteristics of the technology that has made it so valuable in during investigation and trial: the durability of DNA permits reliable testing years after the incident, and the polymorphism of DNA sequence systems greatly increases the probability of a conclusive incriminating or exculpatory result.[45]

In 1999, the Department of Justice conducted a thorough study of the question of postconviction DNA testing.[46] The report of the study suggests that the requests can be viewed in the following categories: (1) "cases in which biological evidence was collected . . . still exists, [and if] subjected to DNA testing or retesting, exclusionary results will exonerate the petitioner;" (2) "cases in which biological evidence was collected . . . still exists, [and if] subjected to DNA testing or retesting, exclusionary results would support the petitioner's claim of innocence, but reasonable persons might disagree as to whether the results are exonerative;" (3) "cases in which biological evidence was collected . . . still exists, [and if] subjected to DNA testing or retesting, favorable results will be inconclusive;" (4) "cases in which biological evidence was never collected, or cannot be found despite all efforts, or was destroyed, or was preserved in such a way that it cannot be tested;" or (5) "cases in which a request for DNA testing is frivolous."[47] Trial judges will usually encounter cases in the first two categories.

Neither common law standards nor existing court rules or statutes regarding postconviction relief are considered adequate to address the prospect of postconviction DNA testing. First, those standards and rules assume that the defendant already has what is regarded as newly discovered evidence, whereas DNA motions seek relief in the form of conducting tests to obtain such evidence. Second, DNA poses the distinct possibility of completely exonerating a defendant. Third, the durability of DNA suggests that arbitrary time rules or statute limits on postconviction motions may not be appropriate to requests for DNA testing. As a result of those concerns, the federal government and a number of states statutes have recently enacted statutes to specifically address postconviction DNA testing motions.[48]

The standards for postconviction testing of federal prisoners have been established by statute.[49] If a prisoner meets the ten listed criteria, a district judge must order DNA testing. The requirements are[50]:

1) the defendant must assert actual innocence of the offense;
2) the specific evidence to be tested must have been secured in relation to the investigation or prosecution of the offense of conviction;
3) DNA testing was not performed or the defendant must be requesting DNA testing using a new method or technology that is substantially more probative than the prior DNA testing;
4) the evidence to be tested must be in the possession of the government and have been subject to a chain of custody and retained under conditions sufficient to ensure that it has not been tampered with, contaminated or altered;
5) the proposed DNA testing is reasonable in scope, uses scientifically sound methods, and is consistent with accepted forensic practices;
6) the defendant identifies a theory of defense that is not inconsistent with an affirmative defense presented at trial and that would establish actual innocence;
7) the identity of the perpetrator was at issue in the trial;
8) the proposed DNA testing of the specific evidence may produce new material evidence that would support the theory of defense and raise a reasonable probability that the defendant did not commit the offense;
9) the defendant certifies that he will provide a DNA sample for purposes of comparison; and
10) the motion is made in a timely fashion.

The forty-eight States that have postconviction testing statutes have similar criteria but there are significant variations. State statutory schemes especially differ as to the classes of defendants who may apply, whether identity of the perpetrator is at issue, and the minimum requirement "materiality".[51] These statutes pose factual issues that often cannot be resolved without an evidentiary hearing.[52]

In states without specific DNA testing statutes or rules, the courts must rely on the general procedures governing motions for postconviction relief. Initially, the defendant in these situations is seeking postconviction discovery in the form of evidentiary samples and testing of those samples. Some courts have held that the right to some postconviction relief necessarily implies a right to postconviction discovery.[53] Other state courts have held that *Brady* v. *Maryland*, guaranteeing a defendant the constitutional right to be informed of exculpatory evidence,[54] carries with it the concomitant right to obtain such evidence even after conviction.[55]

The United States Supreme Court recently considered the question of whether there is a federal constitutional right to postconviction DNA testing, a matter that is especially important in states that have not enacted statutes or rules regulating postconviction DNA testing. In *District Attorney's Office v. Osborne*[56] the Supreme Court specifically held that *Brady v. Maryland* does not apply to postconviction issues and that the federal due process clause does not guarantee postconviction DNA testing. The Supreme Court found Alaska's general rules regarding postconviction discovery and newly-discovered evidence were not constitutionally "inadequate." The result of the *Osborne* decision is to leave the procedures for access to postconviction DNA testing of state prisoners entirely to the states.

The track record of DNA's impact on the criminal justice process indicates that it will continue to play an important role in postconviction as well as preconviction procedures. Justice Stephen Breyer recently surveyed DNA's impact on our criminal justice system and stated:

> DNA evidence promises not only to make future criminal trials more reliable, but also to permit the re-evaluation of past convictions, perhaps convictions that were secured many years ago. When should those convictions be reexamined? Are present reopening procedures adequate, in light of both of the added certainty that DNA evidence can provide and of the

numbers of closed cases in which potentially determinative DNA evidence might be obtained? Must the boundaries of preexisting legal rights be reshaped better to avoid the risk of imprisoning a defendant who is in fact innocent? Are new statutes needed?[57]

Access to potentially exonerating postconviction DNA testing pits our need for judicial efficiency (motivated by a desire for finality) against our constitutionally and humanely motivated desire for certainty of guilt.

---

[1] Kreeger, Lisa R. and Danielle M. Weiss, *Forensic DNA Fundamentals For The Prosecutor: Be Not Afraid* 3, Am. Prosecutors Research Inst. (2003), available on line at http://www.ndaa.org/pdf/forensic_dna_fundamentals.pdf (last visited December 14, 2011).

[2] Imwinkelried, Edward J. *The Relative Priority That Should Be Assigned to Trial Stage DNA Issues*, in *DNA And The Criminal Justice System: The Technology Of Justice*, ed. David Lazer, (2004), at 92-93.

[3] *Id.*, at 93.

[4] For descriptions of the development of DNA testing and its use in the criminal justice system, see *Modern Scientific Evidence: The Law and Science of Expert Testimony*, (eds. David L. Faigman, Michael J. Saks, Joseph Sanders, and Edward K. Cheng), 2009-2010 edition, §§ 31:1 et seq.; Imwinkelried, Edward J., *The Relative Priority That Should Be Assigned to Trial Stage DNA Issues*, in *DNA And The Criminal Justice System: The Technology Of Justice*, ed. David Lazer, (2004), at 91-101; and Moriarty , Jane Campbell and Michael J. Saks, *Forensic Science: Grand Goals, Tragic Flaws, and Judicial Gatekeeping*, Judges' J., Fall 2005, p. 16 (2005), at 19, 24-25.

[5] The material in this section is based on the overview found in National Institute of Justice, U.S. Department Justice, *About Forensic DNA*, available online at http://www.dna.gov/basics/ (last visited November 20, 2011).

[6] Cormier, Karen, Lisa Calandro and Dennis Reeder, *Evolution of DNA Evidence for Crime Solving: A Judicial and Legislative History,* Forensic Mag., June-July 2005, at 13, available online at http://www.forensicmag.com/articles.asp?pid=45 (last visited December 14, 2011).

[7] *Andrews v. State*, 533 So.2d 841, 842 (Fla. Dist. Ct. App. 1988). For a historical review of the use of DNA evidence, see Cormier, Karen, Lisa Calandro and Dennis Reeder, *Evolution of DNA Evidence for Crime Solving: A Judicial and Legislative History*, Forensic Mag., June-July 2005, at 13, available online at http://www.forensicmag.com/article/evolution-dna-evidence-crime-solving-judicial-and-legislative-history (last visited December 14, 2011).

[8] *Andrews v. State*, 533 So. 2d at 843 (Fla. Dist. Ct. App. 1988).

[9] *State v. Woodall*, 385 S.E.2d 253 (W. Va. 1989).

[10] See, e.g., *United States v. Yee*, 134 F.R.D. 161 (N.D. Ohio 1991).

[11] Cormier, Karen, Lisa Calandro and Dennis Reeder, *Evolution of DNA Evidence for Crime Solving: A Judicial and Legislative History*, Forensic Mag., June-July 2005, at 13-14, available online at http://www.forensicmag.com/articles.asp?pid=45 (last visited December 14, 2011).

[12] See Murphy, Erin, *The New Forensics: Criminal Justice, False Certainty, and the Second Generation of Scientific Evidence*, 95 Cal. L. Rev. 721, 793-94 (2007) (arguing that because of "the government's domination of forensic science," "rather than simply selecting and advocating for the theory that suits it best, the government should bear a burden of presenting evidence and disclosing results derived from all legitimate, competing theories").

[13] Kreeger, Lisa R., and Danielle M. Weiss, *Forensic DNA Fundamentals For The Prosecutor: Be Not Afraid* 3, Am. Prosecutors Research Inst. (2003), at 19, available online at http://www.ndaa.org/pdf/forensic_dna_fundamentals.pdf (last visited December 14, 2011).

[14] National Research Council of the Nat'l Acad's, *Strengthening Forensic Science in the United States: A Path Forward* (2009), Executive Summary at 3-12, 5-3.

[15] In *Commonwealth v. Bizanowicz*, 945 N.E.2d 356 at 405-406 (Mass. 2011) for example "The DNA expert testified that the likelihood of a random individual having the same profile was one in 101.5 quadrillion in the Caucasian population, one in 1.503 quintillion in the African American population, and one in 329.8 quadrillion in the Hispanic population. The DNA expert stated that a quadrillion is one million times the population of the earth."

[16] Kreeger. Lisa R. and Danielle M. Weiss, *Forensic DNA Fundamentals For The Prosecutor: Be Not Afraid,* Am. Prosecutors Research Inst. (2003), at 19, available online at http://www.ndaa.org/pdf/forensic_dna_fundamentals.pdf (last visited December 14, 2011).

[17] See *Commonwealth v. Bizanowicz, supra* at 407, stating that "the use of the DNA analysis involved here is generally accepted within the scientific community. . . . There is no scientific debate over the methodology by which such DNA matches are obtained or their validity."; and *VanPelt v. State,* 2009 WL 4980326 (Ala.Crim.App. 2009).

[18] *State v. Bander,* 208 P.3d 1242 (Wash. App. 2009) (with an excellent description of DNA testing and probability testimony).

[19] Kreeger, Lisa R. and Danielle M. Weiss, *Forensic DNA Fundamentals For The Prosecutor: Be Not Afraid,* Am. Prosecutors Research Inst. (2003), available online at http://www.ndaa.org/pdf/forensic_dna_fundamentals.pdf (last visited December 14, 2011).

[20] *Id.,* at 14-15.

[21] *Id.,* at 19.

[22] *Id.,* at 18.

[23] *Id.,* at 17.

[24] *Id.*

[25] *Id.,* at 18.

[26] *Id.*

[27] Lester, Katherine C., *The Affects of Apprendi v. New Jersey on the Use of DNA Evidence at Sentencing – Can DNA Alone Convict of Unadjudicated Prior Acts?,* 17 Wash. & Lee J. Civil Rts. & Soc. Just. 267 (2010).

[28] *Commonwealth v. Matei,* 892 N.E.2d 826 (Mass.App.Ct. 2008).

[29] See, e.g., *State v. Boles,* 933 P.2d 1197 (Ariz. 1997); *Young v. State,* 879 A.2d 44 (Md. 2005); *State v. Ellis,* 799 N.W.2d 267 (Neb. 2011); *State v. Lang,* 129 Ohio St.3d 512 (2011). Cf. *United States v. Davis,* 602 F.Supp.2d 658 (D. Md. 2009).

[30] *United States v. Hair,* 2011 WL 333236 (N.D. Okla. 2011).

[31] *People v. Humphrey,* 2011 WL 1671560 (Cal. App. 3 Dist.).

[32] See generally Koehler, Johnathan J., *Error and Exaggeration in the Presentation of DNA Evidence at Trial,* 34 Jurimetrics J. 21 (1993) (discussing how experts and attorneys may misrepresent and misinterpret estimates, resulting in overstated statements regarding the strength and

implications of DNA evidence); Thompson, William C., *Guide to Forensic DNA Evidence* in *Expert Evidence: A Practitioner's Guide To Law, Science, And The FJC Manual*, eds. Bert Black and Patrick W. Lee (1997).

[33] Thompson, William C., Franco Taroni & Colin G.G. Aitken, *How the Probability of a False Positive Affects the Value of DNA Evidence*, 48 J. Forensic Sci. 47 (2003).

[34] Lieberman, Joel D., et al., *Gold Versus Platinum: Do Jurors Recognize the Superiority and Limitations of DNA Evidence Compared to Other Types of Forensic Evidence?*, 14 Psychol. Pub. Pol'y & L. 27, 31 (2008).

[35] *Id.*

[36] *Id.* (citing Carl W. Gilmore, *Challenging DNA in Paternity Cases: Finding Weaknesses in an Evidentiary Goliath*, 90 Ill. B. J. 472, 474 (2002)).

[37] MacKnight, Kamrin T. , *The Polymerase Chain Reaction (PCR): The Second Generation of DNA Analysis Methods Takes the Stand*, 20 Santa Clara Computer & High Tech. L. J. 95 (2003); Mellon, Jennifer N. , Note, *Manufacturing Convictions: Why Defendants Are Entitled to the Data Underlying Forensic DNA Kits*, 51 Duke L. J. 1097 (2001).

[38] Thompson, William C. , *Tarnish on the "Gold Standard:" Understanding Recent Problems in Forensic DNA Testing*, Champion Mag., Jan.-Feb. 2006, at 10.

[39] David, Johnston, *Report Criticizes Scientific Testing at F.B.I. Crime Lab*, N.Y. Times, Apr. 16, 1997, at A1.

[40] See Bykowicz Julie and Justin Fenton, *City Crime Lab Director Fired: Database Update Reveals Employees' DNA Tainted Evidence, Throwing Lab's Reliability into Question*, Sun (Baltimore, Md.), Aug. 21, 2008, at 1A; Dao, James , *Lab's Errors in '82 Killing Force Review of Virginia DNA Cases*, N.Y. Times, May 7, 2005, at A1; Griffy, Leslie, *Crime Lab in Spotlight: Senate Committee Hears Testimony Faulting DA's Internal Investigation*, San Jose Mercury News, Jan. 24, 2008, at 1B; Hastings, Deborah , *Memo: Chemist May Have Altered Evidence*, Mobile Reg., Apr. 21, 2004, at A5; Hunter, George, *Detroit Shuts Down Error-Plagued Crime Lab*, Detroit News, Sept. 26, 2008, at 1A; Roma Khanna and Steve McVicker, *Police Lab Tailored Tests to Theories, Report Says: Investigators Hope to Establish Whether Mistakes Were Deliberate*, Houston Chron., May 12, 2006, at A1; Mills, Steve and Maurice Possley, *Report Alleges Crime Lab Fraud: Scientist Is Accused of Providing False Testimony*, Chi. Trib., Jan. 14, 2001, at A1; Teichroeb, Ruth, *Rare Look Inside State Crime Labs*

Reveals Recurring Problems, Seattle Post-Intelligencer, July 22, 2004, at A1; Willing, Richard, *Errors Prompt States to Watch over Crime Labs*, USA Today, Mar. 31, 2006, at 3A.

[41] Thompson, William C., *The Potential for Error in Forensic DNA Testing (and How That Complicates the Use of DNA Databases for Criminal Identification)*, Council for Responsible Genetics national conference, *Forensic DNA Databases and Race: Issues, Abuses and Actions,* June 19-20, 2008, New York University, available online at www.gene- watch.org (last visited November 21, 2011).

[42] Carlson, Darren K. , *Americans Conclusive About DNA Evidence*, Gallup, Nov. 15, 2005, http://www.gallup.com/poll/19915/Americans-Conclusive-AboutDNA-Evidence.aspx (last visited December 14, 2011).

[43] See Malcom, Brooke G., Comment, *Convictions Predicated on DNA Evidence Alone: How Reliable Evidence Became Infallible*, 38 Cumb. L. Rev. 313, 338 (2008) (urging consideration of the proposition that DNA evidence alone, without corroboration, is not sufficient for conviction).

[44] See generally Nat'l Inst. of Justice, U.S. Dep't Of Justice, *Convicted By Juries, Exonerated By Science: Case Studies In The Use Of DNA Evidence To Establish Innocence After Trial* (1996), available online at http://www.ncjrs.gov/pdffiles/dnaevid.pdf (last visited December 14, 2011); Nat'l Comm'n On The Future Of DNA Evidence, U.S. Dep't Of Justice, Postconviction *DNA Testing: Recommendations For Handling Requests* (1999), available online at http://www.ncjrs.gov/pdffiles1/nij/177626.pdf (last visited December 14, 2011).

[45] Imwinkelried, Edward J. *The Relative Priority That Should Be Assigned to Trial Stage DNA Issues*, in *DNA And The Criminal Justice System: The Technology Of Justice*, ed. David Lazer, MIT press (2004), at 92-93, 96.

[46] Nat'l Comm'n on the Future of DNA Evidence, U.S. Dep't Of Justice, Postconviction *DNA Testing: Recommendations For Handling Requests* (1999), at iii, vi, xiii, available online at www.ncjrs.gov/pdffiles1/nij/177626.pdf (last visited December 14, 2011).

[47] *Id,*. at xiii-xiv.

[48] Ariz. Rev. Stat. Ann. § 13-4240 (2001); Ark. Code Ann. §§ 16-112-201 To - 208 (2006); Cal. Penal Code § 1405 (West Supp. 2009); Colo. Rev. Stat. Ann. §§ 18-1-411 To -416 (West 2004 & Supp. 2008); Conn. Gen. Stat. Ann. § 54-102kk (West Supp. 2008); Del. Code Ann. Tit. 11, § 4504 (2007); Fla. Stat. Ann. §§ 925.11, 943.3251 (West Supp. 2009); Ga. Code Ann. § 5-

5-41 (1995 & Supp. 2008); Idaho Code Ann. §§ 19-4901 To -4902 (2004); 725 Ill. Comp. Stat. Ann. 5/116-3 (West 2002 & Supp. 2008); Ind. Code Ann. §§ 35-38-7-1 To -19 (West 2004); Kan. Stat. Ann. § 21-2512 (2007); Ky. Rev. Stat. Ann. §§ 422.285, .287 (LexisNexis 2005 & Supp. 2008); La. Code Crim. Proc. Ann. Arts. 924, 926.1 (2008 & Supp. 2009); Me. Rev. Stat. Ann. Tit. 15, §§ 2136-2138 (2003 & Supp. 2008); Mich. Comp. Laws Ann. § 770.16 (West 2006); Minn. Stat. Ann. §§ 590.01-.04, .06 (2000); Mo. Rev. Stat. §§ 547.035, 650.055 (2008); Mont. Code Ann. §§ 46-21-110, 53-1-214 (2007); Neb. Rev. Stat. §§ 29-4119 To -4123 (2003); Nev. Rev. Stat. § 176.0918 (LexisNexis 2006); N. J. Stat. Ann. § 2A:84A-32A (West Supp. 2008); N.M. STAT. ANN. § 31-1A-2 (West Supp. 2008); N.Y. Crim. Proc. Law § 440.30 (McKinney 2005); Ohio Rev. Code Ann. §§ 2953.71 To -.83 (LexisNexis 2002); Okla. Stat. Ann. Tit. 22, §§ 1371-1371.2 (2009); Or. Rev. Stat. §§ 138.690-.698 (2007); 42 Pa. Const. Stat. § 9543.1 (2006); R.I. Gen. Laws §§ 10-9.1-11 To -12 (Supp. 2008); Tenn. Code Ann. §§ 40-30-301 To -313 (2006); Tex. Code Crim. Proc. Ann. Arts. 64.01-.05 (Vernon 2006); Utah Code Ann. §§ 78B-9-301 To 304 (2008); Va. Code Ann. § 19.2-327.1 (2008); Wash. Rev. Code Ann. § 10.73.170 (LexisNexis 2007); Va. Code Ann. § 15-2B-14 (LexisNexis 2004 & Supp. 2008); Wis. Stat. Ann. §§ 974.07 (West 2007).

[49] 18 U.S.C §3600 *et seq.*

[50] See *United States v. Pugh,* 2009 WL 2256019 (N.D. Fla. 2009)

[51] For an excellent description of State statutes and their variability, see Stone, J.H. Dingfelder, *Facing the Uncomfortable Truth: The Illogic of Post-Conviction Testing for Individuals Who Pleaded Guilty,* 45 U.S.F. L. Rev. 47 (2010).

[52] See, e.g., *Commonwealth v. DiBenedetto,* 941 N.E.2d 580 (Mass. 2011).

[53] See, e.g., *People v. Callace,* 573 N.Y.S.2d 137, 139-40 (Gen. Term. 1991).

[54] *Brady v. Maryland,* 373 U.S. 83 (1963).

[55] See, e.g., *Sewell v. State,* 592 N.E.2d 705 (Ind. Ct. App. 1992); *Mebane v. State,* 902 P.2d 494 (Kan. Ct. App. 1995); *State v. Thomas,* 586 A.2d 250 (N.J. Super. Ct. App. Div. 1991); *Dabbs v. Vergari,* 570 N.Y.S.2d 765 (Sup. Ct. 1990); *Commonwealth v. Brison,* 618 A.2d 420 (Pa. Super. Ct. 1992).

[56] *Dist. Attorney's Office v. Osborne,* 557 U.S. ___, 129 S. Ct. 2308 (2009).

[57] Breyer, Stephen, *Furthering the Conversation About Science and Society,* in *DNA And The Criminal Justice System: The Technology Of Justice,* ed. David Lazer, (2004) at 13, 16.

Chapter 7

Fingerprint Evidence

Fingerprint comparison has been accepted as evidence in criminal prosecutions for over one hundred years.[1] Courts have accepted the proposition that each person's fingerprint is unique and that fingerprint comparison is almost infallible as a means of forensic identification. Fingerprint experts often declare a positive identification, rather than a probability of identity.[2] Recently, that assumption of infallibility has been seriously undermined by new scientific analysis. Postconviction DNA testing has resulted in proof of wrongful convictions that were based on seemingly reliable non-DNA forensic scientific evidence, and most disturbing is new scientific evidence that fingerprint comparisons may not be entitled to the great weight that criminal courts and jurors have long ascribed to it.

Analysis of the images left by prints on the fingers, palms or soles is more properly known as "friction ridge analysis." Simply put, it is an examiner's comparison of impressions left by ridges on the skin in two samples. It has traditionally been used to make an identification of a person, such as during an arrest or death investigation, or to prove than an individual touched a surface where one of the ridge impressions was left. Early work was by a simple visual analysis of patent, or obvious, prints left at the scene of a crime.

Skin is never completely dry or clean. Dirt or oil, or even sweat, creates prints whenever a solid surface is touched. If hands are stained, they will leave a patent (visible) print. Latent fingerprints are invisible to the naked eye, but the forensic scientist can visualize them though a variety of means, originally called "dusting." Modern forensic scientists now have a range of techniques for finding latent prints, cleaning up and enhancing print images, and rapidly finding a match from a database using computer technology. Friction ridge analysis is usually performed in crime laboratories, which may or may not be accredited. The training of latent print analysts varies greatly, from a formal training program to a one or two week course to simple on-the job training. No specific certification or training is required but some professional organizations have developed manuals for the training of analysts.[3]

The Fingerprinting Process

Fingerprints are reproduced images of the ridged surfaces on the skin that result when oil is transferred from the skin onto the surface of the area which was touched. Such impression evidence at the scene is generally latent (invisible to the naked eye) or patent (visible).[4] The quality of impression evidence and its eventual analysis depend a great deal on the procedures used to collect, preserve, and enhance the evidence discovered at the scene.

There are generally three types of techniques for making latent fingerprints visible: physical, chemical, and instrumental.[5] The basic physical process for visualizing fingerprints at a scene is "dusting" the suspected area with a powder that then adheres to the oils or other matter left by the ridges. This process is most effective on smooth surfaces that do not absorb the oils. The prints revealed by the dusting can be photographed directly. More often the prints are "lifted" from the surface using tape and that taped image is then pressed onto and transferred to a printed card.

A common chemical technique is called "cyanoacrylate fuming," or more colloquially "super glue fuming."[6] Fingerprints leave traces of amino acids, fatty acids, and proteins which will react to the fumes produced when superglue is heated. That reaction forms a sticky, white material that clings to the ridges of fingerprints, making them visible. Items to be tested are placed inside an air tight chamber, a few drops of "super glue" are placed into a heating tray inside the chamber, and the reaction leaves white outlines of the ridges which can then be photographed directly or dusted, lifted and transferred. This chemical process is especially effective on textured or other surfaces that are not very susceptible to physical visualization. The reaction is not permanent so the print must be photographed or transferred soon after development. A print visualized by a super glue fuming technique is shown in the following photograph.

Other chemicals also react with the chemical in the fingerprint residue and the most common chemical technique for porous surfaces today involves ninhydrin.[7] The chemical reaction of the ninhydrin with the oils from the hand reveals prints in a high-contrast purple tone. Ninhydrin development occurs slowly at room temperature and humidity. Various treatments are then used to enhance the prints, including treatment with metal-based reagents to intensify the prints.

Other techniques have been developed and tested and each may be more appropriate in a given case depending on the conditions and the materials. For example, a recent development of an instrumental technique for fingerprint detection involves the use of a scanning Kelvin microprobe.[8] That device maps the changes in electrical impulses left when the skin comes into contact with some surfaces and displays the electrochemical images of the patterns of that contact. It requires no physical or chemical change in the suspected surface. Another even more recent development is Micro-X-ray fluorescence.[9] Body salts excreted in sweat contain sodium, potassium and chlorine that are deposited along the patterns present in a fingerprint. An image of the fingerprint can be visualized by shining a thin beam of X-rays onto it without disturbing the sample. The chemical elements emit radiation at a "signature" frequency revealed in a spectrograph.

The other part of the fingerprinting process involves imaging and recording fingerprints of a known individual for later comparison. Inked fingerprint cards have long been accepted as the standard means for recording and storing fingerprint data and evolved into an accepted international standard for the exchange of fingerprint identification between criminal justice agencies. The FBI, working with the American National Standards Institute (ANSI), has developed detailed specifications for taking fingerprints that are used by virtually all police agencies in the United States.[10] The techniques for taking and recording the prints are important and have also been described in detail by the FBI.[11] The impressions are recorded on a standard fingerprint identification card. The upper ten impressions are taken individually of the thumb, index, middle, ring, and little fingers of each hand. These are referred to as the "rolled" impressions because the fingers are rolled from one side of the fingernail to the other, in order to obtain all available ridge detail. The impressions at the bottom of the card are taken simultaneously without rolling, printing all of the fingers of each hand at a forty-five degree angle and then the thumbs. These are referred to as "plain," "slapped," or "flat" impressions. The plain impressions are used to verify the sequence and accuracy of the rolled impressions.

More recently, the FBI and many local agencies use an inkless digital system for recording fingerprints called "live scan." Fingerprints are scanned to produce digital images which can be electronically transmitted to the FBI and or other investigating agencies. The technology replaces the ink rolling process and can avoid common problems with ink fingerprints such as smudging, smearing, and using too much or too little ink. The FBI has developed complex standards for digital scanning devices as well.[12] The federal government uses the "live scan" process exclusively and the States are moving to it as well.

Digital devices are not without their own problems. Different types of digital scanners are available. The scanners measure the difference between the ridges and valleys using various elements such as optical or thermal differences. However, when a finger touches or rolls onto a surface, the skin may deform based on the pressure applied by the user or by various skin conditions. There is also concern that the projection of an irregular three dimensional finger onto a two dimensional scanner may introduce distortion. Non-contact three dimensional fingerprint scanners have been developed that compensate for many of these problems.[13]

The FBI manages the nation's fingerprint identification system and database called Integrated Automated Fingerprint Identification System (IAFIS).[14] IAFIS is the largest biometric database in the world, containing the fingerprints of more than 55 million persons. The fingerprints and corresponding criminal history information are submitted by state, local, and federal law enforcement agencies, now mostly in digital format.

Fingerprint Analysis

The forensic science community has long regarded friction ridge analysis as a primary method for assessing "individualization," the conclusion that a suspect fingerprint impression comes, unambiguously, from a single person.[15] The technique used to examine fingerprints goes by the acronym ACE-V, for "Analysis, Comparison, Evaluation, and Verification."[16]

The analysis phase of an unknown print requires the examiner to consider the many factors that may affect the detail in the latent print including: the condition of the skin (aging, damage to the skin scars, diseases, and masking attempts); the type and amount of residue (sweat, oil, blood, paint, etc.); the mechanics of the touch (pressure on the surface of the skin, flexibility of the ridges, furrows, and creases, etc.); the surface which was touched (texture, rigidity, shape, condition, and background); the development technique; the capture technique (photograph or lifting material); and the percentage of the surface available for comparison.[17] The examiner also analyzes the known prints for factors that can affect its quality. If either print does not have sufficient detail for either identification or exclusion, the prints are considered "of no value" or "not suitable" for comparison.

The comparison phase consists of visually measuring and comparing the corresponding details in the suspect print and a known print. The observations might include "the overall shape of the latent print, anatomical aspects, ridge flows, ridge counts, shape of the core, delta location and shape, lengths of the ridges, minutia location and type, thickness of the ridges and furrows, shapes of the ridges, pore position, crease patterns and shapes, scar shapes, and temporary feature shapes."[18]

The evaluation phase requires the examiner to consider the extent of the agreement of the ridge formations in the two prints and the sufficiency of the detail present to establish an identification ("source determination").[19] A "source determination" is made when the examiner concludes that there is sufficient quantity and quality of detail in agreement between the latent print and the known print. A "source exclusion" is made when there is disagreement between the latent and known prints. If the detail is insufficient for either, it is deemed an "inconclusive comparison."[20]

The verification phase requires that another qualified examiner repeat the observations and come to the same conclusion. However, it is not a "blind" comparison since the standard practice allows the second examiner to be aware of the conclusion of the first examiner.[21]

In spite of the seeming formality of the fingerprint analysis process adopted by qualified examiners, the reality is that the assessment of fingerprint identification is nevertheless a subjective human interpretation. As the National Academies Report stated:

> Although some Automated Fingerprint Identification Systems (AFIS) permit fully automated identification of fingerprint records related to criminal history (e.g., for screening job applicants), the assessment of latent prints from crime scenes is based largely on human interpretation. Note that the ACE-V method does not specify particular measurements or a standard test protocol, and examiners must make subjective assessments throughout. In the United States, the threshold for making a source identification is deliberately kept subjective, so that the examiner can take into account both the quantity and quality of comparable details. As a result, the outcome of a friction ridge analysis is not necessarily repeatable from examiner to examiner. . . .
>
> This subjectivity is intrinsic to friction ridge analysis, as can be seen when comparing it with DNA analysis. . . . For these reasons, population statistics for fingerprints have not been developed, and friction ridge analysis relies on subjective judgments by the examiner. Little research has been directed toward developing population statistics, although more would be feasible.[22]

Fingerprint examiners regard their expertise as a matter of qualitative rather than quantitative analysis. They claim that the ability to see details in prints and the ability to compare features in prints is an "acquired skill" gained through experience and a lengthy apprenticeship.[23] They deny that it is possible to establish numerical scores or thresholds based on corresponding features because they do not determine which features are relevant until they make their initial "analysis and comparison."[24]

Fingerprint examiners report a positive identification when they conclude that two different persons could not have produced the latent print. This is a subjective assessment. Although it has been suggested that examiners would be more accurate to use statistics to assign match probabilities based on population distributions of certain friction ridge features, current examiners generally refuse to do so. They claim that published statistical models only count corresponding minutiae and do not incorporate elements of clarity. The fingerprint examiner community discourages its members from testifying in terms of the probability of a match and they testify with absolute certainty that the prints could not possibly have come from two different individuals.[25]

Fingerprint Testimony under *Frye* and *Daubert* Analyses

The challenge of *Daubert* should be significant if it is to be applied to fingerprinting. On the one hand, most if not all of the claims made by or on behalf of fingerprint examiners enjoy unquestioning belief among the lay public, including the bench and the bar. On the other hand, little conventional science exists to support the generally accepted claims regarding fingerprint identification. Although there is debate about the number of points of similarity in fingerprints that are sufficient to declare a match, there is no generally accepted scientific or court-recognized minimum standard.[26] Proficiency testing that has been conducted does not support the zero error rate claimed by fingerprint examiners. In fact, many of the most basic tenets of fingerprint identification have never been subjected to empirical analysis. Most modern researchers who have examined fingerprinting comparison have concluded that the broad claims of fingerprint identification accuracy cannot be substantiated.[27] As one commentator put it, the "gold standard" of fingerprinting identification may be more akin to "fool's gold."[28]

The summary assessment of fingerprint analysis in the National Academies Report was somewhat less critical but certainly casts doubt on the ready acceptance of fingerprint expert testimony:

> Historically, friction ridge analysis has served as a valuable tool, both to identify the guilty and to exclude the innocent. Because of the amount of detail available in friction ridges, it seems plausible that a careful comparison of two impressions can accurately discern whether or not they had a common source. Although there is limited information about the accuracy and reliability of friction ridge analyses, claims that these analyses have zero error rates are not scientifically plausible.

ACE-V provides a broadly stated framework for conducting friction ridge analyses. However, this framework is not specific enough to qualify as a validated method for this type of analysis. ACE-V does not guard against bias; is too broad to ensure repeatability and transparency; and does not guarantee that two analysts following it will obtain the same results. For these reasons, merely following the steps of ACE-V does not imply that one is proceeding in a scientific manner or producing reliable results. . . .

. . . Better documentation is needed of each step in the ACE-V process or its equivalent. At the very least, sufficient documentation is needed to reconstruct the analysis, if necessary. By documenting the relevant information gathered during the analysis, evaluation, and comparison of latent prints and the basis for the conclusion (identification, exclusion, or inconclusive), the examiner will create a transparent record of the method and thereby provide the courts with additional information on which to assess the reliability of the method for a specific case. Currently, there is no requirement for examiners to document which features within a latent print support their reasoning and conclusions.

Error rate is a much more difficult challenge. Errors can occur with any judgment-based method, especially when the factors that lead to the ultimate judgment are not documented. Some in the latent print community argue that the method itself, if followed correctly (i.e., by well-trained examiners properly using the method), has a zero error rate. Clearly, this assertion is unrealistic, and, moreover, it does not lead to a process of method improvement. The method, and the performance of those who use it, are inextricably linked, and both involve multiple sources of error (e.g., errors in executing the process steps, as well as errors in human judgment). Some scientific evidence supports the presumption that friction ridge patterns are unique to each person and persist unchanged throughout a lifetime. Uniqueness and persistence are necessary conditions for friction ridge identification to be feasible, but those conditions do not imply that anyone can reliably discern whether or not two friction ridge impressions were made by the same person. Uniqueness does not guarantee that prints from two different people are always sufficiently different that they cannot be confused, or that two impressions made by the same finger will also be sufficiently similar to be discerned as coming from the same source. The impression left by a given finger will differ every time, because of inevitable variations in pressure, which change the degree of contact between each part of the ridge structure and the impression medium. None of these variabilities—of features across a population of fingers or of repeated impressions left by the same finger—has been characterized, quantified, or compared.[29]

Haber and Haber were less diplomatic in their review of fingerprint analysis and the comparison of multiple fingerprint conclusions, stating, "We have reviewed available scientific evidence of the validity of the ACE-V method and found none."[30] And Professor Jennifer Mnookin summarized the claims of absolute certainty by fingerprint examiners in light of *Daubert*:

Given the general lack of validity testing for fingerprinting; the relative dearth of difficult proficiency tests; the lack of a statistically valid model of fingerprinting; and the lack of validated standards for declaring a match, such claims of absolute, certain confidence in identification are unjustified. . . . Therefore, in order to pass scrutiny under *Daubert*, fingerprint identification experts should exhibit a greater degree of epistemological humility. Claims of 'absolute' and 'positive' identification should be replaced by more modest claims about the meaning and significance of a 'match.'[31]

On the other hand, it seems logical that States that still use the *Frye* analysis will have little difficulty with new fingerprinting information because fingerprint identification is certainly "generally accepted" and has been for a long time. Most of the claims made by fingerprint examiners enjoy widespread belief among members of both the public and the bar. In a sense, this points up the significant limitation of the *Frye* test, in that the criminal justice systems using that test take a very long time to react to changes in science, which often can take place in a short period of time.

Fingerprinting may face some challenges in *Frye* states, however. In the capital case of *Maryland v. Rose*,[32] the State trial judge applied Maryland's version of the *Frye* rule and, in a very detailed opinion, held that fingerprint testimony was not admissible and that the ACE-V methodology "was the type of procedure *Frye* was intended to banish, that is, a subjective, untested, unverifiable identification procedure that purports to be infallible."[33] The Court in that case held a lengthy evidentiary hearing on admissibility, rejecting the prosecution argument that no hearing was necessary under *Frye*:

> The State's primary argument is that history favors acceptance of latent print identifications. Indeed, such identifications have been admitted for nearly one hundred years. So established is such evidence that the State opposed the Defendant's request for a *Frye-Reed* hearing. Moreover, the State requested that the Court take judicial notice of the reliability of latent print identification evidence. . . .
>
> The State is correct that fingerprint evidence has been used in criminal cases for almost a century. While that fact is worthy of consideration, it does not prove reliability. For many centuries, perhaps for millennia, humans thought that the earth was flat. The idea has a certain intuitive appeal. Indeed, there still exists a Flat Earth Society for people who cling to the idea the earth is not an orb. But science has proved that the earth is not flat; and, it is the type of fact of which a court can take judicial notice.[34]

Daubert should clearly be a more difficult admissibility test for fingerprinting. That has not been the case. Following the State judge's exclusion of fingerprint evidence in the *Rose* case, the federal prosecutor had Rose indicted by a grand jury in federal court, where the *Daubert* standard would apply. In her brief ruling granting the government's motion in limine seeking to admit fingerprint evidence, even without a *Daubert* evidentiary hearing, the federal District Court judge relied primarily on the 4th Circuit holding in *United States v. Crisp*[35] and simply held that "fingerprint identification evidence based on the ACE-V methodology is generally accepted in the relevant scientific community, has a very low incidence of erroneous misidentifications, and is sufficiently reliable to be admissible under Fed. R. Ev. 702 generally and specifically in this case."[36]

The judge in that case had the benefit of the National Academies Report but found that the Report "did not conclude that fingerprint evidence was unreliable such as to render it inadmissible under Fed. R. Ev. 702"[37] and she specifically rejected the Haber study error rate results, holding that "there is nothing to contradict the conclusion reached by many courts and other experts that the incidence of error in the sense of erroneous misidentification . . . is extremely rare."[38] Perhaps, as recently suggested by Professor Simon Cole, the *Frye* standard may prove to be a more stringent test for fingerprinting than *Daubert.* [39]

The federal *Rose* decision exemplifies the resistance of courts to any challenge to the admissibility of fingerprint testimony. Like the Fourth Circuit in *Crisp*, the Third Circuit in *United States v. Mitchell*[40] and the Fifth Circuit in *United States*[41] have held that trial judges are not even required to hold a *Daubert* or *Frye* hearing on a fingerprint challenge absent "novel" issues and several States have followed suit.[42] And most courts that have re-examined fingerprint identification under *Daubert* have either held that it passed *Daubert* muster[43] or have just continued to give it a superficial review and approval.[44] Very few have rejected or limited fingerprint examiner testimony after a *Daubert* review.[45] In *New Hampshire v. Langill,*[46] the New Hampshire Supreme Court held that the failure to conduct a blind verification phase under ACE-V was not a basis upon which fingerprint testimony could be excluded. In *United States v. Llera Plaza I,*[47] vacated and superseded on reconsideration in *United States v. Llera Plaza II,*[48] the federal district judge did an interesting about-face in his *Daubert* analysis of fingerprint evidence, eventually admitting it.[49] However, in view of the mounting scholarly evidence that fingerprinting may lack scientific validation, some courts have found the issue of the reliability of fingerprint comparisons is at least admissible as a jury question.[50] In a case which may signal at least some willingness to re-examine fingerprint testimony, the district judge in *United States v. Aman*[51] considered the *Daubert* problems posed by recent scientific developments. Contrasting the findings of the National Academies Report with the overwhelming prior acceptance of fingerprint testimony by the courts, the judge stated:

But of course, a history of judicial and expert community acceptance does not obviate the government's burden to demonstrate in this case reliability of the expert's testimony under *Daubert.* The NRC [NAS] Report devotes significant attention to friction ridge analysis, noting the "subjective" and "interpret[ive]" nature of such examination. . . .
Additionally, the examiner does not know, *a priori,* which areas of the print will be most relevant to the given analysis, and small twists or smudges in prints can significantly alter the points of comparison. This unpredictability can make it difficult to establish a clear framework with objective criteria for fingerprint examiners. And unlike DNA analysis, which has been subjected to population studies to demonstrate its precision, studies on friction ridge analysis to date have not yielded accurate population statistics. In other words, while some may assert that no two fingerprints are alike, the proposition is not easily susceptible to scientific validation.
Furthermore, while fingerprint experts sometimes use terms like "absolute" and "positive" to describe the confidence of their matches, the NRC has recognized that a zero-percent error rate is "not scientifically plausible."[52]

In the end however the judge, like many before and since, could not bring himself to overcome precedent and held that the concerns with fingerprint testimony did not preclude its admission but only presented issues for the jury:

The absence of a known error rate, the lack of population studies, and the involvement of examiner judgment all raise important questions about the rigorousness of friction ridge analysis. To be sure, further testing and study would likely enhance the precision and reviewability of fingerprint examiners' work, the issues defendant raises concerning the ACE–V method are appropriate topics for cross-examination, not grounds for exclusion. . . .
Furthermore, it can hardly be questioned that the ACE–V method has achieved widespread acceptance in the fingerprint examination community. . . . In sum, the ACE–V method, although perhaps not worthy of the pedestal on which it has

been historically placed, is sufficiently reliable to overcome *Daubert* 's bar to admissibility.[53]

It may be that the strong pro-prosecution bias of judges evaluating fingerprint admissibility in criminal cases will continue to allow fingerprint testimony to be admitted in spite of its scientific shortcomings. The rather blind acceptance of fingerprint evidence is the product of years of assumptions about its validity. Any change may only result from published DNA exonerations of persons convicted on the basis of fingerprint identification. One such case was the FBI's total misidentification of fingerprints in a multiple murder terrorism case as those of an Oregon attorney, Brandon Mayfield, only to find later that foreign police had properly identified the prints as those of an Algerian terrorist.[54] Indeed, the federal judge in the *Rose* case felt it necessary to dismiss the *Mayfield* case as "extremely rare" and even claimed that it demonstrates the validity of ACE-V because the Spanish police caught the error.[55]   The Innocence Project has disclosed other wrongful convictions based at least in part on erroneous fingerprint evidence. [56]

Any erosion of the admissibility of fingerprint evidence is likely to be slow. However, the federal courts and those State courts that have adopted *Daubert* will eventually face the necessity to re-evaluate the scientific basis for fingerprinting's assumptions about uniqueness. Ultimately the courts will have to reexamine the question of whether fingerprint comparison, without scientific standards of point similarity, is perhaps more art (or "judgment" as its proponents claim) than science. States still using the *Frye* analysis may take longer to reassess fingerprint evidence. By definition, the "general acceptance" of fingerprinting will only erode as even more scientists begin to doubt its validity and as *Daubert* courts start to doubt its admissibility.

---

[1] For a description of the evolution and history of fingerprint identification, see Cole, Simon A., *Fingerprint Identification and the Criminal Justice System: Historical Lessons for the DNA Debate* in *DNA And The Criminal Justice System. The Technology Of Justice*, ed. David Lazer (2004)

[2] *Id.*

[3] See International Association for Identification, *Friction Ridge Skin Identification Training Manual,* available at www.theiai.org (last visited December 23, 2009); and Scientific Working Group on Friction Ridge Analysis, *Training to Competency for Latent Print Examiner* (2002), available online at www.SWGFAST.org (last visited December 14, 2011).

[4] See generally Maltoni, David, Darri Maio, Anil K Jain, & Salil Prabbakar, *Handbook of Fingerprint Recognition* (2009); R. Hawthorne, Mark, *Fingerprints: Analysis and Understanding* (2008); *Advances in Fingerprint Technology,* eds. Henry C. Lee and Robert E Gaensslen, (2nd ed., 2001); Stoney, David A., *The Scientific Basis of Expert Testimony on Fingerprint Identification,* §§ 32.21 *et seq,* in *Modern Scientific Evidence: The Law and Science of Expert Testimony,* eds. David L. Faigman, Michael J. Saks, Joseph Sanders, and Edward K. Cheng, (2009-2010 edition).

[5] Stoney, *id.*

[6] *Advances in Fingerprint Technology,* eds. Henry C. Lee and Robert E Gaensslen, (2nd ed., 2001).

[7] *Id.*; Stoney, David A., *The Scientific Basis of Expert Testimony on Fingerprint Identification,* in *Modern Scientific Evidence: The Law and Science of Expert Testimony,* eds. David L. Faigman, Michael J. Saks, Joseph Sanders, and Edward K. Cheng, (2009-2010 edition) at § 33.28.

[8] See Williams, G., H. McMurray, and D. Worsley, *Latent Fingerprint Detection Using a Scanning Kelvin Microprobe,* 46 J. Forensic Sci. 1005 (2001).

[9] Worley, Christopher G. , Sara S. Wiltshire, Thomasin C. Miller, George J. Havrilla and Vahid Majidi, *Detection of Visible and Latent Fingerprints Using Micro-X-ray Fluorescence Elemental Imaging,* 51 J. Forensic Sci. 57 (2005).

[10] National Institute of Standards and Technology, U.S. Department of Commerce , *American National Standard for Information Systems— Data Format for the Interchange of Fingerprint, Facial, & Other Biometric Information,* NIST Special Publication No. 500-271, ANSI/NIST-ITL 1-2007 (2007), available online at http://fingerprint.nist.gov/standard/index.html (last visited December 14, 2011).; and see *FBI Biometric Specifications,* available online at http://www.fbibiospecs.org/biospecs.html (last visited December 14, 2011).

[11] FBI Criminal Justice Information Services, U.S. Department of Justice, *Taking Legible Fingerprints*, available online at http://www.fbi.gov/hq/cjisd/takingfps.html (last visited December 14, 2011).

[12] See Brislawn, Christopher M., *Fingerprints Go Digital*, 42 Notices of the American Mathematical Society 1278 (1995), available online at http://www.ams.org/notices/199511/brislawn.pdf (last visited December 14, 2011).

[13] Sun, Y., J. Paik, A. Koschan, D.L. Page, and M.A. Abidi, *Point Fingerprint: A New 3-D Object Representation Scheme*, IEEE Trans. on Systems, Man, and Cybernetics-Part B: Cybernetics, Vol. 33, No. 4, pp. 712-717, (August 2003).

[14] FBI Criminal Justice Information Services, U. S. Department of Justice, *Integrated Automated Fingerprint Information System*, available online at http://www.fbi.gov/hq/cjisd/iafis.htm (last visited Decemember 14, 2011).

[15] Nat'l Research Council of the Nat'l Acads., *Strengthening Forensic Science in the United States: A Path Forward* (2009) at 136.

[16] *Id.*, at 137-139; Haber, Lyn and Ralph N. Haber, *Scientific Validation of Fingerprint Evidence under Daubert*, 7 Law, Probability and Risk 87 (2008); Ashbaugh, David R., *Quantitative-Qualitative Friction Ridge Analysis: An Introduction to Basic and Advanced Ridgeology* (1999); Vanderkolk, J, *ACE-V: A Model*, 54 J. Forensic Ident. 45 (2002); Triplett, Michele and Lauren Cooney, *Etiology of ACE-V and Its Proper Use: An Exploration of the Relationship Between ACE-V and the Scientific Method of Hypothesis Testing*, 56 J. Forensic Ident. 345 (2006).

[17] Nat'l Research Council of the Nat'l Acads., *Strengthening Forensic Science in the United States: A Path Forward* (2009) at 137-138.

[18] *Id.*, at 138.

[19] Scientific Working Group on Friction Ridge Analysis, Study and Technology, *Friction Ridge Examination Methodology for Latent Print Examiners*. (2002), available online at http://www.swgfast.org/Friction_Ridge_Examination_Methodology_for_Latent_Print_Examiners_1.01.pdf (last visited December 14, 2011).

[20] Nat'l Research Council of the Nat'l Acads., *Strengthening Forensic Science in the United States: A Path Forward* (2009) at 138.

[21] *Id.*

[22] *Id* at 139-140. See also Haber, Lyn and Ralph N. Haber, *Scientific Validation of Fingerprint Evidence under Daubert*, 7 Law, Probability and Risk 87 (2008).

[23] *Id*, at 140.

[24] *Id.*

[25] *Id.*, at 141-142.

[26] The details of fingerprinting and fingerprinting comparison, as well as some of its limitations, are described in Stoney, David A., *The Scientific Basis of Expert Testimony on Fingerprint Identification*, in *Modern Scientific Evidence: The Law and Science of Expert Testimony*, eds. David L. Faigman, Michael J. Saks, Joseph Sanders, and Edward K. Cheng, (2009-2010 edition).

[27] *Modern Scientific Evidence: The Law and Science of Expert Testimony*, (eds. David L. Faigman, Michael J. Saks, Joseph Sanders, and Edward K. Cheng), 2009-2010 edition, §§33:1 *et seq*; Epstein, Robert, *Fingerprints Meet Daubert: The Myth of Fingerprint "Science"*, 75 S. Cal. L. Rev. 605 (2002); Cole, Simon A., *More Than Zero: Accounting for Error in Latent Fingerprint Identification*, 95 J. Crim. L. & Criminology 985 (2005); Saks, Michael J. and Jonathan J. Koehler, *The Coming Paradigm Shift in Forensic Identification Science*, 309 Science 892 (2005); Benedict, Nathan, *Fingerprints and the Daubert Standard for Admission of Scientific Evidence: Why Fingerprints Fail and a Proposed Remedy*, 46 Ariz. L. Rev. 519 (2004): Cole, Simon A., *Grandfathering Evidence: Fingerprint Admissibility Rulings from Jennings to Llera Plaza and Back Again*, 41 Amer. Crim. L. Rev. 1189 (2004); Cole, Simon A., *The Prevalence and Potential Causes of Wrongful Conviction by Fingerprint Evidence*, 37 *Golden Gate Univ. L. Rev.* 39 (2006).

[28] Malcom, Brooke G., *Convictions Predicated On DNA Evidence Alone: How Reliable Evidence Became Infallible*, 38 Cumb. L. Rev. 313 (2008).

[29] Nat'l Research Council of the Nat'l Acads., *Strengthening Forensic Science in the United States: A Path Forward* (2009) at 142-144 (footnotes omitted).

[30] "[W]e report a range of existing evidence that suggests that examiners differ at each stage of the method in the conclusions they reach. To the extent that they differ, some conclusions are invalid. We have analysed the ACEV method itself, as it is described in the literature. We found that these descriptions differ, no single protocol has been officially accepted by the profession and the standards upon which the method's conclusions rest have

not been specified quantitatively. As a consequence, at this time the validity of the ACE-V method cannot be tested." Haber, Lyn and Ralph N. Haber, *Scientific Validation of Fingerprint Evidence under Daubert*, 7 Law, Probability and Risk 87 (2008), at 19; and see Nat'l Research Council of the Nat'l Acads., *Strengthening Forensic Science in the United States: A Path Forward* (2009).

[31] Mnookin, Jennifer, *The Validity of Latent Fingerprint Identification: Confessions of a Fingerprinting Moderate*, 7 Law, Probability and Risk 111 (2008).

[32] *State v. Rose*, Case No. K06-0545 (Md. Balt. Co. Cir. Oct. 19, 2007), available online at http://www.baltimoresun.com/media/acrobat/2007-10/33446162.pdf (last visited December 14, 2011).

[33] *Id.*, at 31.

[34] *Id.*, at 22, 24.

[35] *United States. v. Crisp*, 324 F.3d 261 (4th Cir. 2003) holding that it was not an abuse of discretion to admit expert fingerprint identification testimony in a criminal case under the *Daubert* standard.

[36] *United States v. Rose*, No. CCB-08-0149 (D. Md., December 8, 2009), available online at http://www.mdd.uscourts.gov/Opinions/Opinions/Brian%20Rose%20Mem-FINAL.pdf (last visited December 14, 2011).

[37] *Id.*, at 5.

[38] *Id.*, at 6.

[39] ". . . latent print individualization may have survived its *Daubert* trials only to end up in the "Fryeing pan." Further, it may contradict the conventional wisdom that *Daubert* is a more stringent admissibility threshold than *Frye*, especially for unpopular litigants with unpopular causes." Cole, Simon A., *Out of the Daubert Fire and Into the Fryeing Pan? Self-Validation, Meta-Expertise and the Admissibility of Latent Print Evidence in Frye Jurisdictions*, 9 Minn. J. L. Sci. & Tech. 453, 537 (2008).

[40] *United States. v. Mitchell*, 365 F.3d 215 (3d Cir. 2004).

[41] *United States v. John*, 597 F.3d 263 (5th Cir. 2010).

[42] See, e.g., *State v. Johnson*, 2010 WL 5464926 (La.App. 1 Cir. 2010); *Revis v. State*, ___ So.3d ___, 2011 WL 109641 (Ala.Crim.App. 2011); *Markham v. State*, 984 A.2d 262 (Md. App. 2009).

[43] See, e.g., *United States. v. Crisp*, 324 F.3d 261 (4th Cir. 2003); *U.S. v. Scott*, 403 Fed.Appx. 392 (11th Cir. 2010);*U.S. v. Havvard*, 117 F.Supp.2d 848 (2000).

[44] *United States. v. Frias*, 2003 WL 296740 (S.D. N.Y 2003), modified in part, 2003 WL 352502 (S.D. N.Y 2003); *U.S. v. Sullivan*, 246 F. Supp.2d 700 (E.D. Ky. 2003); U.S. v. Cruz-Rivera, 2002 WL 662128 (D.P.R. 2002); *United States. v. Hernandez*, 299 F.3d 984 (8th Cir. 2002), cert. denied, 537 U.S. 1134 (2003); *U.S. v. Navarro-Fletes*, 49 Fed. Appx 732 (9th Cir. 2002); *U.S. v. Martinez-Cintron*, 136 F. Supp.2d 17 (D.P.R. 2001); *United States v. Cline*, 188 F. Supp 2d 1287 (D. Kan. 2002), aff'd 349 F.3d 1276 (10th Cir. 2003); *United States v. Rogers*, 26 Fed. Appx 171 (4th Cir. 2001); *United States v. Reaux*, 2001 WL 883221 (E.D. La. 2001); *United StatesS. v. Joseph*, 2001 WL 515213 (E.D. La. 2001).

[45] See, e.g., *Jacobs v. Government of Virgin Islands*, 53 Fed. Appx. 651 (3d Cir. 2002).

[46] *New Hampshire v. Langill*, 157 N.H. 77, 945 A.2d 1 (N.H. 2008).

[47] *U. S. v. Llera Plaza I* ,179 F. Supp.2d 492 (E.D. Pa. 2002).

[48] *U.S. v. Llera Plaza II* , 188 F. Supp.2d 549 (E.D. Pa. 2002).

[49] For an analysis of these two conflicting fingerprint opinions, see Mark P. Denbeaux and D. Michael Risinger, *Kumho Tire and Expert Reliability: How the Question You Ask Gives the Answer You Get*, 34 Seton Hall L. Rev. 15 (2003).

[50] See, e.g., *United States v. Cerna*, 2010 WL 3448528 (N.D.Cal. 2010); *State v. Bickart*, 963 A.2d 183 (Me. 2009) (palmprints); and more generally Epstein, Robert, *Fingerprints Meet Daubert: The Myth of Fingerprint "Science'*, 75 S. Cal. L. Rev. 605 (2002) at 650.

[51] *United States v. Aman*, 748 F.Supp.2d 531 (E.D. Va. 2010).

[52] *Id.* at 540.

[53] *Id.* at 541-542.

[54] Office of the U.S. Inspector General, A *Review of the FBI's Handling of the Brandon Mayfield Case*, (March 2006), available online at http://www.justice.gov/oig/special/s0601/PDF_list.htm (last visited December 14, 2011).

[55] *United States. v. Rose*, No. CCB-08-0149 (D. Md., December 8, 2009), available online at http://www.mdd.uscourts.gov/Opinions/Opinions/Brian%20Rose%20Mem-FINAL.pdf (last visited December 14, 2011).

[56] See the reported cases of *Gene Bibbins*, available online at http://www.innocenceproject.org/Content/53.php (last visited December 14, 2011); and *Stephan Cowans*, available online at http://www.innocenceproject.org/Content/73.php (last visited December 14, 2011).

Chapter 8

Handwriting Comparison

Comparison of handwriting samples, or questioned document examination as its practitioners call it, was an early form of identification and is one of the oldest types of forensic evidence. It broadly involves the comparison of documents and printing and writing to identify persons who are the source of the writing, to reveal alterations, or to identify the source of typewritten marks.[1] This chapter focuses primarily on handwriting analysis. The science is based on "the asserted ability to determine the authorship *vel non* of a piece of handwriting by examining the way in which the letters are inscribed, shaped and joined, and comparing it to exemplars of a putative author's concededly authentic handwriting."[2] Handwriting examiners claim that no two people write alike and that no one person writes the same way twice.[3] They argue, therefore, that no two writings are ever identical.[4] Although it was offered in courts even before the twentieth century, it was not widely accepted as scientific evidence until it became part of the cornerstone of the prosecution case in *State v. Hauptmann*, the Lindbergh kidnapping case.[5]

In America, the handwriting analysis system was developed and promoted by Albert S. Osborne in the early 1900s and it has remained virtually unchanged since.[6] After the *Hauptmann* case, it appears to have been almost unanimously accepted as reliable and admissible.[7] As with several other such routinely accepted types of forensic scientific evidence, *Daubert* has led scientists and the courts to reexamine questions of the reliability and admissibility of handwriting comparison expert testimony.

Questioned Document Principles and Procedures

Handwriting analysis involves the comparison of a questioned item with an item of known origin. Certain requirements must be met before a handwriting comparison can be made.[8] The writing must be of the same type (e.g., handwritten or hand printed) and the text must be of a comparable sort (e.g., similar letter and word combinations). Special situations involve forgery, which is an attempt to imitate another's writing, and disguise, which is an attempt to change writing style to prevent identification. The bases for comparison are the features or attributes that are common to both samples. The characteristics of the writings are also identified as class characteristics (the style that the writer was taught), individual characteristics (the writer's personal style), and other gross or subtle characteristics. The attributes used for comparison of handwriting are twenty one so-called discriminating elements.[9] The comparison is based on the principal that, although individuals have variations within their own writing, no two persons write the same way. The analysis compares variability among writers and variability within a single person's writing, as shown in the samples. Determining that two samples were written by the same person means concluding that the degree of variability is more consistent with individual writing variations than with variations between two different persons.

Beyond these basic principles there is no dispute and no claim that there is an identified or accepted system for analyzing handwriting, and that the analysis and conclusions are subjective evaluations made by handwriting examiners.[10] The emphasis, therefore, has been on training and testing persons to be considered handwriting experts. The American Society for Testing and Materials (ASTM) has developed a number of standards.[11] The American Board of Forensic Document Examiners is a trade organization that provides for certification.[12] Although that organization requires an undergraduate degree in some field, there is no formal educational or training requirement otherwise, and most handwriting analysts are trained in forensic laboratories.

D. Michael Risinger summed up the contentions of the handwriting analysts as follows:

> Handwriting identification experts believe they can examine a specimen of adult handwriting and determine whether the

author of that specimen is the same person as or a different person than the author of any other example of handwriting, as long as both specimens are of sufficient quality and not separated by years or the intervention of degenerative disease. They further believe that they can accomplish this result with great accuracy, and that they can do it much better than an average literate person attempting the same task. They believe they can obtain these accurate findings as the result of applying an analytical methodology to the examination of handwriting, according to certain principles which are reflected in the questioned documents literature. They believe that this literature explains how to examine handwriting for identifying characteristics, and that by applying the lessons taught by this literature in connection with their experiences in various training exercises and in real world problems, they learn to identify handwriting dependably.[13]

Risinger and others disagree and express significant scientific concerns with handwriting analysis testimony.

Scientific Concerns with Handwriting Analysis Testimony

The basic principles of handwriting analysis are generally accepted as plausible scientific hypotheses. However, scientists point out that this plausibility is based on intuition rather than scientifically established evidence. They point out that these conclusions are accepted as axiomatic by handwriting examiners when they have never been thoroughly tested using scientific methods.[14] Determining whether each person's handwriting is truly unique would necessitate a study of a large number of randomly chosen persons and the categorization and measurement of the multitude of possible variations.[15] There are no standardized measurements and there is not even a public record of handwriting samples which can be scientifically used to develop such measurements or to test the basic underlying theories of handwriting analysis.[16] No formal empirical testing has been completed.[17] The scant studies which have been undertaken do not provide statistical support for uniqueness.[18]

Criticism of the claimed expertise of handwriting examiners is more intense and has been the subject of heated debate among scholars and scientists. In 1989, D. Michael Risinger and two other law professors published the results of their literature search which asserted that there was no reliable study that established that document examiners can accurately identify or exclude authorship by handwriting comparison.[19] The conclusion was hotly disputed by handwriting examiner organizations, but no contrary study was found.[20]

The Forensic Sciences Foundation designed and administered handwriting examiner proficiency tests for government crime laboratories. The original tests were criticized as non-scientific because they were administered only to a select group of volunteer laboratories and did not use original documents.[21] The 1975 tests resulted in 89% of the laboratories correctly identifying the writer of a specimen letter.[22] The proficiency tests were again undertaken in 1984 and 74% of the responding 23 volunteer laboratories reached the correct result.[23] Tests in 1985, 1986 and 1987 revealed correct identification in only 41%, 13%, and 52%, respectively, of the responses.[24] The examiner organization disputes the interpretation of these results.[25] Two subsequent Forensic Sciences Foundation tests were administered in 1987 and 1989. Risinger interpreted the unpublished 1987 test results as showing that 94% to 97% of the "easy" identifications were correctly made by the respondents, while only 41% of the "harder" identifications were correctly made.[26] Risinger interpreted the unpublished 1989 results as showing that 41% of respondents made false positive identifications.[27]

In 1994, the FBI sponsored handwriting examiner proficiency studies, which were conducted by Professor Moshe Kam and his colleagues. The first study was designed to test whether a small group of FBI document examiners could more correctly identify handwriting authors than a group of college students with no handwriting training. The results showed overwhelmingly good results by the trained examiners "indicating that handwriting identification expertise exists."[28] Subsequently, Kam and his colleagues designed a proficiency test and administered it to professional examiners, trainees, and laypersons. The results were only published in the aggregate but Kam claimed that the results "lay to rest the debate over whether or not the professional document examiners possess writer-identification skills absent in the general population,"[29] However, the study still showed that the professional erroneously declared an identification in 6.5% of the cases.[30] There were significant criticisms of the study[31] and a further study was conducted by Kam and colleagues in 1998 to explain the effect that monetary incentives may have had on the test results.[32] One final Kam study was undertaken which most closely approximated a typical identification task and compared results between professional examiners and laypersons. The reported results indicated that trained examiners performed significantly better in identifying the genuiness of signatures than laypersons and that the error rates exhibited by the professionals were much smaller than those of the laypersons.[33]

A study examining proficiency in determining the genuiness of signatures was conducted in 2002 and found that professional examiners were wrong in 3.4% of the cases.[34] Perhaps the most significant scientific advancement in handwriting analysis legitimacy comes from a recent study funded by the Department of Justice. Professor Sargar Srihari and his colleagues collected handwriting samples from 1568 persons and analyzed them using computer algorithms to extract common features.[35] They concluded that the computer was able to distinguish writers with a high degree of confidence.[36] This scientific method may lead to a much more definitive scientific basis for the expertise claimed in handwriting analysis.

The NAS report found value in handwriting comparison testimony but recommended further scientific study:

> The scientific basis for handwriting comparisons needs to be strengthened. Recent studies have increased our understanding of the individuality and consistency of handwriting and computer studies and suggest that there may be a scientific basis for handwriting comparison, at least in the absence of intentional obfuscation or forgery. Although there has been only limited research to quantify the reliability and replicability of the practices used by trained document examiners, the committee agrees that there may be some value in handwriting analysis.[37]

Handwriting Analysis under *Daubert*

Daubert started a reevaluation of handwriting testimony which led to even more inquiries after *Kumho*. Some courts are no longer so sure about the admissibility of handwriting analysis evidence. In the pre-*Kumho* case of *United States v. Starzecpyzel*[38] the court held an extensive *Daubert* hearing on the reliability of handwriting comparison evidence. After a detailed analysis, the judge rejected the claim that handwriting analysis has a scientific basis and stated that "Were the Court to apply *Daubert* to the proffered FDE [forensic document examiner] testimony, it would have to be excluded. This conclusion derives from a straightforward analysis of the suggested *Daubert* factors -- testability and known error rate, peer review and publication, and general acceptance."[39]   However, the judge went on to hold that "while scientific principles may relate to aspects of handwriting analysis, they have little or nothing to do with the day-to-day tasks performed by FDEs" and that because it is not a "science," handwriting expert testimony is not subject to the *Daubert* requirements.[40] He allowed the handwriting expert to testify as a technical or experience based expert.[41]

After *Kumho*, in *United States v. Fujii*, an American court excluded handwriting analysis testimony for the first time since the Lindbergh case,[42] and it was followed in *United States v. Saelee*.[43] While other courts have begun to express some reservations, they have not excluded handwriting analysis testimony altogether. Even when the testimony about handwriting comparison is far from conclusive, some courts have allowed it as being helpful to the jury.[44] Notwithstanding the doubts about the scientific basis for handwriting comparison testimony, courts have still found it admissible for the most part. In 2003, the Fourth Circuit expressly ruled that handwriting comparison testimony was admissible under *Daubert* in *United States v. Crisp*.[45] The Court there held that "The fact that handwriting comparison analysis has achieved widespread and lasting acceptance in the expert community gives us the assurance of reliability that *Daubert* requires. Furthermore, as with expert testimony on fingerprints, the role of the handwriting expert is primarily to draw the jury's attention to similarities between a known exemplar and a contested sample."[46] The Court seemed to almost abdicate the "gatekeeper" role for trial judges when it concluded that "To the extent that a given handwriting analysis is flawed or flimsy, an able defense lawyer will bring that fact to the jury's attention, both through skillful cross-examination and by presenting expert testimony of his own."[47] In *United States v. Mooney*,[48] the 1st Circuit reached a similar result without much explanation. For the most part, courts have continued, on one basis or another, to allow handwriting comparison testimony, although the testimony of particular witnesses has been excluded.[49]

Much like fingerprint testimony, the court system appears reluctant to actually apply a *Daubert* analysis to handwriting evidence which has been a standard tool in the prosecution's evidence arsenal for such a long time. It may well take a highly publicized post conviction DNA exoneration of a person who was convicted based on handwriting examiner testimony to change the trend. In the meantime, however, the good news is that the handwriting examiner community appears to be taking its scientific obligations more seriously and seeking to establish a true scientific basis for the claimed expertise. The principal prospect for such evidence may lie in recent efforts to use computer analysis to compile reliable databases of handwriting samples and quantifiable features and characteristics.

---

[1] National Research Council of the National Academies, *Strengthening Forensic Science in the United States: A Path Forward* (2009), p. 163

[2] Risinger, D. Michael, *Handwriting Identification, in Modern Scientific Evidence: The Law and Science of Expert Testimony*, eds. David L. Faigman, Michael J. Saks, Joseph Sanders, and Edward K. Cheng, (2009-2010 edition) at §§34.1, *et seq* at 453; see also Morris, Ron N., *Forensic Handwriting Identification: Fundamental Concepts And Principles* 129-42 (2000).

[3] Risinger, D. Michael, *Handwriting Identification, in Modern Scientific Evidence: The Law and Science of Expert Testimony*, eds. David L. Faigman, Michael J. Saks, Joseph Sanders, and Edward K. Cheng, (2009-2010 edition) at, §34:12, at 569.

[4] *Id.*.

[5] *State v. Hauptmann*, 180 A. 809, 822 (N.J. 1935).

[6] See Risinger, D. Michael , *Handwriting Identification, in Modern Scientific Evidence: The Law and Science of Expert Testimony*, eds. David L. Faigman, Michael J. Saks, Joseph Sanders, and Edward K. Cheng, (2009-2010 edition) §34:3, at 455-459; Lyssitzyn, Christine Beck, *Forensic Evidence in Court: A Case Study Approach* (2007), at 247.

[7] Moriarty, Jane Campbell & Michael J. Saks, *Forensic Science: Grand Goals, Tragic Flaws, and Judicial Gatekeeping*, Judges' J., Fall 2005, p. 16, 21 (2005); Risinger, D. Michael , *Handwriting Identification, in Modern*

Scientific Evidence: The Law and Science of Expert Testimony, eds. David L. Faigman, Michael J. Saks, Joseph Sanders, and Edward K. Cheng, (2009-2010 edition) §34:3, at at 455-459; Risinger, D. Michael, Mark P. Denbeaux & Michael J. Saks, *Exorcism of Ignorance as a Proxy for Rational Knowledge: The Lessons of Handwriting Identification "Expertise"*, 137 U. Pa. L. Rev. 731 (1989).

[8] National Research Council of the National Academies, *Strengthening Forensic Science in the United States: A Path Forward* (2009), pp. 165-166.

[9] Huber, Roy A. and A. M. Headrick, *Handwriting Identification: Facts and Fundamentals* (1999).

[10] See Risinger, D. Michael, *Handwriting Identification, in Modern Scientific Evidence: The Law and Science of Expert Testimony*, eds. David L. Faigman, Michael J. Saks, Joseph Sanders, and Edward K. Cheng, (2009-2010 edition) §34:3, at 455-459; Lyssitzyn, Christine Beck, *Forensic Evidence in Court: A Case Study Approach* (2007), at 249.

[11] See, e.g., *Standard Descriptions of Scope of Work Relating to Forensic Document Examiners*, ASTM E444-09 (2009); *Standard Terminology for Expressing Conclusions of Forensic Document Examiners*, ASTM E1658 - 08 (2008); *Standard Guide for Minimum Training Requirements for Forensic Document Examiners*, ASTM E2388 - 05 (2005).

[12] American Board of Forensic Examiners, online at http://www.abfde.org/Index.html (last visited December 14, 2011).

[13] Risinger, D. Michael, *Handwriting Identification, in Modern Scientific Evidence: The Law and Science of Expert Testimony*, eds. David L. Faigman, Michael J. Saks, Joseph Sanders, and Edward K. Cheng, (2009-2010 edition) §34.10 at 563-564, citing Albert S. Osborne, *Questioned Documents* 6 (2d ed. 1929); and Ellen, David, *The Scientific Examination of Documents: Methods and Techniques* 9 (1989).

[14] *Id.*, at 568-569.

[15] Lyssitzyn, Christine Beck, *Forensic Evidence in Court: A Case Study Approach* (2007), at 251.

[16] Saks, Michael J. and Holly VanderHaar, *On the "General Acceptance" of Handwriting Identification Principles,* 50 J. Forensic. Sci. 119 (2005).

[17] Risinger, D. Michael , *Handwriting Identification, in Modern Scientific Evidence: The Law and Science of Expert Testimony*, eds. David L. Faigman, Michael J. Saks, Joseph Sanders, and Edward K. Cheng, (2009-2010 edition) §34.14 at 579.

[18] R. J. Muehlberger, et al, *A Statistical Examination of Selected Handwriting Characteristics*, 22 J. For. Sci. 206 (1977); Srihari, Sargur N., Sung-Hyuk Cha, Hina Arora, Sangjik Lee, *Individuality of Handwriting: A Validation Study*, Sixth International Conference on Document Analysis and Recognition, ICDAR'01, (2001), available online at http://www.cedar.buffalo.edu/papers/articles/Individuality_Handwriting_200 1.pdf (last visited December 14, 2011).

[19] Risinger, D. Michael , Mark P. Denbeaux, and Michael J. Saks, *Exorcism of Ignorance as a Proxy for Rational Knowledge: The Lessons of Handwriting Identification "Expertise"*, 137 U. Pa. L. Rev. 731 (1989).

[20] Galbraith, Oliver, Craig Galbraith, and Nanette Galbraith, *The "Principle of the Drunkard's Search" as a Proxy for Scientific Analysis: The Misuse of Handwriting Test Data in a Law Journal Article*, 1 Int'l J. Forensic Document Examiners 7 (1995). For a full discussion of the ensuing debate, see Risinger, D. Michael , *Handwriting Identification, in Modern Scientific Evidence: The Law and Science of Expert Testimony*, eds. David L. Faigman, Michael J. Saks, Joseph Sanders, and Edward K. Cheng, (2009-2010 edition) §34.14, at 581-643.

[21] Risinger, D. Michael, *Handwriting Identification, in Modern Scientific Evidence: The Law and Science of Expert Testimony*, eds. David L. Faigman, Michael J. Saks, Joseph Sanders, and Edward K. Cheng, (2009-2010 edition) §34.14 *et seq.*

[22] *Id.*

[23] *Id.*

[24] *Id.*

[25] Galbraith, Oliver, Craig Galbraith, and Nanette Galbraith, *The "Principle of the Drunkard's Search" as a Proxy for Scientific Analysis: The Misuse of Handwriting Test Data in a Law Journal Article*, 1 Int'l J. Forensic Document Examiners 7 (1995).

[26] Risinger, D. Michael , *Handwriting Identification, in Modern Scientific Evidence: The Law and Science of Expert Testimony*, eds. David L. Faigman, Michael J. Saks, Joseph Sanders, and Edward K. Cheng, (2009-2010 edition) §34.14 *et seq.*

[27] *Id.*

[28] Kam, Moshe J., Wetstein, and R. Conn, *Proficiency of Professional Document Examiners in Writer Identification*, 39 J. For. Sci. 5 (1994),

abstract available online at http://www.ncjrs.gov/App/Publications/
abstract.aspx?ID=146638 (last visited December 14, 2011).

[29] Kam, Moshe, G. Fielding and Robert Conn, *Writer Examination by
Professional Document Examiners*, 42 J. For. Sci. 778 (1997).

[30] *Id.*

[31] The criticisms included the use of monetary incentives for the layperson
subjects, aggregation of results, and other concerns. See Risinger, D.
Michael , *Handwriting Identification, in Modern Scientific Evidence: The
Law and Science of Expert Testimony*, eds. David L. Faigman, Michael J.
Saks, Joseph Sanders, and Edward K. Cheng, (2009-2010 edition) §34.29.

[32] Kam, Moshe, Gabriel Fielding and Robert Conn, *Effects of Monetary
Incentives on Performance in Document Examination Proficiency Tests*, 43
J. For. Sci. 1000 (1997).

[33] Kam, Moshe, K. Gummadidala, G. Fielding, and R. Conn, *Signature
Authentication by Forensic Document Examiners*, 46 J. For. Sci. 884 (2001).

[34] Sita, J,, B. Found and D. Rogers, *Forensic Handwriting Examiners'
Expertise for Signature Comparison*, 47 J. Forensic Sci. 1117 (2002).

[35] Srihari, Sargur N., Sung-Hyuk Cha, Hina Arora & Sangjik Lee, *Individuality
of Handwriting*, 47 J. Forensic Sci. 856, 871 (2002).

[36] *Id.*

[37] National Research Council of the National Academies, *Strengthening
Forensic Science in the United States: A Path Forward* (2009), pp. 166-167.

[38] *United States v. Starzecpyzel*, 880 F. Supp. 1027, 42 Fed. R. Evid. Serv. 247
(S.D. N.Y. 1995).

[39] *Id.*

[40] *Id.*

[41] *Id.* The distinction was later rejected in *Kumho*.

[42] *United States v. Fujii*, 152 F. Supp.2d 939, *942* (N.D. Ill. 2000). The Court
held that "[c]onsidering the questions about handwriting analysis generally
under *Daubert*, the lack of any evidence that the identification of
handprinting is an expertise that meets the *Daubert* standards and the
questions that have been raised, which the government has not attempted to
answer, about its expert's ability to opine reliably on handprinting
identification in dealing with native Japanese writers taught English printing
in Japan, the court grants the defendant's motion."

[43] *United States v. Saelee*, 162 F. Supp.2d 1097 (D. Alaska 2001). In a broader
decision than *Fujii*, the *Saelee* Court found that the government could not

establish that handwriting identification was "the product of reliable methods".

[44] *United States v. Hines*, 55 F. Supp.2d 62, 67-68 (D. Mass. 1999) (holding that expert testimony about general similarities and differences between the evidentiary sample and defendant's exemplar was admissible but that the expert could not testify to the conclusion that the defendant was the author because it lacked empirical validation); *People v. Todmann*, 2010 WL 684009 (V.I. 2010) (upholding a trial judge's exclusion of handwriting testimony that the defendant "may have" signed the document because it was "far too speculative to be of any assistance to the jury, and will most likely mislead the jurors"). Cf. *Miller v. State*, ___A.3d ___, 2011 WL 4363938 (Md. 2011) (allowing ambiguous testimony that a comparison of handwriting samples showed characteristics "which prevents [defendant's] elimination as a suspect in this case").

[45] *United States v. Crisp*, 324 F.3d 261 (4th Cir. 2003).

[46] *Id.*

[47] *Id.*

[48] *United States v. Mooney*, 315 F.3d 54, 60 Fed. Evid. Serv. 60 (1st Cir. 2002).

[49] See, e.g., *United States v. Brooks*, 81 Fed. R. Evid. Serv. 381 (E.D. N.Y. 2010). For an extremely detailed description of post-*Daubert* cases dealing with handwriting comparison, see Risinger, D. Michael , *Handwriting Identification*, in *Modern Scientific Evidence: The Law and Science of Expert Testimony*, eds. David L. Faigman, Michael J. Saks, Joseph Sanders, and Edward K. Cheng, (2009-2010 edition) at §§34.4 -34.9.

Chapter 9
Hair Analysis

Hair analysis can be a forensic tool because human hairs are routinely shed and can be discovered at a crime scene. Examination of hair found at the scene and compared with hair from a known source may be helpful to the extent that it reflects similarities. The extent of the similarity in those samples and the examiner's ability to discover and compare those similarities is the principal issue when hair analysis is offered in a criminal case. Microscopic hair examination and analysis has been undertaken for over a century but has limited capability to identify individuals. Recent developments in DNA testing have greatly expanded the ability of hair sample examination to make individual identifications.

Microscopic Hair Analysis

Traditionally, forensic evidence comparing human hair was based on a microscopic comparison of the evidentiary sample with a known sample from the defendant.[1] To make a microscopic hair comparison, a control group of hairs from a known source must be properly collected by pulling or combing hairs from a subject.[2] That requires a total of fifty hairs from different areas of the scalp or a total of twenty-five hairs from a pubic region.[3] The samples are then examined macroscopically for gross feature comparison, such as color, form and thickness. In the microscopic stage, hairs are mounted on slides using a mounting medium that has the same refractive index as the hair. The hair analyst then attempts to identify the part of the body from which the hair might have come, based on certain area characteristics.

Features of the hair are divided into "major and secondary characteristics." Major characteristics include color, treatment, pigment aggregation, shaft form, pigment distribution, medulla appearance, hair diameter, medullary index, and the presence or absence of a root or shaft. Secondary characteristics include cuticular margin, pigment density, pigment size, tip shape, and shaft diameter.[4] The examiner then formulates an opinion as to exclusion or consistency.

Although used by investigative agencies, including the FBI,[5] it is uniformly recognized that microscopic hair comparisons do not constitute a basis for an absolute identification.[6] It can be useful, however, as exclusionary evidence, but for identification the most that it can show is a "class" identification, that a hair is consistent with having originated from a particular person but would also be consistent with many others.[7] Prosecutorial and expert claims of a "match" based on hair analysis are gross overstatements of the capabilities of microscopic hair analysis.[8] It is clear that substantial errors have occurred using microscopic hair analysis.[9] In one recent case, a man served sixteen years in prison after he was convicted of rape based in part on the testimony of a police forensic analyst that "she believed each person's hair was unique and that she could identify the unique characteristics" of the hair, and that hairs found near the victim matched the defendant's hair. The defendant was eventually exonerated by post conviction DNA testing.[10] In a subsequent portion of a civil action, the 10th circuit characterized her testimony as "bogus."[11] In another case, a defendant was sentenced to serve over 3,000 years in prison after his conviction for rape, sodomy, and other charges based in part on an analyst testimony that he compared hairs from the crime scene with the defendant's hair and found similar characteristics that he had seen in "less than 5 percent" of hair samples he had examined. The defendant was exonerated by DNA testing after serving over three years of his sentence.[12]

Nevertheless, courts have even recently allowed hair analysis testimony as generally accepted evidence.[13] Many other courts have begun to exclude such testimony, at least when the analyst attempts to suggest that there is an individual identification by comparison.[14] The NAS Report assessed the state of microscopic hair analysis:

> No scientifically accepted statistics exist about the frequency with which particular characteristics of hair are distributed in

the population. There appear to be no uniform standards on the number of features on which hairs must agree before an examiner may declare a "match."

. . .

The committee found no scientific support for the use of hair comparisons for individualization in the absence of nuclear DNA.[15]

DNA Analysis of Hair Samples

The advent of DNA, and particularly the mtDNA method, has changed the field of forensic hair analysis completely. If the evidence sample has a root, typical and much more definitive nuclear DNA can, of course, be used.[16] The mtDNA method, on the other hand, is not nearly as discriminating as the usual nuclear DNA, since it is based on mitochondria in human cells, which are shared by maternal relatives.[17] Thus siblings will be indistinguishable based on mtDNA comparison.[18] In spite of that limitation, the value of mtDNA comparison lies in the fact that mitochondria are found outside the nuclei of human cells and exist in shafts of hair that have no roots attached.[19] Where there is no root, as is often the case, mtDNA is very effectively used to supplant, or at least support, a microscopic hair analysis.[20] With the limitations on the accuracy of microscopic comparisons, mtDNA analysis can give the court a much more substantial basis for admitting hair analysis as a significant part of a prosecution.[21]

In *State v. Pappas,* the Supreme Court of Connecticut conducted an exhaustive review of the status of mtDNA sequencing for hair analysis comparison.[22] In language that would satisfy either *Frye* or *Daubert,* the court concluded that "the procedures used to extract and chart the chemical bases of mtDNA—extraction, PCR amplification, capillary electrophoresis, and the use of an automated sequencing machine to generate a chromatograph—are scientifically valid and generally accepted in the scientific community."[23]

The use of mtDNA sequencing evidence, for hair and other sample analysis, is becoming widespread and has been accepted by many courts.[24] The trend is clearly that mtDNA evidence has become the standard for hair analysis testimony and that microscopic analysis alone may no longer be sufficiently reliable for admission, regardless of the qualifiers placed on the testimony by the analyst.

---

[1] See *Modern Scientific Evidence: The Law and Science of Expert Testimony*, eds. David L. Faigman, Michael J. Saks, Joseph Sanders, and Edward K. Cheng, (2009-2010 edition) §30.46.

[2] Scientific Working Group on Materials Analysis (SWGMAT), *Forensic Human Hair Examination Guidelines*, 7(2) Forensic. Sci. Comm. (April 2005), available online at www.fbi.gov/hq/lab/fsc/backissu/april2005/standards/2005_04_standards02. htm (last visited December 14, 2011).

[3] *Id.*

[4] *Id.*

[5] See, e.g., Deedrick, Douglas W. & Sandra L. Koch, *Microscopy of Hair Part 1: A Practical Guide and Manual for Human Hairs*, Forensic Sci. Comm, (Jan. 2004), available online at http://www.fbi.gov/hq/lab/fsc/backissu/jan2004/research/2004_01_research01b .htm (last visited December 14, 2011).

[6] *Id.*

[7] See Moenssens, Andre A., Carol E. Henderson & Sharon G. Portwood, *Scientific Evidence In Civil And Criminal Cases* § 11.13, at 732-34 (5th ed. 2007); National Research Council of the National Academies, *Strengthening Forensic Science in the United States: A Path Forward* (2009), pp. 155-161; Richard E. Bisbing, *The Forensic Identification and Association of Human Hair, in 1 Forensic Science Handbook* 420-21 (Richard Saferstein ed., 2d ed. 2002).

[8] See, e.g., *People v. Moore*, 662 N.E.2d 1215 (Ill. 1996); *People v. Linscott*, 566 N.E.2d 1355 (Ill. 1991).

[9] At least one court has found that *Daubert* required the exclusion of microscopic hair analysis evidence and overturned a conviction based on it. *Williamson v. Reynolds*, 904 F. Supp 1529 (E.D. Okla. 1995), *aff'd sub nom. Williamson v. Ward*, 110 F.3d 1508 (10th Cir. 1997); see Moriarty, Jane Campbell and Michael J. Saks, *Forensic Science: Grand Goals, Tragic Flaws, and Judicial Gatekeeping*, Judges' J., Fall 2005, p. 16 (2005) at 21, ("Of the first seventy-one convictions that were reversed on the basis of DNA testing, twenty-one involved erroneous microscopic identification of hair samples."). See generally Smith, Clive A. Stafford and Patrick D.

Goodman, *Forensic Hair Comparison Analysis: Nineteenth Century Science or Twentieth Century Snake Oil?*, 27 Colum. Hum. Rts. L. Rev. 227 (1996) (questioning the scientific foundation of microscopic hair analysis).

[10] The Innocence Project, *David Johns Bryson*, online at http://www.innocenceproject.org/Content/1701.php (last visited December 14, 2011).

[11] *Bryson v. Gonzales*, 534 F.3d 1282 (10th Cir. 2008).

[12] The Innocence Project, *Timothy Durham*, available online at http://www.innocenceproject.org/Content/90.php (last visited December 14, 2011).

[13] See *State v. West*, 877 A.2d 787 (Conn. 2005); *Bookins v. State*, 922 A.2d 389 (Del. Supr. 2007).

[14] See Gianelli, Paul C. and E. West, *Hair Comparison Evidence*, 37 Crim. L. Bull. 514 (2001).

[15] National Research Council of the National Academies, *Strengthening Forensic Science in the United States: A Path Forward* (2009), at pp. 160-161.

[16] State v. Council, 515 S.E.2d 508, 516 n.12 (S.C. 1999) (citing Brian Huseman, Note, *Taylor v. State, Rule 706, and the DNA Database: Future Directions in DNA Evidence*, 22 Okla. City U. L. Rev. 397 (1997)).

[17] Cheng, Edward K., *Mitochondrial DNA: Emerging Legal Issues*, 13 J. L. & Pol'y 99 (2005).

[18] *Id*., at 106.

[19] *Id*,. at 100.

[20] For descriptions of the mtDNA process as applied to hair analysis, see *State v. Pappas*, 776 A.2d 1091 (Conn. 2001). See also Bieber, Frederick R., *Science and Technology of Forensic DNA Profiling: Current Use and Future Directions*, in *DNA And The Criminal Justice System, supra* note 30, at 32-33; Kiely, Terrence F., *Forensic Evidence: Science And Criminal Law* 79-81, 106-19 (2d ed. 2006); Cheng, Edward K., *Mitochondrial DNA: Emerging Legal Issues*, 13 J. L. & Pol'y 99 (2005), at 107-116; Walker, Marlan D., Note, *Mitochondrial DNA Evidence in State v. Pappas*, 43 Jurimetrics J. 427 (2003) (describing the case of *State v. Pappas*, which admitted mitochondrial DNA identification evidence, and its consequences).

[21] One study found that nearly twelve percent of declared microscopic hair identifications were found to be erroneous after mtDNA testing. Max M.

Houck and Bruce Budowle, *Correlation of Microscopic and Mitochondrial DNA Hair Comparison*, 47 J. Forensic Sci. 964, 966 (2002).

[22] *State v. Pappas*, 776 A.2d at 1100-1113 (Conn. 2001).

[23] *Id.*, at 1108.

[24] *Id.*; see also *United States v. Beverly*, 369 F.3d 516 (6th Cir. 2004); *United States v. Coleman*, 202 F. Supp. 2d 962 (E.D. Mo. 2002); *Wagner v. State*, 864 A.2d 1037 (Md. Ct. Spec. App. 2005); *State v. Underwood*, 518 S.E.2d 231 (N.C. Ct. App. 1999); *State v. Council*, 515 S.E.2d at 516-17.

Chapter 10

Bite Mark Analysis

Bite mark testimony seeks to identify a perpetrator by comparing a cast or image of teeth from a bite mark left on a victim or at a crime scene with a sample of the defendant's teeth. A forensic odontologist offers testimony in which the bite marks are analyzed and compared. The basic premise underlying bite mark forensic evidence is that human dentition is unique and that, when compared within a reasonable time, an expert opinion identifying the person who made both impressions can be made.[1]

Obtaining and Analyzing Odontology Evidence

The American Board of Forensic Odontology has established methods to be used in obtaining and preserving bite mark evidence.[2] Bite marks on human skin can be recorded with a number of accepted techniques, including various forms of photography. Casting three dimension impressions of bite marks is also suggested when feasible. Since the bite marks are a potentially valuable source of suspect DNA, a bite mark is usually swabbed for later DNA analysis as well. The dentition from a suspect to be compared is obtained through dental records, x-rays, or actual physical examination if possible. At least two casts are made and, if possible, a suspect's bite mark into a comparable substance is obtained and casted. Odontologists will make exemplars of the suspect's teeth by anything from a hand-traced outline to xerographic copying to computer imaging.

While there is little dispute about the validity of these techniques, there are significant problems associated with the deterioration of bite marks with the passage of time or contamination from other sources or deformation through the natural healing process. Additionally, problems can arise with the normal changes in a suspect's dentition as well. The eventual comparison is made visually, microscopically, and, in some cases, with digital photography.

The Scientific Validity of Bitemark Testimony

The basic concept of dental uniqueness has been accepted by many courts.[3] Indeed, bite mark evidence in general has received widespread acceptance. In *State v. Timmendequas*,[4] when admitting bite mark evidence, the Supreme Court of New Jersey stated that "[j]udicial opinions from other jurisdictions establish that bite-mark analysis has gained general acceptance and therefore is reliable. . . . Over thirty states considering such evidence have found it admissible and no state has rejected bite-mark evidence as unreliable."[5] Nevertheless, significant questions remain about the scientific validity of bite mark comparison testimony and its continued admissibility under *Daubert* scrutiny.[6]

First, despite its acceptance in various cases, there is significant disagreement among odontologists and other scientists about the basic premise of dental uniqueness. The American Society of Forensic Odontology asserts that the uniqueness premise has been established by at least two studies.[7] And odontologists are convinced that human dentition is unique to each living person.[8] However, The NAS Report states that "the uniqueness of the human dentition has not been scientifically established."[9] That claim is supported by the studies of several other scholars.[10] If human dentition is not unique, there may be very little proper use for bite mark testimony in criminal proceedings.

Beyond the basic question of uniqueness, a number of factors in a particular case may affect the accuracy of bite mark identification.[11] These include such things as the "freshness" of the bite mark impression and its changes over time, temperature or contamination effects at the crime scene, damage to soft tissue around the bite mark, and dental similarities among individuals.[12] A primary concern is often that the impression includes only a limited number of teeth.[13] When experts rely, as they often do, on photographic images of bite marks made at the scene or during an autopsy, the quality of the photography and the enhancement techniques used for comparison can clearly affect the reliability of the odontologist's conclusions.[14] Guidelines have been suggested by the American Board of Forensic Odontology that specifically address many of these factors.[15]

Perhaps the biggest technical evidentiary issues relating to these factors are questions of whether a reliable pattern of bite marks is transferred to human skin when a bite occurs and, if so, whether the skin can retain that pattern for any period of time without undergoing a distortion caused by the biological reaction of the skin to being punctured. The NAS Report was specific and very critical in its findings on these points:

> The ability of the dentition, if unique, to transfer a unique pattern to human skin and the ability of the skin to maintain that uniqueness has not been scientifically established.
> i. The ability to analyze and interpret the scope or extent of distortion of bite mark patterns on human skin has not been demonstrated.
> ii. The effect of distortion on different comparison techniques is not fully understood and therefore has not been quantified.[16]

As to the first point, "[c]entral to bitemark analysis are the characteristics of the skin receiving the mark, because in cases of physical assault having skin injuries, the anatomy and physiology of the skin, and the position of the victim, affect the detail and shape of the bitemark."[17] There is one recent study which attempted to measure the accuracy of human skin as a "substrate," or recording recipient, of bitemarks by using the same dentition to make bites on cadavers. The authors found that no two bites were measurably identical and that there was distortion between the bites of as much as 80%.[18] In a subsequent study of the cadavers, several selected dentition models were used and the investigators found that up to 86% of the models could not be excluded by examination and that, indeed, some of the non-biter dentitions appear to "fit" better than the actual biter's dentition.[19] The odontologists concluded that "this study suggests that an open population postmortem bitemark should be carefully and cautiously evaluated."[20] That assessment has been called "understated."[21]

As to the issue of distortion, from bruising, healing, or other biological skin reactions to injury, the scientific research indicates that there is a significant degree of distortion that takes place in a bite mark impression on the skin with any passage of time.[22] The longer the time interval, the greater the distortion, and it appears that even preservation of the skin does not necessarily lessen the distortion.[23]

In spite of its general admissibility, expert testimony has varied to such a degree that some courts have excluded the testimony altogether. The conclusions that an expert can draw from the evaluation are necessarily limited by the number and quality of corresponding points in the evidentiary sample. Testifying odontologist experts have expressed opinions ranging from stating that the bite mark was "consistent" with the defendant's teeth, to stating that the defendant's teeth "probably" made the bite mark, to conclusively claiming that there was a "match" that was a positive identification of the defendant.[24]

The error rate for odontologist experts appears to be high. An interpretation of results of the latest study by the American Board of Forensic Odontology indicated an error rate of 12.5% out of a possible 27%, meaning that participating odontologists were almost half as wrong as they could be in that study.[25] Of particular concern in criminal cases, the bulk of that error rate was from false positives.[26]

As with all scientific testimony, the qualifications and bias of a particular proffered expert is always an issue. In *Ege v. Yukins*,[27] for example, the District Court for the Eastern District of Michigan found constitutional error in a state court case in which testimony about bite marks was a critical factor in the conviction.[28] The court found that testimony of the government's bite mark expert comparing a photograph of a disputed bite mark on the victim's cheek with a mold of the defendant's teeth made some nine years prior was unreliable, grossly misleading, and "so extremely unfair that its admission violates fundamental concepts of justice."[29] Specifically, the court used the expert's testimony that out of the 3.5 million people residing in the Detroit metropolitan area, the defendant was the only one whose dentition could match the individual who left the possible bite mark on the victim's cheek "was unreliable and not worthy of consideration by a jury."[30] The court specifically noted that "[t]he opinion apparently was based on the mathematical product theory, a proposition that long has been condemned." Other bite mark experts have also been the subject of blistering reviews by the courts.[31]

As in other types of long accepted forensic scientific evidence, postconviction DNA exonerations have called the validity of bite mark evidence into question. In a case that received a great deal of publicity, bite mark evidence from two experts convicted a defendant of capital murder. The defendant was later exonerated by DNA while on death row.[32] Publicity surrounding other murder case DNA exonerations based on bite mark evidence has led to serious public and professional doubts about its validity.[33] The extent to which bite mark evidence will survive *Daubert* scrutiny, especially in light of both these significant and public reversals and the lack of empirical studies on the subject, remains to be seen.

---

[1] For general information about bite mark comparisons, see *Bitemark Evidence* (Robert B.J. Dorion ed., 2004); *Identification from Bitemarks* §§ 37.1 *et seq*, in *Modern Scientific Evidence: The Law and Science of Expert Testimony*, eds. David L. Faigman, Michael J. Saks, Joseph Sanders, and Edward K. Cheng, (2009-2010 edition).

[2] American Board of Forensic Odontology, Inc., *Diplomates Reference Manual* (June 28, 2009), available online at http://www.abfo.org/pdfs/ABFO%20Manual%20-%20revised%2010-28-09-B.pdf (last visited December 14, 2011).

[3] *See, e.g., People v. Milone*, 356 N.E.2d 1350, 1355 (Ill. App. Ct. 1976); *People v. Smith*, 443 N.Y.S.2d 551, 556-57 (Sup. Ct. 1981).

[4] *State v. Timmendequas*, 737 A.2d 55 (N.J. 1999).

[5] *Id.* at 114 (citations omitted).

[6] See Deitch, Adam, *An Inconvenient Tooth: Forensic Odontology is an Inadmissible Junk Science When it is Used to "Match" Teeth to Bitemarks in Skin*, 2009 Wis. L. Rev. 1205 (2009); Kieser, Jules A., *Weighing Bitemark Evidence: A Postmodern Perspective*, 1 J. Forensic Sci. 75 (2005); Kittelson, J. M., J. A. Kieser, D. M. Buckingham, and G. P. Herbison , *Weighing Evidence: Quantitative Measures of the Importance of Bitemark Evidence*, 20 J. Forensic Odonto-Stomatology 31 (2002).

[7] Sweet, David J. , *Human Bitemarks: Examination, Recovery, and Analysis*, in *Manual Of Forensic Odontology* 148 (C. Michael Bowers & Gary L. Bell eds., 3d rev. ed. 1997); Rawson, R. D., R. K. Ommen, and G. J. Kinard, *Statistical Evidence for the Individuality of the Human Dentition*, 29 J. Forensic Sci. 245 (1984), Sognnaes, Reider F., R. D. Rawson, B. M. Gratt, and N. B. Nguyen, *Computer Comparison of Bitemark Patterns in Identical Twins*, 105 J. Am. Dent. Assoc. 449 (1982).

[8] Pretty, Iain,*A Web-Based Survey of Odontologist's Opinions Concerning Bitemark Analysis*, 48 J. Forensic Sci. 117 (2003); Bowers, C. Michael, *Identification From Bitemarks: Scientific Issues*, in *Modern Scientific Evidence: The Law and Science of Expert Testimony*, (eds. David L. Faigman, Michael J. Saks, Joseph Sanders, and Edward K. Cheng), 2009-2010 edition) at §37.8, *et seq*.

[9] Nat 'L Research Council Of The Nat'l Acads., *Strengthening Forensic Science in the United States: A Path Forward* (2009), at 175.

[10] See Bowers, C. Michael, *Problem-Based Analysis in Bite Mark Misidentifications: The Role of DNA*, 159 Forensic Sci. Int'l. (Supp. 1) 104 (May, 2006); Wilkinson, Allen P. and Ronald M. Gerughty, *Bite Mark Evidence: Its Admissibility Is Hard to Swallow*, 12 W. St. U. L. Rev. 519 (1985); Pretty, Iain and M. D. Turnbull, *Lack of Dental Uniqueness Between Two Bite Mark Suspects*, 46 J. Forensic Sci. 1487 (2001); Giannelli, Paul C., *Bite Mark Analysis*, 43 Crim. L. Bull. 930 (2007); Moriarty, Jane Campbell and Michael J. Saks, *Forensic Science: Grand Goals, Tragic Flaws, and Judicial Gatekeeping*, Judges' J., Fall 2005, p. 16 (2005), at 21.

[11] Bowers, C. Michael , *Identification From Bitemarks: Scientific Issues*, in *Modern Scientific Evidence: The Law and Science of Expert Testimony*, eds. David L. Faigman, Michael J. Saks, Joseph Sanders, and Edward K. Cheng, (2009-2010 edition) at §37:12; Rothwell, Bruce M. , *Bitemarks in Forensic Dentistry: A Review of Legal, Scientific Issues*, 126 J Am. Dent. Assoc. 223 (1995).

[12] See Wilkinson, Allen P. and Ronald M. Gerughty, *Bite Mark Evidence: Its Admissibility Is Hard to Swallow*, 12 W. St. U. L. Rev. 519 (1985), at 535-37, 550-52.

[13] See Giannelli, Paul C., *Bite Mark Analysis*, 43 Crim. L. Bull. 930 (2007), at 932.

[14] See Wilkinson, Allen P. and Ronald M. Gerughty, *Bite Mark Evidence: Its Admissibility Is Hard to Swallow*, 12 W. St. U. L. Rev. 519 (1985), at 557-59.

[15] American Board of Forensic Odontology, *Guidelines For Bite Mark Analysis*, 112 J. Am. Dental Assn. 383, 384-86 (1986); see also McClure, Michelle, *Odontology: Bite Marks as Evidence in Criminal Trials*, 11 Santa Clara Comp. & High Tech. L. J. 269, 273-75 (1995) (summarizing the American Board of Forensic Odontology's guidelines).

[16] Nat 'L Research Council Of The Nat'l Acads., *Strengthening Forensic Science in the United States: A Path Forward* (2009), at 175.

[17] Bowers, C. Michael, *Identification From Bitemarks: Scientific Issues*, in *Modern Scientific Evidence: The Law and Science of Expert Testimony*, eds. David L. Faigman, Michael J. Saks, Joseph Sanders, and Edward K. Cheng, (2009-2010 edition) at §37:18 at p. 45.

[18] Bush, Mary A., et al., *Biomechanical Factors in Human Dermal Bitemarks in a Cadaver Model*, 54 J. Forensic Sci. 167 (2009).

[19] Miller, Raymond G. , et al, *Uniqueness of the Dentition as Impressed in Human Skin: A Cadaver Model*, 54 J. Forensic Sci. 909 (2009).

[20] *Id.*, at 913.

[21] Bowers, C. Michael *Identification From Bitemarks: Scientific Issues*, in *Modern Scientific Evidence: The Law and Science of Expert Testimony*, eds. David L. Faigman, Michael J. Saks, Joseph Sanders, and Edward K. Cheng, (2009-2010 edition) at §37:18 at p. 46.

[22] Dailey, J. C. and C. Michael Bowers, *Aging of Bitemarks: A Literature Review*, 42 J. Forensic Sci. 792 (1997).

[23] Rothwell, Bruce R. and A. V. Thien, *Analysis of Distortion in Preserved Bite Mark Skin*, 46 J. Forensic Sci. 573 (2001).

[24] For a review of various reported cases using these qualifiers, see generally Giannelli, Paul C., *Forensic Science*, 33 J. L. Med. & Ethics 535 (2005).

[25] Bowers, C. Michael, *Identification From Bitemarks: Scientific Issues*, in *Modern Scientific Evidence: The Law and Science of Expert Testimony*, eds. David L. Faigman, Michael J. Saks, Joseph Sanders, and Edward K. Cheng, (2009-2010 edition) at §37:13.

[26] *Id.*

[27] *Ege v. Yukins*, 380 F. Supp.2d 852 (E.D. Mich. 2005).

[28] *Id.* at 880.

[29] *Id.* at 880 (quoting *Dowling v. United States*, 493 U.S. 342, 352 (1990)).

[30] *Id.* at 871.

[31] See *Brooks v. State*, 748 So. 2d 736 (Miss. 1999); *Banks v. State*, 725 So. 2d 711 (Miss. 1997); *Harrison v. State*, 635 So. 2d 894 (Miss. 1994).

[32] See *State v. Krone*, 897 P.2d 621 (Ariz. 1995) (en banc); Hansen, Mark, *The Uncertain Science of Evidence*, A.B.A. J., July 2003, at 49, 49-50; Randerson, James, *Bite-Mark Evidence Can Leave a False Impression*, New Scientist, Mar. 13, 2004, at 6, available online at http://www.newscientist.com/article/dn4758-bitemark-evidence-can-leave-

false-impression.html (last visited December 14, 2011).

[33] See Leonard, Wade H., *Brewer Seeks $18M in Damages for Wrongful 1995 Conviction*, Com. Dispatch (Columbus, Miss.), Oct. 12, 2008, at 1A; Levs, Melanie Lasoff, *Bite-Mark Evidence Loses Teeth*, A.B.A. J., May 2008, at 16,   16,   available   online   at http://www.abajournal.com/magazine/bite_mark_evidence_loses_teeth   (last visited December 14, 2011); Santos, Fernanda, *Evidence from Bite Marks, It Turns out, Is Not So Elementary*, N.Y. Times, Jan. 28, 2007, at WK 4.

Chapter 11

Toolmarks, Firearms, and Bullet Lead Comparison

Toolmarks and Firearms

Toolmarks are the impressions left when a hard tool contacts a softer object. The marks may be generated during the manufacturing process, such as when the barrel of a gun is rifled by cutting tools which leave marks on the barrel. The marks may also be generated when a manufactured item, perhaps a tool itself, is used in contact with other substances, such as when a screwdriver or crowbar is used to break into a door or window. In turn, the use of the item generates further marks on surfaces of the tool itself that were not present at the time of manufacture, such as when a gun is repeatedly fired or a screwdriver is used over time on various other items.

When a suspect tool is recovered, examiners look for distinctive features, often microscopically. They seek first to identify "class characteristics," or features that are shared by many similar objects.[1] Then they examine the item microscopically for "individual characteristics," markings which are thought to be unique to the individual tool or firearm.[2] They may also classify some features as "subclass characteristics" when they are common only to a small group of the manufactured items.[3] The analysis then is the comparison of two sets of marks to see if they can be identified by common individual characteristics.

The proffered basis for expert toolmark testimony is that each set of markings is somehow unique.[4] Such testimony has been almost universally accepted.[5] Testimony about a variety of tools has been admitted,[6] including screwdrivers and crowbars,[7] bolt cutters,[8] hammers,[9] pliers,[10] and a punch tool.[11] Testimony about knives has been admitted when used as a tool.[12] A Florida Court did, however, refuse to admit toolmark testimony about a knife when used as a weapon, finding no scientific basis for proffered testimony relating a particular knife to marks made on human cartilage.[13]

In this multitude of cases, the admissibility of testimony of toolmark witnesses seems almost presumed. However, in *United States v. Green*, the judge allowed toolmark evidence but commented that "[t]he more courts admit this type of toolmark evidence without requiring documentation, proficiency testing, or evidence of reliability, the more sloppy practices will endure; we should require more."[14]

Weapons used in the commission of crimes are a prime source of evidence, as investigators seek to identify a particular gun as the unique source of bullets or other ammunition components. Firearms testimony is simply one branch of the larger field of toolmark evidence. As with some other types of toolmarks, firearms examiners assert that marks on firearms and ammunition bear individual characteristics that are particular to one firearm and that can be reproduced only with that firearm. The marks made by tools in the manufacture of guns or ammunition may result in particular corresponding marks on bullets, cartridge cases, and shot shells as they process through the firing mechanism.[15]

Manufacturers cut a groove in the barrel of a gun so that the bullet spins as it travels through the barrel to make it travel straighter when it leaves the barrel. This "rifling" process leaves marks and scrapes on the barrel metal. When a bullet is fired and travels through the barrel, the barrel marks are transferred to and reflected in marks, called "stria," on the fired bullet.[16] As the gun is used repeatedly and as the barrel is cleaned, the marks in the barrel, and the resulting stria on the bullet, may develop more individual characteristics.

Other individual gun characteristics can be imparted to the brass cartridge case of the bullets as they are fired and as they are ejected from some types of guns. As the firing pin strikes the cartridge, it leaves its mark. As the cartridge case is blown back to the breech of the gun, the toolmarks in that area of the gun are impressed on the exterior of the casing. If the gun ejects the casing, the toolmarks of the extractor and ejector parts of the gun are imparted to the exterior of the casing as well.

To compare bullet striations or cartridge impressions, a recovered gun may be test fired so that the test bullet or casing can be compared to a found bullet or casing to see if they originated from the tested gun. As with other toolmarks, a firearms examiner makes initial visual determinations of class characteristics. The markings are then compared with a comparison microscope to see if the individual characteristics correspond.

American courts have admitted firearms comparison testimony routinely for over 130 years, with reported cases beginning with *Wynn v. State*.[17] Any early hesitancy about its admissibility had all but disappeared by the 1930s,[18] when the pioneer firearms scientist Calvin Goddard, perfected the comparison microscope.[19] Expert testimony that a found bullet or cartridge and a test bullet or cartridge originated from the same gun has now been admitted in every U. S. jurisdiction.[20]

Toolmark evidence may be susceptible to a viable *Daubert* challenge. The questions primarily arise in two areas, the claimed uniqueness of toolmarks and the standards by which experts may testify that toolmarks on two items agree or correspond sufficiently to claim a common origin.

On the uniqueness question, the National Academy of Sciences 2008 ballistics report concluded that "The validity of the fundamental assumptions of uniqueness and reproducibility of firearms related toolmarks has not yet been fully demonstrated."[21] The report went on to state that "A significant amount of research would be needed to scientifically determine the degree to which firearms-related toolmarks are unique or even to quantitatively characterize the probability of uniqueness."[22]

The standard, or lack thereof, for determining whether the marks on two items agree is of greater concern. Experts agree that there is no perfect match.[23] The Association of Firearms and Tool Mark Examiners (AFTE) states that the marks must be of "sufficient agreement" and only defines that phrase as "when it exceeds the best agreement demonstrated between tool marks known to have been produced by different tools and is consistent with the agreement demonstrated by tool marks known to have been produced by the same tool."[24] The circularity of this "standard," and the lack of more definite criteria, has been the subject of criticism.[25] And the expertise of firearms and toolmark examiners to make reliable comparisons has been steadfastly defended by its practitioners.[26]

Like fingerprint and other impression testimony, the testimony of toolmark experts is, in the final analysis, subjective but that alone does not render it inadmissible. The 2009 National Academies report is critical of the scientific basis for the type of toolmark and ballistics evidence that has been routinely accepted by the courts because "not enough is known about the variabilities among individual tools and guns" and because "[s]ufficient studies have not been done to understand the reliability and repeatability of the methods."[27] The Academy report found that a "A fundamental problem with toolmark and firearms analysis is the lack of a precisely defined scientific process" and noted the "heavy reliance on the subjective findings of examiners rather than on the rigorous quantification and analysis of sources of variability."[28] However, even when confronted with the Report's findings, some courts have held that ballistics testimony is admissible even without a *Daubert* hearing.[29] Even when *Daubert* hearings or analyses are conducted, they have not resulted in many successful attacks on classic firearms expert testimony.[30]

Some courts have taken notice of the NAS Report and the *Daubert* challenges to ballistics testimony and have at least limited the language of such testimony. In *United States v. Glynn*[31] the federal district judge conducted a *Daubert* hearing and stated that "Based on the *Daubert* hearings this Court conducted . . . , the Court very quickly concluded that whatever else ballistics identification analysis could be called, it could not fairly be called 'science' ," and the court limited the expert to testifying that a firearms match was "more likely than not". And in *United States v. Taylor*[32] the court ruled that the government expert "will not be allowed to testify that he can conclude that there is a match to the exclusion, either practical or absolute, of all other guns."

In two federal cases in Massachusetts, the courts conducted lengthy *Daubert* hearings to determine the admissibility of firearms expert testimony. In *United States v. Montiero*[33] the court reviewed the *Daubert* requirements at length and found that firearms testimony was generally admissible but that the government's proffered witness was not qualified.[34] Moreover, the judge held that even a qualified government expert "may testify that the cartridge cases were fired from a particular firearm to a reasonable degree of ballistic certainty. However, the expert may not testify that there is a match to an exact statistical certainty."[35] Similarly in *United States v. Green*[36] the judge admitted testimony regarding cartridge casings but limited the government expert's testimony to his "observations" and prohibited him from testifying "that the match he found by dint of the specific methodology he used permits 'the exclusion of all other guns' as the source of the shell casings."[37]

Even with this limitation, there are no reported cases that reject the fundamental assumptions of firearm or other toolmark testimony based on a *Daubert* analysis. Of course, such testimony remains subject to attacks on the propriety and reliability of the laboratory procedures utilized or the qualifications of a proposed expert witness in a particular case and may require the trial judge to hold preliminary hearings into those matters to determine if they pose admissibility questions or only go to the weight of the government's evidence.[38] While often holding that issues of reliability go to the weight of the evidence and are therefore jury issues, at least one court has held that a witness who would testify about the unreliability of ballistics analysis was "not an appropriate subject for expert opinion testimony" and the defense would be limited to cross examination of the government's experts.[39]

As in other forensic science fields, the future of firearms identification expert testimony may lie in the availability of better science rather than traditional subjective judgments. The FBI and ATF have developed a computerized system known as the Integrated Ballistic Identification System (IBIS) that automatically digitizes and sorts bullet and shell casing characteristics:

> The ballistic comparison of crime scene bullet or cartridge casing evidence can be automatically compared with other bullet or cartridge casing images previously entered into the system. The ballistic comparison system does not positively identify (match) bullets or casings fired from the same weapon — that must be done by a firearms examiner. However, the system does produce a short list of candidates for the match. The numerical probability of a match is given for each candidate on the list eliminating the need for the examiner to visually compare unlikely candidates. By doing automated searches, the system speeds up and optimizes time spent on comparisons.[40]

IBIS has become a nationwide, and even international, system available to local law enforcement agencies.[41] It has proven to be a reliable computerized tool for initial analysis of firearms.[42] Although the ATF emphasizes that "the system does not make identifications; the firearm examiner must make the identification if two bullets or cartridge cases come from the same firearm,"[43] the automated comparison process can be a substantial step toward probabilistic based testimony rather than subjective "match" opinions. Further refinements of the digital based automated system are being investigated and those may well lead to a more scientific analytical basis for firearms identification testimony.[44]

Bullet Lead Comparison

Bullet lead comparison is of very questionable validity. Analysis of bullet lead for identification purposes is premised on the theory that batches of lead in bullets have unique combinations of arsenic, antimony, tin, copper, bismuth, silver, and cadmium.[45] The theory of compositional analysis of bullet lead (CABL) is that when two bullets have the same ratios of these elements, they came from the same source.[46] However, one batch of lead in the bullet making process produces a large number of bullets, and those bullets may in turn go to a variety of distribution routes.[47]

Several courts initially admitted bullet lead analysis comparison testimony for identification.[48] Subsequently, however, metallurgists and statisticians demonstrated that it is not reliable. An early *Daubert* evaluation in *United States v. Mikos*[49] found that source conclusions based on bullet lead analysis were based on faulty science and were inadmissible.[50] The court allowed the FBI agent in that case to testify as to the chemical similarities in the bullets but not as to any probability that they came from the same source.[51]

The National Research Council of the National Academy of Sciences conducted an earlier study funded by the FBI in 2004 and found that, while the methods for identifying and measuring the elements were sound, the assumptions based on those measurements were simply unsupportable.[52] Initially, the FBI rejected the results of its own funded study,[53] but shortly thereafter, the FBI announced that it had ceased to use bullet lead comparison in its investigations.[54] No state laboratories do such analysis.[55]

Since the FBI decision, analysis of bullet lead comparison testimony under *Daubert* standards has been rejected by courts.[56] Even *Frye* courts have since rejected bullet lead comparisons.[57]

Subsequently, several convictions which had been based on CABL evidence were overturned.[58] Surprisingly, the Ninth Circuit in a *habeas* action recently refused to overturn an old conviction which had been based on CABL testimony, holding that "While the CABL evidence introduced against Berry may have been flawed, we do not find it so arbitrary as to render Berry's trial "fundamentally unfair."[59] The decision probably should be interpreted more as a statement of habeas standards than any endorsement of the use of bullet lead analysis, which remains a sad chapter in the history of forensic science.

---

[1] Nat'l Research Council of the Nat'l Acads., *Strengthening Forensic Science in the United States: A Path Forward* (2009), at 152.

[2] *Id.*

[3] *Id.*

[4] Nat'l Research Council of the Nat'l Acads., *Strengthening Forensic Science in the United States: A Path Forward* (2009), at 150; Biasotti, Alfred, John Murdock, and Bruce R. Moran, Firearms *and Toolmark Identification-Scientific Issues*, §§ 35.6 *et seq*, in *Modern Scientific Evidence: The Law and Science of Expert Testimony*, eds. David L. Faigman, Michael J. Saks, Joseph Sanders, and Edward K. Cheng, (2009-2010 edition).

[5] See *Firearms and Toolmark Identification*, §§ 35.1-5 in *Modern Scientific Evidence: The Law and Science of Expert Testimony*, eds. David L. Faigman, Michael J. Saks, Joseph Sanders, and Edward K. Cheng, (2009-2010 edition); Moriarty, Jane Campbell & Michael J. Saks, *Forensic Science: Grand Goals, Tragic Flaws, and Judicial Gatekeeping*, Judges' J., p. 16.(Fall 2005).

[6] *Id.*; and see Moenssens, Andre A., et al., *Scientific Evidence in Civil and Criminal Cases* (5th ed. 2009 Supp.).

[7] *State v. Brown*, 291 S.W.2d 615 (Mo. 1956); *State v. Wade*, 465 S.W.2d 498 (Mo. 1971); *State v. Eickmeier*, 187 Neb. 491, 191 N.W.2d 815 (1971); *Fletcher v. Lane*, 446 F. Supp. 729 (S.D. Ill. 1978).

[8] *Souza v. United States*, 304 F.2d 274 (9th Cir. 1962).

[9] *State v. Olsen*, 212 Or. 191, 317 P.2d 938 (1957).

[10] *People v. Genrich*, 928 P.2d 799 (Colo. Ct. App. 1996).

[11] *People v. Wilkes*, 280 P.2d 88 (Cal. App 1955).

[12] *State v. Clark*, 156 Wash. 543, 287 P. 18 (1930); but compare the earlier ruling of the same court in *State v. Fasick*, 149 Wash. 92, 270 P. 123 (1928), aff'd 149 Wash. 92, 174 P. 712 (1929).

[13] *Ramirez v. State*, 542 So.2d 352 (Fla. 1989).

[14] *United States v. Green*, 405 F. Supp.2d 104, 107 (D. Mass. 2005).

[15] See generally *Firearms and Toolmark Identification*, §§ 35.1 *et seq*, in *Modern Scientific Evidence: The Law and Science of Expert Testimony*, eds. David L. Faigman, Michael J. Saks, Joseph Sanders, and Edward K. Cheng, (2009-2010 edition); Nat'l Research Council of the Nat'l Acads., *Strengthening Forensic Science in the United States: A Path Forward* (2009) at 150-161; Hocherman, Gil, Arie Zeichner, and Tzipi Kahana *Firearms - A Review: 2001-2004*, 14th Interpol Forensic Science Symposium Report at 47 (2004).

[16] See *Expert Evidence to Identify Gun From Which Bullet or Cartridge Was Fired*, 26 A.L.R.2d 892 (1965); *Admissibility of Testimony That Bullet Could or Might Have Come From Particular Gun*, 31 A.L.R.4th 486 (1992); Nat'l Research Council Of The Nat'l Acads,, *Ballistic Imaging* (2008) .

[17] *Wynn v. State*, 56 Ga. 113, 1876 WL 2941 (1876).

[18] See *Evans v. Commonwealth*, 230 Ky. 411, 19 S.W.2d 1091 (1929) and the discussion of that opinion in Moessens, Andre, et al, *Scientific Evidence in Civil and Criminal Cases* §6.18; and see *Firearms and Toolmark Identification*, in *Modern Scientific Evidence: The Law and Science of Expert Testimony*, eds. David L. Faigman, Michael J. Saks, Joseph Sanders, and Edward K. Cheng, (2009-2010 edition) at §35.3.

[19] Goddard, Calvin H., *Scientific Identification of Firearms and Bullets* (1926) Northwestern University; and see Fred E. Inbau, *Scientific Evidence in Criminal Cases*, 24 Am. Inst. Crim. L. & Criminology 825 (1933-1934); Tom A. Warlow, *Firearms, the Law and Forensic Ballistics,* 2nd ed. (2004).

[20] *Expert Evidence to Identify Gun From Which Bullet or Cartridge Was Fired,* 26 A.L.R.2d 892 (1965); *Admissibility of Testimony That Bullet Could or Might Have Come From Particular Gun,* 31 A.L.R.4th 486 (1992); and see *Firearms and Toolmark Identification,* in *Modern Scientific Evidence: The Law and Science of Expert Testimony,* eds. David L. Faigman, Michael J. Saks, Joseph Sanders, and Edward K. Cheng, (2009-2010 edition)at §35.3.

[21] Nat'l Research Council of the Nat'l Acads., *Ballistic Imaging* (2008) at p. 3.

[22] *Id.*

[23] See Biasotti, Alfred A., *A Statistical Study of the Individual Characteristics of Fired Bullets,* 4 J. Forensic Sci. 34 (1959).

[24] American Federation of Firearms and Toolmark Examiners, *Theory of Identification, Range if Striae Comparison Reports and Modified Glossary Definitions - An AFTE Criteria for Identification Committee Report,* 24 J. Assoc. of Firearm and Tool Mark Examiners 336 (1992). Further discussions of criteria appear in Masson, J. J.,*Confidence Level Variations in Firearms Identification Through Computerized Technology,* 29 J. Assoc. of Firearm and Tool Mark Examiners 42 (1997); and J. Miller and M. M. McLean, *Criteria for Identification of Toolmarks,* 30 J. Assoc. of Firearm and Tool Mark Examiners 15 (1998).

[25] Schwartz, Adina , *A Systemic, Challenge to the Reliability and Admissibility of Firearms and Toolmark Identification,* 6 Colum. Sci. & Tech. L. Rev. 2 (2005).

[26] Nichols, Ronald G., *Defending the Scientific Foundations of the Firearms and Tool Mark Identification Discipline: Responding to Recent Challenges,* 522 J. Forensic Sci. 586 (2007).

[27] Nat'l Research Council of the Nat'l Acads., *Strengthening Forensic Science in the United States: A Path Forward* (2009) at 154.

[28] *Id* at 155.

[29] See, e.g., *Commonwealth v. Heang,* 942 N.E.2d 927 (Mass. 2011) (stating that "Although the NAS report called into question the exactitude with which a forensic ballistics expert could declare a 'match,' there was no evidence before the judge suggesting that firearms examiners could not assist the jury by using their technical expertise to observe and compare toolmarks found on projectiles and cartridge cases"); *State v. Green,* 2009 WL 3353595 (Ohio App. 2 Dist. 2009); *People v. Melcher,* 2011 WL 4432935 (Cal.App. 1 Dist. 2011); *State v. Fuentes,* 228 P.3d 1181 (N.M. Ct. App. 2011) (holding that as to firearms analysis "the reliability of the science in question could properly be taken for granted"); *Jones v. United States,* ___ A.3d ___ , 2011 WL 3847414 (D.C. App 2011) (in response to the defense assertion that it could show that ballistics was no longer generally accepted in the scientific community, the court stated that "This assertion is simply not true").

[30] See, e.g., *Turner v. State,* ___ N.E.2d ___-, 2011 WL 4479926 (Ind. 2011) ; *Commonwealth v. Powell,* 940 N.E.2d 521 (Mass. App. Ct. 2011); *United States v. Pugh,* 80 Fed. R. Evid. Serv. 950 (S.D. Miss. 2009); *State v. Adams,*

713 S.E.2d 251, 2011 WL 1938270 (N.C.App. 2011); *State v. Onunwor*, 2010 WL 4684717 (Ohio App. 8 Dist. 2010).

[31] *United States v. Glynn*, 578 F.Supp.2d 567 (S.D. N.Y 2008). But see *United States v. Givens*, 912 N.Y.S.2d 855 (2010) citing Glynn only as precedent for the blanket admission of firearms testimony.

[32] *United States v. Taylor*, 663 F.Supp.2d 1170 (D. N.M. 2009).

[33] *United States v. Monteiro*, 407 F. Supp. 2d 351 (D. Mass. 2006).

[34] *Id.*

[35] *Id.*

[36] *United States v. Green*, 405 F. Supp. 104 (D. Mass. 2005).

[37] *Id.*, at 108-09.

[38] See, e.g., *State v. Torres*, 222 P.3d 409 (Ha. 2009).

[39] *United States v. Taylor*, 704 F.Supp.2d 1192 (D.N.M. 2009).

[40] Bureau of Alcohol, Tobacco, Firearms and Explosives, *Automated Firearms Ballistic Technology*, available online at http://www.nibin.gov/about/program-overview/automated-firearms-ballistics-technology.html (last visited November 24, 2011).

[41] Bureau of Alcohol, Tobacco, Firearms and Explosives, *National Integrated Ballistic Information Network*, available online at http://www.nibin.gov/ (last visited November 24, 2011); and see, e.g., California Department of Justice, *NIBIN Program - Automated Firearms Evidence Imaging*, available online at www.crime-scene-investigator.net/CAnibin.pdf (last visited November 24, 2011).

[42] Puente, Leo´n, Fernando, *Automated Comparison of Firearm Bullets*, 156 Forensic Science International 40 (2006).

[43] Bureau of Alcohol, Tobacco, Firearms and Explosives, *Automated Firearms Ballistic Technology*, available online at http://www.nibin.gov/about/program-overview/automated-firearms-ballistics-technology.html (last visited November 24, 2011).

[44] See, e.g., Chu, Wei, et al, *Pilot Study of Automated Bullet Signature Identification Based on Topography Measurements and Correlations*, 55 J. Forensic Sci. 341 (March 2010).

[45] See generally *Bullet Lead Analysis* §§ 36.1 *et seq*, in *Modern Scientific Evidence: The Law and Science of Expert Testimony*, eds. David L. Faigman, Michael J. Saks, Joseph Sanders, and Edward K. Cheng, (2009-2010 edition); Bohan, Thomas L., *Scientific Evidence and Forensic Science Since Daubert: Maine Decides to Sit out the Dance*, 56 Me. L. Rev. 101, 139 (2004).

[46] See *Bullet Lead Analysis* §§ 36.1 *et seq*, in *Modern Scientific Evidence: The Law and Science of Expert Testimony*, eds. David L. Faigman, Michael J. Saks, Joseph Sanders, and Edward K. Cheng, (2009-2010 edition)§ 36:1.

[47] For a general description of the theory of bullet lead analysis, see Koons, Robert D. and JoAnn Buscaglia, *Forensic Significance of Bullet Lead Comparisons*, 50 J. Forensic Sci. 1(2005); and Kiely, Terrence F., *Forensic Evidence: Science and the Criminal Law* (2d ed. 2005) at 199-212.

[48] See e.g., *United States. v. Davis*, 103 F.3rd 660, 46 Fed. R. Evid. Serv. 189 (8th Cir. 1996); *State v. Ware*, 338 N.W.2d 707 (Ia. 1983); *State v. Noel*, 157 N.J. 141, 723 A.2d 602 (1999); *State v. Grube*, 126 Idaho 377, 883 P.2d 1069 (1994); Kiely, Terrence F., *Forensic Evidence: Science and the Criminal Law* (2d ed. 2005), at p. 235; and *Bullet Lead Analysis*, in *Modern Scientific Evidence: The Law and Science of Expert Testimony*, eds. David L. Faigman, Michael J. Saks, Joseph Sanders, and Edward K. Cheng, (2009-2010 edition) §36.2, at 728-729.

[49] *United States v. Mikos*, No. 02 CR 137, 2003 WL 22922197 (N.D. Ill. 2003).

[50] *Id.* at *6.

[51] *Id.*

[52] Nat'l Research Council of the Nat'l Acads., Comm. On Scientific Assessment Of Bullet Lead Elemental Composition Comparison, *Forensic Analysis: Weighing Bullet Lead Evidence* (2004), available online at http://books.nap.edu/openbook/0309090792/html/index.html (last visited December 14, 2011).

[53] FBI Press Release, *National Academy of Sciences Releases FBI-Commissioned Study on Bullet Lead Analysis*, (February 10, 2004), available online at http://www.fbi.gov/news/pressrel/press-releases/national-academy-of-sciences-releases-fbi-commissioned-study-on-bullet-lead-analysis (last visited December 14, 2011).

[54] FBI Press Release, FBI Laboratory Announces Discontinuation of Bullet Lead Analysis, (September 10, 2005), available online at http://www.fbi.gov/news/pressrel/press-releases/fbi-laboratory-announces-discontinuation-of-bullet-lead-examinations (last visited December 23, 2011); and see Charles Piller, *FBI Abandons Controversial Bullet-Matching Technique*, L.A. Times, Sept. 2, 2005, at A38.

[55] *Bullet Lead Analysis*, in *Firearms and Toolmark Identification*, in *Modern Scientific Evidence: The Law and Science of Expert Testimony*, eds. David L.

Faigman, Michael J. Saks, Joseph Sanders, and Edward K. Cheng, (2009-2010 edition) at 731.

[56] See, e.g., *Ragland v. Com.*, 191 S.W.3d 569 (Ky. 2006).

[57] See, e.g., *Clemons v. State*, 392 Md. 339, 896 A.2d 1059 (2006).

[58] See *Ragland v. Com.*, 191 S.W.3d 569 (Ky. 2006); *Clemons v. State*, 392 Md. 339, 896 A.2d 1059 (2006); *State v. Behn*, 868 A.2d 329, (N.J. Super. Ct. App. 2005).

[59] *United States v. Berry*, 624 F.3d 1031 (9th Cir. 2011) at 1040.

Chapter 12

Fire, Explosion and Arson Evidence

The primary use of forensic science evidence relating to fires and explosions is to attempt to identify the source of the fire and to determine whether, and what type of, an accelerant was used to start or spread a fire or cause an explosion. It is an unusual forensic science first because the fire or explosion being investigated by its nature tends to destroy the physical evidence that could be used to trace its origin. One result of that difference is that the number of criminal arson cases actually pursued by the government, especially in the absence of a homicide, is relatively small.[1]

The field is also unusual in that most of the experts who offer fire origin testimony, known as "cause and origin investigators," are not scientists, have little or no scientific training, and attempt to testify primarily based on their technical knowledge in the field. Perhaps for that reason, many of the cases in this area that followed early on the heels of *Daubert* reflected an attempt by these practitioners to avoid the applicability of *Daubert* criteria on the ground that their testimony was "technical" rather than "scientific." That argument was supported, at least in part, by the decision of the 11th Circuit in *Michigan Millers Mut. Ins. Corp. v. Benfield*,[2] holding that the "experienced based" testimony of a local fire investigator was not subject to *Daubert* scrutiny and could be presented to the jury. That same court had authored a similar opinion in *Carmichael v. Samyang Tire, Inc.*,[3] which was then subsequently reversed by the Supreme Court in *Kumho Tire Co., Ltd. v. Carmichael.*[4] The Supreme Court in the *Kumho* case unanimously held that the substantive basis for testimony of "technical" experts were subject to the same constraints as to validity as "scientific" experts. Since then, *Daubert* objections to fire cause and origin testimony have dramatically increased and the admission of such testimony, at least in civil cases, has been curtailed.

Fire Cause and Origin Investigation

The preferred methodology for fire investigations is set forth in a code adopted by the National Fire Protection Association.[5] That guide has been accepted as the proper standard both by investigators[6] and by many courts when determining *Daubert* challenges to fire cause and origin testimony.[7] Origins of fires are, of course, difficult to determine since practitioners in the field recognize that no two fires will burn alike. So-called "test burns" have been used to try to document common characteristics of fires in a structure before the fire engulfs the entire area, called "flashover." But such information is primarily used for safety and prevention purposes and is of little or no value in the reconstruction of an actual fire.[8] However, those studies of test burns have served to confirm many of the investigative procedures in the National Fire Protection Association guide and to dispel many of the myths preciously used by investigators.[9] The field investigations initially focus on observations about how and where the fire appears to have spread. All investigators agree that fire behaves based on the "fire triangle" of heat, fuel and oxygen.[10] Heat rises and many investigators' observations are targeted toward finding a V shaped pattern in the remains that will lead them to the origin of the fire at the bottom of the "V." Where, however, a fire has spread to the point where other ignitions occur, there may be additional "V" patterns and there is significant disagreement about the ability of fire investigators to determine the first origin in such circumstances.[11]

Cause determinations, especially for accelerants, proceed on a much stronger scientific footing. The presence of an accelerant is most often detected by smell. Some agencies use dogs to direct an investigator to a location for further investigation.[12] Others use commercially available electronic sniffers to detect area for possible investigation, similar to devices that had been used to detect combustible gases in mines. Gasoline or other petroleum based products, of course, are the dominant form of accelerants used in intentionally set fires. Once an accelerant is detected, the task then is to attempt to individualize the particular accelerant. Fire debris is examined in the laboratory to identify common petroleum based products. The industry standard is to use gas chromatography.[13] Based on the results of the gas chromatography, petroleum products may be identified generally by classification, such as gasoline, according to a recognized petroleum distillate classification system.[14] Further individualization within any particular class is difficult if not impossible.[15] Thus, although fire investigators may be able to locate the origin of a fire, and can probably determine the general type or class of any accelerant that was present in fire debris, they are not able to individualize cause or origin with any more particularity.

The NAS report expressed its findings and doubts about the validity of fire cause and origin testimony:

. . . much more research is needed on the natural variability of burn patterns and damage characteristics and how they are affected by the presence of various accelerants. Despite the paucity of research, some arson investigators continue to make determinations about whether or not a particular fire was set. However, according to testimony presented to the committee, many of the rules of thumb that are typically assumed to indicate that an accelerant was used . . . have been shown not to be true. Experiments should be designed to put arson investigations on a more solid scientific footing.[16]

Cause and Origin Testimony Under *Daubert* Standards

Since the *Kumho* case made it clear that *Daubert* standards were to be applied to fire cause and origin testimony, a number of courts have refused to admit such testimony. For example, in *Weisgram v. Marley*, the 8th Circuit found error in the admission of a fire investigator's testimony because it lacked sufficient scientific foundation and because no testing had been performed to substantiate his conclusions or theory.[17] Other courts reached similar results after conducting a *Daubert* analysis.[18]

On the other hand, some proffered fire cause and origin testimony has been admitted after the court applied similar *Daubert* scrutiny. For example, in *Allstate Insurance Company v. Hugh Cole Builder, Inc.,* the court reviewed the scientific and factual basis for an expert to testify as to the location and cause of a house fire and determined that the testimony was based on reliable principles and that he had appropriately applied those principles to the observable facts at the scene.[19] Other courts have similarly admitted fire cause and origin testimony, although some without rigorous application of *Daubert* criteria.[20]

In spite of the critical findings in the NAS Report, courts have still held that fire origin testimony is sufficiently reliable for admission in criminal cases. In *United States v. Aman*, the district judge stated:

> In any event, although the NRC sensibly suggests that further development of the principles and methods of fire investigation would improve the precision of such experts' findings, the NRC's critique does not change the result that, for all of the reasons already stated, the NFPA 921 methodology is sufficiently reliable to withstand *Daubert* scrutiny.[21]

On the other hand, Judge Nancy Gertner , who is one of the few federal judges who has given serious credence to the NAS Report, held in *United States v. Henshie*, that trial counsel was ineffective for not demanding a *Daubert* hearing on the admissibility of fire origin testimony, stating:

> . . . a number of articles in legal journals and cases cast a critical eye on the scientific reliability of arson evidence, methodologies, and techniques. Ordinarily competent counsel would have understood that men and women had been convicted, sentenced, perhaps even executed, on the basis of flawed arson evidence and taken appropriate steps to litigate the issues using all the tools available.[22]

At the same time, both *Hebshie* and *United States v. Myers*[23] are extremely critical of expert testimony from the handlers of dogs that supposedly have the ability to detect accelerants.

Fire Cause and Origin Testimony in Criminal Cases

Reputable scholars have asserted that *Daubert* criteria are being applied by the courts primarily to exclude expert testimony offered by plaintiffs in civil cases and that courts rarely, if ever, rigorously apply *Daubert* standards to expert testimony proffered by prosecutors in criminal cases.[24] Perhaps no area of forensic evidence more clearly demonstrates what some believe to be the discriminatory application of *Daubert* to criminal cases than fire cause and origin testimony.

There appear to be no reported criminal cases in which courts have completely excluded fire cause and origin testimony from prosecution experts on the basis of its scientific invalidity under *Daubert*. On the other hand, several courts in criminal cases have specifically allowed such testimony. In *United States v. Norris*, the 5th Circuit upheld a trial court decision to allow a government expert videotape of a reproduced burn and held that *Daubert* only applied to the expert's qualifications, which were found to be appropriate.[25] In *United States v. Gardner*, the 7th Circuit approved prosecution fire cause and origin testimony with virtually no real discussion of *Daubert* standards.[26] In *United States v. Diaz*, the First Circuit found no clear error in the admission of government expert testimony as to the cause of the fire in an arson case.[27]

State courts where most arson cases are tried appear to have similarly routinely held that fire cause and origin testimony is generally admissible under *Daubert*. In *Commonwealth v. Goodman*, the court upheld the admission of prosecution fire cause and origin testimony even though the National Fire Protection Association's investigation protocol was not followed.[28] In *State v. Interest of W.T.B.*, the Louisiana Court of Appeals affirmed a juvenile conviction based on testimony from an investigator, following a lead from his canine accelerant sniffer, that the fire patterns indicated an accelerant was used. The only reported case in which a state court has even limited government fire cause and origin testimony in a criminal prosecution is *State v. Campbell*, in which the court found that such testimony was admissible but that the investigator's statement that the defendant started the fire was improperly admitted.[29]

The Willingham Case

The reliability of fire origin testimony in criminal cases has come under severe criticism as a result of the highly publicized case of Todd Willingham, who was executed in Texas for the alleged murder of his three children by setting fire to his own home where the children were sleeping. He was convicted based on testimony from a Texas fire marshal investigator that the fire in Willingham's home had burned "fast and hot" and had been started using a liquid accelerant. He relied on his observations that there were char patterns in the floor in the shape of "puddles," multiple starting points of the fire, "crazed glass" damage, and a positive test for "mineral spirits," all indicating to him that the fire had been ignited with the help of a liquid accelerant. He also testified that Willingham's statement that he had run out of the house to avoid the fire was not believable because he did not have burns consistent with that story. On appeal, the Texas Court of Criminal Appeals summarized the fire origin expert testimony in simple terms, "An expert witness for the State testified that the floors, front threshold, and front concrete porch were burned, which only occurs when an accelerant has been used to purposely burn these areas. This witness further testified that this igniting of the floors and thresholds is typically employed to impede firemen in their rescue attempts."[30] Willingham's habeas corpus petition to the federal court was denied[31] and his last petition for certiorari to the United States Supreme Court was denied on November 3, 2003.[32]

Prior to Willingham's execution, a fire origin expert working *pro bono* for the defense made a detailed report finding that the conclusions of arson made by the fire investigators were invalid, and stated:

The Fire Investigation Report of the Texas State Fire Marshal's office in this case is a remarkable document. On first reading, a contemporary fire origin and cause analyst might well wonder how anyone could make so many critical errors. However when the report is looked at in the context of its time and in light of a few key advances that have been made in the fire investigation field in the last dozen years, it becomes obvious that the report more or less simply reflects the shortcomings in the state of the art prior to the beginning of serious efforts to introduce standards and to test old theories that had previously been accepted on faith. . . .

As will be shown later, most of the conclusions reached by the Fire Marshal would be considered invalid in light of current knowledge.[33]

The Hurst report was sent to the Texas Board of Pardons and Paroles and to Texas Governor Rick Perry. The Board voted unanimously to recommend denial of clemency, which the Governor did, and Willingham was executed on February 17, 2004.

Willingham's execution in spite of the Hurst report quickly generated press coverage detailing the controversy over the validity of the fire origin expert testimony in his case, including a statement by Hurst that "[t]here's nothing to suggest to any reasonable arson investigator that this was an arson fire".[34] Three other experts also reached a similar conclusion.[35] In 2006, the Innocence Project asked the newly formed Texas Forensic Science Commission[36] to review the Willingham case and another case. The Commission eventually commissioned its own review by another reputable fire origin expert, Dr. Craig Beyler. In his August 2009 report, Beyler concluded:

The investigations of the Willis and Willingham fires did not comport with either the modern standard of care expressed by NFPA 921, or the standard of care expressed by fire investigation texts and papers in the period 1980–1992. The investigators had poor understandings of fire science and failed to acknowledge or apply the contemporaneous understanding of the limitations of fire indicators. Their methodologies did not comport with the scientific method or the process of elimination. A finding of arson could not be sustained based upon the standard of care expressed by NFPA 921, or the standard of care expressed by fire investigation texts and papers in the period 1980–1992.[37]

Of the Fire Marshal who testified in Willingham's case, Beyler was extremely critical:

His statistics of the fraction of fires which are in fact arson are remarkable and far exceed any rational estimate. It reflects his predisposition to find arson in his cases. This directly violates NFPA 921 and professional norms in general. His quotations that "The fire tells a story, I am just the interpreter," and "the fire does not lie, it tells me the truth," are hardly consistent with a scientific mindset and is more characteristic of mystics or psychics. The quotes separate the findings from his own judgment and seek to make him not responsible for his own interpretation. It seems to deny the role of rational reasoning. It is an expression of fire investigation as a mystical art rather than an application of science and reason. [38]

A lengthy media report brought further national attention to the case[39] and a political firestorm ensued. Prosecutors and politicians reacted strongly against the Beyler report and just days before Beyler was to present his findings to the Commission, Governor Perry replaced four of its members with new appointees, including naming a vocal opponent of the report as Chair.[40] The political maneuvering to prevent an official report that Willingham was wrongfully executed intensified with the announced candidacy of Governor Perry for President. A "final" report of the Commission was eventually issued on April 15, 2011 in which the Commission critically reviewed the Willingham evidence and recommended a series of education and training improvements for fire investigators.[41] It did not make any findings regarding the conduct of the fire investigators in the case because State claimed it had no jurisdiction to do so. On July 29, 2011 the Texas Attorney General issued an opinion restricting the Commission's jurisdiction[42] and the Commission then issued a "Final Report Addendum" in which it adopted the Attorney General's restricted view of the Commission's jurisdiction and effectively ended the investigation:

> The Opinion contains two conclusions that restrict the Commission from proceeding with further investigation or reaching a finding of negligence and/or misconduct in this case. The first is that the FSC is prohibited from taking any action with respect to evidence offered or entered into evidence before September 1, 2005. The second is that the FSC's authority is limited to laboratories, facilities, or entities

that were accredited by DPS at the time the forensic analysis took place. [43]

Regardless of the political maneuvering that was triggered by the scientific examination of the fire origin testimony in the *Willingham* case, the case will affect the future credibility of fire origin testimony in criminal cases. If anything, the political actions may have intensified the awareness of the case in the eyes of the public. That awareness may well be reflected in jurors, and may even rub off on judges when performing their gatekeeping role.

---

[1] Lentini, John J., *Fires, Arson and Explosions - Scientific Status* in *Modern Scientific Evidence: The Law and Science of Expert Testimony*, eds. David L. Faigman, Michael J. Saks, Joseph Sanders, and Edward K. Cheng, (2009-2010 edition) at §39.21 at 205.

[2] *Michigan Millers Mut. Ins. Corp. v. Benfield*, 140 F.3d 915, 49 Fed. R. Evid. Serv. 549 (11th Cir. 1998).

[3] *Carmichael v. Samyang Tire, Inc.,* 131 F.3d 1433, 48 Fed. R. Evid. Serv. 334 (11th Cir. 1997), rev'd *sub nom Kumho Tire Co., Ltd. v. Carmichael*, 526 U.S. 137 (1999).

[4] *Id.*

[5] National Fire Protection Association (NFPA), *Guide for Fire and Explosion Investigation* (Pub. No. 921 2008), available for purchase online at www.nfpa.org (last visited December 14, 2011).

[6] See Lentini, John J., *Fires, Arson and Explosions - Scientific Status* in *Modern Scientific Evidence: The Law and Science of Expert Testimony*, eds. David L. Faigman, Michael J. Saks, Joseph Sanders, and Edward K. Cheng, (2008-2009 edition) at §38.2, p. 109.

[7] See, e.g., *Travelers Property & Casualty Corp. v. General Electric Co.*, 150 F.Supp.2d 360 (D. Conn. 2001); *Royal Ins. Co. of America v. Joseph Daniel Const., Inc.*, 208 F.Supp2d 423 (S.D. N.Y. 2002); *American Family Ins. Group v. JVC Americas Corp.*, 2001 WL 1618454 (D. Minn. 2001); *Allstate In. Co. v. Hugh Cole Builder, Inc.*, 137 F.Supp.2d 1283 (M.D. Ala. 2001); *Ziegler v. Fisher-Price, Inc.*, 2003 WL 1889021 (N.D. Ia. 2003); *Booth v. Black & Decker, Inc.*, 166 F.Supp2d 215 (E.D. Pa. 2001); *Tunnell v. Ford Motor Co.*, 320 F.Supp.2d 707 (W.D. Va. 2004).

[8] Lentini, John J., *Fires, Arson and Explosions - Scientific Status* in *Modern Scientific Evidence: The Law and Science of Expert Testimony*, eds. David L. Faigman, Michael J. Saks, Joseph Sanders, and Edward K. Cheng, (2009-2010 edition) at §39.23.

[9] *Id.*

[10] *Id*, at §38.31

[11] *Id.* See *Fire Investigation Handbook*, ed. Francis Brannigern, National Bureau of Standards Handbook 134 (1980), available online at http://fire.nist.gov/bfrlpubs/fire80/PDF/f80004.pdf (last visited December 14, 2011).

[12] See *United States. v. Marji*, 158 F.3d 60 (2d Cir 1998), upholding the use of a dog alert evidence to assist in accelerant detection.

[13] American Society for Testing Materials (ASTM), *Standard Practice for Sampling of Headspace Vapors from Fire Debris Samples*, ASTM E1388-05 (2005), available for purchase online at http://webstore.ansi.org/RecordDetail.aspx?sku=ASTM+E1388-05 (last visited December 14, 2011).

[14] American Society for Testing Materials (ASTM), *Standard Test Method for Ignitable Liquid Residues in Extracts from Fire Debris Samples by Gas Chromatography-Mass Spectrometry*, ASTM E1618-06E1 (2006), available for purchase online at http://webstore.ansi.org/RecordDetail.aspx?sku=ASTM+E1618-11 (last visited December 14, 2011).

[15] Lentini, John J. , *Fires, Arson and Explosions - Scientific Status* in *Modern Scientific Evidence: The Law and Science of Expert Testimony*, eds. David L. Faigman, Michael J. Saks, Joseph Sanders, and Edward K. Cheng, (2009-2010 edition) at §39.52.

[16] Nat'l Research Council of the Nat'l Acads., *Strengthening Forensic Science in the United States: A Path Forward* (2009) at 173.

[17] *Weisgram v. Marley*, 169 F.3d 514 (8th Cir. 1999), aff'd, 528 U.. 440 (2000).

[18] See e.g.,, *Pride v. BIC Corp.*, 218 F.3d 566 (6th Cir. 2000); *Werner v. Pittway Corp.*, 90 F.Supp2d 1018 (W.D. Wis. 2000); *Comer v. American Elec. Power*, 63 Supp2d 927 (N.D. Ind. 1999); *Knotts v. Black & Decker, Inc.*, 204 F.Supp.2d 1029 (N.D. Ohio 2002); *Truck Ins. Exchange v. MagneTek, Inc.*, 360 F.3d 1206 (10th Cir. 2004).

[19] *Allstate Ins. Co. v. Hugh Cole Builder, Inc.*, 137 F.Supp.2d 1283 (M.D. Ala. 2001).

[20] See e.g. *Zeigler v. Fisher-Price, Inc.*, 261 F. Supp.2d 1047 (N.D. Iowa 2003); *Zeigler v. Fisher-Price, Inc.*, 302 F.Supp.2d 999 (N.D. Ia. 2004);

Hynes v. Energy West, Inc., 211 F.3d 1193 (10th Cir. 2000); *Thurman v. Missouri Gas Energy*, 107 F.Supp2d 1046 (W.D. Mo. 2000).

[21] *United States v. Aman*, 748 F.Supp.2d 531 (E.D. Va.2010).

[22] *United States v. Hebshie*, 754 F.Supp.2d 89 (D. Mass. 2010).

[23] *United States v. Myers*, 2010 WL 2723196 (S.D. W.Va. 2010).

[24] See Berger, Margaret A., *Expert Testimony in Criminal Proceedings: Questions Daubert Does Not Answer*, 33 Seton Hall L. Rev. 1125 (2003); Findley, Keith A., *Innocents at Risk: Adversary Imbalance, Forensic Science, and the Search for Truth*, 38 Seton Hall L. Rev. 893, 929-950 (2008), available online at http://ssrn.com/abstract-1144886 (last visited January 1, 2009); Groscup, Jennifer L., et al., *The Effects of Daubert on the Admissibility of Expert Testimony in State and Federal Criminal Cases*, 8 Psychol.. Pub. Pol"y & L. 339 (2002); Neufeld, Peter J., *The (Near) Irrelevance of Daubert to Criminal Justice and Some Suggestions for Reform*, 95 Am. J. Pub. Health 107 (2005); Risinger, D. Michael, *Navigating Expert Reliability: Are Criminal Standards of Certainty Being Left on the Dock?*, 64 Alb. L. Rev. 99 (2000).

[25] *United States v. Norris*, 217 F.3d 262 (5th Cir. 2000).

[26] *United States v. Gardner*, 213 F.3d 1049 (7th Cir. 2000).

[27] *United States v.. Diaz*, 300 F.3d 66 (1st Cir. 2002).

[28] *Commonwealth v. Goodman*, 54 Mass. App. Ct. 385, 765 N.E.2d 792 (2002).

[29] *State v. Campbell*, 2002 WL 398029 (Ohio Ct. App. 1st Dist. 2002).

[30] *Willingham v. State*, 897 S.W.2d 351 (Tex. Ct. Crim. App 1995).

[31] *Willingham v. Johnson*, (N.D. Tex. 2001), not reported, available, in part, online at http://www.clarkprosecutor.org/html/death/US/willingham899.htm, (last visited November 26, 2011).

[32] *Willingham v. Dretke*, 540 U.S. 986 (2003).

[33] Hurst, Gerald, *Cameron Todd Willingham Report of D. Gerald Hurst*, Feb. 13, 2004, available online at http://www.scribd.com/doc/37712737/Gerald-Hurst-s-Report-on-Todd-Willingham-Arson-Investigation (last visited November 26, 2011).

[34] Mills, Steve and Maurice Possley, *Man Executed on Disproved Forensics*, Chicago Tribune, (Dec. 9, 2004) available online at http://www.chicagotribune.com/news/nationworld/chi-0412090169dec09,0,1173806.story (last visited November 26, 2011)

[35] *Id.*

[36] Vernon's Ann. Texas C.C.P. Art. 38.01 (2005). The Commission website is online at http://www.fsc.state.tx.us/ (last visited November 26, 2011).

[37] Beyer, Craig L., *Analysis of the Fire Investigation Methods and Procedures Used in the Criminal Arson Cases Against Ernest Ray Willis and Cameron Todd Willingham* (August 17, 2009), available online at http://www.innocenceproject.org/Content/The_Texas_Forensic_Science_Co mmission_and_the_Willingham_Case.php (last visited November 26, 2011).

[38] *Id.*

[39] Grann, David, *Trial by Fire: Did Texas Execute an Innocent Man?*, The New Yorker (Sept. 7, 2009) available online at http://www.newyorker.com/reporting/2009/09/07/090907fa_fact_grann?yrail (last visited November 26, 2011). See also Mills, Steve, *Report Questions if Fire Was Arson*, Chicago Tribune, (Aug. 25, 2009) available online at http://www.chicagotribune.com/news/chi-090825willingham,0,7297380.story (last visited November 26, 2011).

[40] See Turner, Allen, *Panel Cites 'Flawed Science' in Arson Case*, Houston Chronicle (July 24, 2010), available online at http://www.chron.com/news/houston-texas/article/Flawed-science-cited-in-arson-case-leading-to-1718240.php?plckFindCommentKey=CommentKey:9694e74b-0c4f-49d4-b368-22e307f00188 (last visited November 26, 2011).

[41] Texas Forensic Science Commission, *Final Report of the Texas Forensic Science Commission: Willingham/Willis Investigation* (Apr. 15, 2011), available online at http://www.fsc.state.tx.us/reporting.html (last visited November 26, 2011).

[42] Texas Attorney General Opinion No. GA-0866, *Investigative Authority of the Texas Forensic Science Commission* (July 29, 2011) available online at www.fsc.state.tx.us/documents/11.pdf (last visited November 26, 2011).

[43] Texas Forensic Science Commission, *Addendum to the April 15, 2011 Report of the Texas Forensic Science Commission: Willingham/Willis Investigation* (Oct. 28, 2011), available online at http://www.fsc.state.tx.us/reporting.html (last visited November 26, 2011).

Chapter 13

Bloodstain Pattern Evidence

Bloodstains and bloodstain patterns are often the subject of forensic science testimony in assault or homicide cases. It is important for investigators to understand how a particular stain and pattern occurred. Initially, the investigative question can simply be whether a particular stain is blood or not. More complex is the question of what can be learned from a pattern of blood stains or spattering. It is used to form the basis for testimony about such issues as the sequence of events, the distance from which a victim was shot, claims of self defense, and any number of other homicide or assault dynamics. It may include determination of whether a stain resulted from arterial spurting, blood dripping, expirated (coughed) blood, back spatter, angular deposits, flight paths, or many other characteristics of the blood path that led to the recorded bloodstain pattern.

Bloodstains

Investigators often view, record and collect blood from a crime scene. The question sometimes is whether the particular substance is indeed a bloodstain or some other substance. The presence or absence of blood can be an important piece of evidence. Investigators may want to make presumptive tests to see if a stain is indeed blood at the scene. Several chemicals may be used to make such field determinations,[1] the most common of which is luminol.[2] Luminol is the same chemical used in the glow of popular light sticks. Criminal investigators use the same reaction to detect traces of blood at crime scenes. Luminol powder is mixed with hydrogen peroxide and a hydroxide. When the solution is sprayed on blood, the iron from the hemoglobin in the blood acts as a catalyst for the reaction that produces a blue glow.

Unfortunately, luminol is also known to produce false positives, indicating that the stain is blood when it is some other substance.[3] Notwithstanding that significant problem, some courts have admitted evidence that field tests with luminol revealed the presence of blood.[4] However, a more appropriate ruling is one reflected in *Ayers v. State*, in which the court ruled that evidence about a luminol reaction is not admissible unless additional tests confirmed that the stain was human blood.[5] Further refinements to the forensic use of luminol are being studied.[6] In the meantime, however, luminol should be regarded as a field test which is only presumptive for disclosing the presence of blood and whenever possible the sample should be recovered and preserved for more definitive serology or DNA testing.

Blood Spattering Patterns

The most common bloodstain testimony relates to conclusions drawn from the pattern of blood spattering at a crime scene. The role of blood pattern analysis has been defined by its practitioners as follows:

> . . . BPA [blood pattern analysis] focuses on the analysis of the size, shape and distribution of bloodstains resulting from bloodshed events as a means of determining the types of activities and mechanisms that produced them . . .
> BPA is a discipline that uses the fields of biology, physics and mathematics. BPA may be accomplished by direct scene evaluation, and/or careful study of scene photographs (preferably color photographs with a measuring device in view) in conjunction with detailed examination of clothing, weapons, and other objects regarded as physical evidence. Details of hospital records, postmortem examination, and autopsy photographs also provide useful information and should be included for evaluations and study.[7]

The basic mechanical premise of blood pattern analysis has been stated as follows:

Acts of extreme violence often create a dispersion of blood volumes forces from a wound site. Gunshot and other high energy impacts, such as blunt force beatings, may disperse blood volumes along relatively flat trajectories.

Molecular cohesion creates surface tension at the boundaries of these blood volumes. Surface tension causes the drop volumes to assume nearly spherical shapes in free flight. These drops result in bloodstain evidence being deposited on the floor, walls, ceiling or other surfaces or objects within a crime scene. Interpretation of the resulting stain patterns may permit an analyst to approximate the three-dimensional point of origin.[8]

Forms of blood pattern analysis have been part of criminal investigations for over a century.[9]

Notwithstanding the claimed basis of the practice in "biology, physics and mathematics," there are no formal educational requirements for persons claiming to be experts in blood pattern analysis. Some professional organizations, such as the International Association for Identification (IAI) and the Scientific Working Group on Bloodstain Pattern Analysis (SWGSTAIN), recommend training and workshops, but those requirements are minimal. For certification, the IAI requires as little as 240 hours of workshop training.[10] SWGSTAIN's guidelines for minimum training would recognize an analyst who had a "High school diploma or equivalent and four years of job-related experience."[11] The NAS report was critical of these seemingly minimalist qualification requirements and the subjective nature of blood pattern analysts in general:

This emphasis on experience over scientific foundations seems misguided, given the importance of rigorous and objective hypothesis testing and the complex nature of fluid dynamics. In general, the opinions of bloodstain pattern analysts are more subjective than scientific. In addition, many bloodstain pattern analysis cases are prosecution or defense driven, with targeted requests that can lead to context bias.[12]

Indeed, much blood pattern testimony is offered through police officers based on little education in fluid dynamics and limited hard evidence. For example in *Richter v. Hickman*[13] the Ninth Circuit sitting *en banc* conducted a *habeas* review of a murder conviction that was based on the testimony of a police officer presented by the prosecution as a blood spatter expert. The crucial issue was the location of the victim when he had been shot. The officer testified that the victim could not have been killed in the place or manner described by the defendant. He "drew his conclusions from an analysis of photographs, nearly a year after the events in question" and "all I have had is these photos which are lacking. I mean, they are dark and not clear, but I was not able to see in viewing the photos anything consistent with" the defendant's version of events.[14]   The Ninth Circuit held that the defense counsel's failure to consult a blood spatter expert who would have, based on a post-conviction affidavit, strongly rebutted the officer's testimony, was ineffective assistance of counsel entitling the defendant to a new trial. However, the United States Supreme Court later granted certiorari and reversed the Ninth Circuit in *Harrington v. Richter*.[15] The Supreme Court held that *habeas* review of Richter's conviction was precluded by statute and that it was not "reasonably likely" that the defense expert's testimony would have changed the verdict.

The NAS Report summarized its highly critical assessment regarding bloodstain pattern analysis:

> Scientific studies support some aspects of bloodstain pattern analysis. One can tell, for example, if the blood spattered quickly or slowly, but some experts extrapolate far beyond what can be supported. Although the trajectories of bullets are linear, the damage that they cause in soft tissue and the complex patterns that fluids make when exiting wounds are highly variable. For such situations, many experiments must be conducted to determine what characteristics of a bloodstain pattern are caused by particular actions during a crime and to inform the interpretation of those causal links and their variabilities. For these same reasons, extra care must be given to the way in which the analyses are presented in court. The uncertainties associated with bloodstain pattern analysis are enormous.[16]

Nevertheless, the legal history of bloodstain pattern testimony from such experts has been characterized by almost routine acceptance of qualifications and findings of admissibility. Courts are willing to qualify experts on minimal credentials, even after *Daubert*.[17] For example, in *State v. Davolt*, the Arizona Supreme Court approved the trial court's qualification of a police detective as an expert bloodstain pattern analyst in a death penalty case because "Detective Harry's training in blood splatter analysis consisted of attending classes on crime scene management, a class on homicide investigation, and watching two training videos on blood splatter analysis as part of his advanced officer training at the Lake Havasu Police Department. While this training is not extensive, it is significantly more extensive than the average person has received and is sufficient to allow the testimony to be heard by the jury."[18]

The case of *Holmes v. State* demonstrates the courts' reluctance to disallow blood pattern analysis evidence and to allow a witness with minimal credentials to be qualified as an expert.[19] There the Court considered the Texas rule that "evidence derived from a scientific theory, to be considered reliable, must satisfy three criteria in any particular case: (a) the underlying scientific theory must be valid; (b) the technique applying the theory must be valid; and (c) the technique must have been properly applied on the occasion in question." The appellate court found however that the prosecution was not required to produce any evidence of the theory or technique of blood pattern analysis because they decided that, after a review of other mostly pre-*Daubert* legal opinions, "we take judicial notice of the validity of blood spatter analysis and hold that the State was not required, and will not be required in the future, to produce evidence on the first two criteria." [20] They also approved the trial court's qualification of a local police officer who had "45-50 hours" of instruction at a conference as an expert in blood pattern analysis.[21]

And recently in *Wines v. Commonwealth*[22] the Supreme Court of Kentucky approved the admission of blood spatter testimony from a medical examiner in a way that suggested that it was almost like lay observations:

> The subject of her testimony - the very general observation that weapons repeatedly brought into contact with blood will tend to accumulate blood and transfer it to surrounding

surfaces-was not far removed from common sense and common experience, and was surely within the competence of someone as familiar with blood in general and as specifically trained in blood-spatter phenomena as the medical examiner. This general testimony, therefore, did not require a more extensive foundation than the one provided, as might have been the case, for example, had the medical examiner opined that a particular blood pattern was the result of cast-off.

It appears that *Daubert* has not yet reached the courts' ken regarding blood spatter testimony.

---

[1] Sutton, T. Paulette *Presumptive Testing for Blood*, in *Scientific and Legal Applications of Bloodstain Pattern Analysis* (ed. Stuart H. James, CRC Press (1991).

[2] See Lytle, L. T. and D. G. Hedgecock, *Chemiluminescence in the Visualization of Forensic Bloodstains*, 23 J. Forensic Sci. 550 (1978).

[3] Quickenden, Terence I. and J. I. Creamer, *A Study of Common Interferences With the Forensic Luminol Test for Blood*, 16 Journal of Bioluminescence and Chemiluminescence 295 (2001); Laux, Dale L., *Effects of Luminol on the Subsequent Analysis of Bloodstains*, 36 J. Forensic Sci. 1512 (1991); *Rivera v. State*, 2005 WL 16193 (Tex. Ct. App 2005); and see Kiely, Terrence F., *Forensic Evidence: Science And Criminal Law* (2d ed. 2006) at p. 390.

[4] *State v. Canaan*, 265 Kan. 835, 964 P.2d 681 (1998); *State v. Maynard*, 954 S.W.2d 624 (Mo. Ct. App. 1997); *Murphy v. State*, 941 N.E.2d 568 (Ind.App. 2011).

[5] *Ayers v. State*, 334 Ark. 258 , 975 S.W.2d 88 (1998).

[6] Quickenden, Tereence I. and Paul D. Cooper, Increasing *the Specificity of the Forensic Luminol Test for Blood*, 16 Luminesence 251 (2001), available online at http://mason.gmu.edu/~pcooper6/papers/1.pdf (last visited December 14, 2011).

[7] James, Stuart H., Paul E. Kish, and T. Paulette Sutton, *Principles of Bloodstain Pattern Analysis: Theory and Practice*, CRC Press (2005) at pp. 1-2.

[8] Fischer, William C., *Defining the "Address" of Bloodstains and Other Evidence at the Crime Scene* in *Scientific and Legal Applications of*

Bloodstain Pattern Analysis, ed. Stuart H. James, CRC Press (1991) at pp. 1-2.

[9] For a detailed history of forensic blood and blood pattern analysis, see James, Stuart H., Paul E. Kish, and T. Paulette Sutton, *Principles of Bloodstain Pattern Analysis: Theory and Practice*, CRC Press (2005) at pp. 3-6; .and see also Anita Wonder, *Blood Dynamics*, Academic Press (2001).

[10] International Association for Identification, *Bloodstain Pattern Examiner Certification Requirements*, available online at http://www.theiai.org/certifications/bloodstain/requirements.php (last visited December 14, 2011).

[11] Scientific Working Group on Bloodstain Pattern Analysis, *Guidelines for the Minimum Educational and Training Requirements for Bloodstain Pattern Analysts*, available online at http://www.fbi.gov/about-us/lab/forensic-science-communications/fsc/jan2008/standards/2008_01_standards01.htm/ (last visited December 14, 2011).

[12] Nat'l Research Council of the Nat'l Acads., *Strengthening Forensic Science in the United States: A Path Forward* (2009) at 178.

[13] *Richter v. Hickman*, 578 F.3d 944 (9th Cir. 2009).

[14] *Id* at fn4.

[15] *Harrington v. Richter*, ___ U.S. ___, 131 S. Ct. 770 (2011).

[16] Nat'l Research Council of the Nat'l Acads., *Strengthening Forensic Science in the United States: A Path Forward* (2009) at 178-179.

[17] See generally Kiely, Terrence F., *Forensic Evidence: Science And Criminal Law* (2d ed. 2006) at pp. 398- 405.

[18] *State v. Davolt*, 207 Ariz. 191, 84 P.3d 456, 475 (2004).

[19] *Holmes v. State*, 135 S.W.3d 178 (Tex. Ct. App 2004).

[20] *Id* at 195.

[21] *Id* at 183-184.

[22] *Wines v. Commonwealth*, 2009 WL 1830805 (Ky. 2009).

Chapter 14

Human Scent Evidence

Canine Tracking Evidence

For some time, police have used the heightened olfactory sense of dogs to train them to detect particular odors, such as narcotics or explosives, and even to trace humans as in the folklore "bloodhound" scenario. Courts have almost uniformly allowed the government to rely upon trained dog scent responses to provide probable cause for searches, especially in narcotics or explosives cases. Sensory trained dogs have also been used by police to assist in the location of human cadavers. Although their accuracy in such human cadaver situations varies by dog and handler and has been tested to have ranges of 57% to 100%, they are nevertheless a valuable investigative tool for police investigations.[1] The leap from valuable investigative technique to admissible evidence used to prove guilt is another matter.[2]

Dog evidence to identify the scent of a human has been offered at trial by the prosecution in a variety of cases.[3] Many courts originally held that evidence that a trained tracking dog connected the defendant to a crucial piece of physical evidence in the case was generally reliable and admissible if a proper foundation was laid.[4] A proper foundation was considered to be:

> 1) that the dog is of ... [a breed and pedigree] characterized by acuteness of scent and power of discrimination, (2) that the dog has been accustomed and trained to pursue the human track, (3) that the dog has been found by experience in actual cases to be reliable in such tracking, (4) that the dog was placed on the trail at a spot where the alleged participant or

participants in the crime were known to have been, and (5) that the dog was placed on the trail within the period of his efficiency.[5]

Other courts have long been skeptical of dog tracking evidence as admissible evidence of guilt for a variety of reasons.[6] Some have felt that it was a form of hearsay, as the Supreme Court of Montana said in *State v. Storm*:

> Dogs and other dumb animals do not qualify as witnesses in the courts of this state. They know not the nature of an oath. They may not be sworn. They cannot be cross-examined. They testify only through professed interpreters whose translations and conclusions are always hearsay.[7]

Courts have also expressed the general proposition "that the life and liberty of a free citizen ought not to be put in jeopardy on the testimony of dogs"[8] and have described such evidence as propagation of the "bloodhound myth."[9] Most importantly, even before *Daubert* there was substantial concern about the scientific reliability of the dog scent identification of humans.[10]

Post-*Daubert* analysis of dog scent evidence has not been generally positive when it comes to human scent identification by dogs. For example in *Winfrey v. State* the Texas high court reviewed a murder conviction based on testimony that a dog scent lineup in which dogs apparently identified the defendant's scent on clothes of the victim. The court set aside the conviction and stated:

> Law-enforcement personnel have long utilized canines in crime management. For example, dogs have been employed for detecting narcotics and explosives, for tracking trails, in 883*883 search-and-rescue operations, for locating cadavers, and for discriminating between scents for identification purposes. In thousands of cases, canines and their handlers have performed with distinction. Despite this success, we acknowledge the invariable truth espoused by Justice Souter that "[t]he infallible dog, however, is a creature of legal fiction." *Illinois v. Caballes,* 543 U.S. 405, 411, 125 S.Ct. 834, 160 L.Ed.2d 842 (2005) (Souter J., dissenting). . . .

Accordingly, we conclude that scent-discrimination lineups, when used alone or as primary evidence, are legally insufficient to support a conviction.[11]

Subsequently in *State v. Dominguez*[12] and in *State v. Smith*[13] dog scent identifications were excluded from evidence as "not scientifically reliable".

Human Decomposition Odors - The Anthony Case

In the recent highly publicized trial in the *Casey Anthony* case[14], the government nevertheless tried to take human scent identification to another level. The defendant in that case was charged with the murder of her child, whose remains were discovered several weeks after her initially unreported disappearance. The prosecution theorized that the defendant had killed her daughter, placed the body in the trunk of her car, and then dumped the body where the remains were later found. To support that theory, the prosecution offered the testimony of a forensic anthropologist, a Dr. Vass, who claimed that he had perfected a process of "human decomposition odor analysis" by which he could identify whether the scent of a decomposing human body was in the air, without any necessity for dog involvement. The police gathered air from the trunk in metal cans and Vass used gas chromatography to identify the gases present in the sample. Vass reported that 79.2% of the gases were consistent with those of a decomposing human body.[15]

Florida is a *Frye* State and the trial judge conducted a hearing on admissibility. Vass did not testify that his theory was generally accepted but insisted that it was "scientifically valid."[16] He cited his two published articles describing his research.[17] The defense presented the testimony of an expert in chemistry and biochemistry, a Dr. Furton. Furton testified that the concept "odor signatures of human composition" is not generally accepted n the scientific community and that "there are no scientifically validated methods capable of identifying the presence of human remains based on the presence or absence of specific chemical residues."[18] The prosecutor also submitted an article from a Greek chemical engineer, Dr. Miltiades Statheropoulos, who had studied the gases given off by the bodies of two men which were recovered after spending 3-4 weeks decomposing in the Mediterranean Sea.[19] The Statheropoulos article recognized its limitations based on a study of the volatile organic compounds given off by these two cadavers that had been in sea water for a month and also stated that "So far in the literature, there is not enough work to relate VOCs with human decomposition." The trial judge quoted from the Statheropoulos article extensive in his opinion, but apparently not for its scientific value. Ultimately, the judge admitted the Vass testimony, using an unusual interpretation of *Frye* that while the technique used by the expert must be generally accepted, the expert's opinion need not be. Thus, the judge reasoned, since the gas chromatography and mass spectrometry equipment used to detect the gases was generally accepted the expert's claimed ability to analyze the data from those instruments need not be. [20] The judge stated:

> Here, it is quite apparent Dr. Vass' opinions are based upon the results of the GC-MS and his knowledge and experience. Both Dr. Vass and Dr. Furton looked at the same data from the GC-MS but arrived at differing opinions. These different opinions can be based upon the expert's knowledge and experience in the area of human decomposition. The disagreement between the experts is best resolved by the trier of fact the jury. This is where both the defense and the state will have the opportunity to controvert the experts' findings and conclusions. [21]

The judge ruled that the Vass conclusion from the testing was admissible with the limitation that he could not state that the gases were "solely" those of a human decomposing body.[22]

The judge's opinion, however, amazingly went further than allowing Vass to give his database conclusions also included some comments that would later be a factor in what the jury heard. The judge held:

> As pointed out in Dr. Statheropoulos' article, the odor of putrefaction is characteristic and familiar to the front line criminal experts such as police investigators, forensic pathologists, anthropologists, entomologists, crime scene technicians and other medical and non-medical professionals. *It is simply common sense* that, to some extent, all of us have organoleptic expertise. Generally, we exercise the powers of

> sight, smell, and feel in our daily lives to detect odors and smells. . . . Thus, Dr. Vass, based upon his background and experience could offer testimony concerning the odor he smelled emanating from the sealed container. (emphasis added) [23]

The judge in effect ruled that Dr. Vass, and apparently others, were lay experts whose noses can detect the odor of a dead human body as distinguished from any other odors, including that of other dead mammals.

When the case went before the jury, Vass not only testified to his conclusions from the organic compound testing, but also was allowed to state that his olfactory senses were so attuned that he immediately knew the captured air was from a place where there had been a decomposing human:

> Vass recalled jumping back after opening the can of air. He said he could not believe such a tiny can could contain such a strong odor. He went on to say the odor was consistent with what he knows to be the smell of human decomposition, and went as far as to say he could not think of anything other than a dead and decomposing body that would explain the results he got from the samples he analyzed. [24]

Following the judge's lead in the opinion, the prosecution was also even allowed to present the testimony of a tow truck driver that when he was towing the defendant's car, he could "smell a dead body in the closed trunk."[25]

Ultimately, the jury acquitted Ms. Anthony. The trial judge's opinions and rulings will never be subjected to appellate review. The case is, however, illustrative from a forensic science evidence viewpoint. The Vass "human decomposition odor analysis" testimony would clearly not be admissible under *Daubert* criteria. There are no standards, there has been no testing of his theory, no error rate determination has been even undertaken, and the theory is certainly not yet generally accepted in the scientific community. With that state of affairs, it would seem even less likely to be admissible in a *Frye* State. The judge's interpretation of *Frye* as only requiring that the instrumentation be generally accepted for conclusions from that data to be admissible is not a "generally accepted" interpretation in the legal community. His further rationale allows the personal testimony of basically any first responder or criminalist, or even a tow truck driver, to testify as a lay expert that they have such highly developed olfactory senses that they can immediately identify the smell of a decomposing human body, even inside a closed car trunk. That opinion would strain even the most ardent rejecters of the *Kumho* ruling. In the end, what the *Anthony* case rulings demonstrate is the lengths to which judges will go to allow the admission of virtually any "scientific" evidence offered by the prosecution. It may also demonstrate that jurors, if confronted with a defense that has the resources to rebut such testimony, will find it overreaching and not to be, as the judge said, based on "common sense."

---

[1] See, e.g., Lasseter, A., K. Jacobi, R. Farley, and L. Hensel, *Cadaver Dog and Handler Team Capabilities in the Recovery of Buried Human Remains in the Southeastern United States*, 48 J Forensic Sci. 617 (2003); Komar, D., *The Use of Cadaver Dogs in Locating Scattered, Scavenged Human Remains: Preliminary Field Test Results*, 44 J Forensic Sci. 405 (1999).

[2] See, e.g. *United States v. Myers*, 2010 WL 2723196 (S.D.W.Va. 2010), applying *Daubert* and finding "scant, if any, evidence regarding the general acceptance, standard, or testing of canine searches used for identifying ignitable liquids" in a case involving possession of a "Molotov cocktail".

[3] For an early history of the admissibility issues in dog scent cases, see *Terrell v. State*, 239 A.2d 128 (Md. App. 1968).

[4] See, e.g., *United States v. Gates*, 680 F.2d 1117 (6th Cir. 1982); *State v. Roscoe*, 700 P.2d 1312 (Ariz. 1984); *United States v. McNiece*, 558 F.Supp. 612 (E.D.N.Y. 1983); *People v. Craig*, 86 Cal.App.3d 905 (1978).

[5] *State v. Roscoe, supra* at 221-222.

[6] See *Brott v. State*, 97 N.W. 593 (Neb.1903).

[7] *State v. Storm*, 238 P.2d 1161 (Mont. 1951) ("Irrespective of the rule obtaining elsewhere, we here hold that in this jurisdiction such so-called "bloodhound testimony" is incompetent and inadmissible on the trial of any person accused of crime and it is so declared.")

[8] See, e.g. *People v. McPherson*, 271 N.W.2d 228 (Mich. App. 1978).

[9] *State v. Storm, supra*: McWhorter, J.C., *The Bloodhound as Witness*, 54 Am. L. Rev.109 (1920); *People v. Cruz*, 643 N.E.2d 636   (Ill. 1994) ("We

continue to adhere to the principle that bloodhound evidence is inadmissible to establish any factual proposition in a criminal proceeding in Illinois.").

[10] Taslitz, Andrew E., *Does the Cold Nose Know? The Unscientific Myth of the Dog Scent Lineup*, 42 Hastings L.J. 17 (1990) (a comprehensive study of dog scent lineups, concluding that the uniqueness and stability of human odor had not been established and that scent lineups should not be admissible).

[11] *Winfrey v. State*, 323 S.W.3d 875 (Tex. Crim. App. 2010).

[12] *State v. Dominguez*, 2011 WL 3207766 (Tex. App. 2010).

[13] *State v. Smith*, 335 S.W.3d 706 (Tex. App. 2011).

[14] *State v. Anthony*, Ninth Judicial Circuit of Florida, Case No. 48-2008-CF-015606-O (2011), motions and orders available online at http://www.ninthcircuit.org/news/High-Profile-Cases/Anthony/orders&motions.shtml (last visited December 6, 2011).

[15] *Id., Motion to Exclude Unreliable Evidence* (Dec. 29, 2010).

[16] *Id, Order Denying Motion to Exclude Unreliable Evidence* (May 7, 2011).

[17] Vass, Arpad A., Rob R. Smith, Cyril V. Thompson, Michael N. Burnett, Dennis A. Wolf, Jennifer A. Synstelien, Nishan Dulgerian, and Brian A. Eckenrode, *Decompositional Odor Analysis Database*, 49 J. Forensic Sci. 1 (2004); Vass, Arpad A., Rob R. Smith, Cyril V. Thompson, Michael N. Burnett, Nishan Dulgerian, and Brian A. Eckenrode, *Odor Analysis of Decomposing Buried Human Remains*, 52 J. Forensic Sci. 384 (2008).

[18] *State v. Anthony, supra, Order Denying Motion to Exclude Unreliable Evidence* (May 7, 2011).

[19] Statheropoulos, Miltiades, C. Spiliopoulou, A. Agapiou, *A Study of Volatile Organic Compounds Evolved from the Decaying Human Body*, 153 Forensic Sci. Int'l 147 (2005).

[20] *State v. Anthony, supra, Order Denying Motion to Exclude Unreliable Evidence* (May 7, 2011).

[21] *Id.*, at p. 21.

[22] *Id.*, at pp.21-22.

[23] *Id.*, at pp.19-20.

[24] As reported by local news media in Fell, Jacqueline , Adam Longo and Kelli Cook, *Day 11: Expert smelled death in air samples from Casey Anthony's car*, Central Florida News, June 8, 2011, available online at http://www.cfnews13.com/article/news/2011/june/257538/ (last visited December 8, 2011).

[25] As reported by local news media in Fell, Jacqueline , Adam Longo and Kelli Cook, *Day 4: George Anthony questioned about smell in Casey's car*, Central   Florida   News,   May   27,   2011,   available   online   at http://www.cfnews13.com/article/news/2011/may/252672/Day-4:-George-Anthony-questioned-about-smell-in-Caseys-car (last visited December 8, 2011).

Chapter 15

Juror Expectations about Scientific Evidence

The "CSI Effect" Myth

Decisions about the admissibility of forensic science evidence assume even larger importance to the extent that jurors consider such evidence to be especially critical to their ultimate decision about guilt. It is widely perceived, especially by prosecutors and other law enforcement agencies, that modern juries give a great deal of weight to scientific evidence. They complain that jurors today demand more from the prosecution in the way of scientific evidence and that they will wrongfully acquit defendants when such evidence is not presented. Most of the blame for these expectations is heaped on a single television show, *CSI* (and its spin-offs), to the degree that it has become known, both in the popular media and in legal circles, as the "*CSI* effect."[1] One commentator even refers to it as the *CSI* "infection" of jurors.[2] However, while jurors clearly do have increased expectations and even demands for scientific evidence, it is far too simplistic to attribute those expectations and demands to a particular television show—or even to the a particular medium of television—and that to do so, distracts judges and lawyers from the important adjustments that need to be made in criminal trial practice to accommodate these new jurors.

Some commentators have speculated that there has been no increase in juror expectations or demands about scientific evidence, and the claimed *CSI* effect could be nothing more than "sour grapes" by prosecutors who were rationalizing losses[3] or attorneys for both sides just trying to influence jurors during voir dire.[4] Empirical studies of jurors were conducted in 2006 and 2009 to determine whether current juries expect and demand scientific evidence and, if so, whether it is related to their television watching habits.[5] The studies found that jurors do indeed expect prosecutors to present scientific evidence and that, especially in cases in which the rest of the evidence is circumstantial, they will demand scientific evidence before they will return a verdict of guilty.[6] However, the studies also found that, contrary to the common media characterizations, these increased expectations and demands for scientific evidence were *not* related to watching *CSI* or similar television programs.[7] Subsequent and other researchers have come to a similar conclusion.[8] Moreover, statistical studies have found no increase in acquittal rates that correlates to the onset or persistence of CSI or similar shows.[9]

The "Tech" Effect

If it is not watching *CSI*, then what is causing these increased expectations and demands? It has long been understood by social scientists that juror perceptions of the criminal justice system are influenced by characterizations of that system in television and other media. An early theory for that influence was the "cultivation theory," posited over thirty years ago by George Gerbner.[10] He theorized that television programs develop or "cultivate" the public's perceptions of societal reality.[11] Indeed, he regarded television as such a strong force in our society that it was the source of our perceptions of reality.[12] Gerbner found that one strong message that television communicated to the public was about crime and an overestimated likelihood of becoming a victim of crime in a "mean world."[13]

The problem with the cultivation theory as a means of explaining the impact of popular culture on individual perceptions of reality, especially as it relates to a claimed *CSI* effect, is that it is seriously technologically outdated. Thirty years is an enormous amount of time technologically. Television no longer has the overwhelming media impact on our culture today that it did when Gerbner made his observations, with a multitude of other media, including the internet, now available and being used by the population. Even within television, the media has changed dramatically. Since Gerbner's time, television offerings have increased dramatically from the three networks he saw to the hundreds of cable channels available today.

It certainly remains true that portrayals of crime and criminal justice on television impact the perception of law and, in particular, criminal justice in our popular culture.[14] However, today the medium of television conveys only a few of the many messages about crime and criminal justice that potential jurors receive. Perhaps more importantly, television itself is no longer the overpowering media influence in our society that it once was.[15] Postmodern society is globalized and interconnected, not only by goods and commerce, but by "changing, swirling, and colliding" media messages and other cultural forces that frame our perceptions of crime and criminal justice in a myriad of different messages and media.[16] The 2006 study concluded that "[r]ather than any direct "*CSI* effect" from watching certain types of television programs, . . . juror expectations of and demands for scientific evidence are the result of broader changes in popular culture related to advancements in both technology and information distribution. . . . that could be more accurately referred to as the 'tech effect.'"[17]

A unique feature of the rapid development of new scientific technology is that it has led to applications that have almost immediately become part of popular culture. Ordinary citizens know about and use their own personal and business applications of this technology. They may use a personal laptop, a high-powered business computer, or perhaps a brightly colored cellular phone with some of the capabilities of both types of computers. They may have a satellite-driven global positioning system on the dash of their car, or perhaps it is incorporated into that satellite-driven cellular phone as well. They may even use a mail-in or portable DNA kit to determine the parentage of their child. They also know that this new technology can be used in criminal courts. They have learned from the media about the now hundreds of wrongly convicted defendants who have had their innocence proven with DNA. They have watched countless television and films with news or fictional depictions of police solving crimes with some new technology, whether that technology is real or imagined. The 2009 juror study found that there was a connection between the sophistication of the technology equipment jurors used and their demands for scientific evidence.[18] This supports the idea of a "tech effect" as opposed to a "CSI effect."

The sources of this tech effect, and the various sociological theories which might explain it, are relevant to criminal justice professionals only to the extent that we might tailor our reactions to it in court.[19] If we appreciate the complexity of the tech effect, then law enforcement personnel and defense lawyers must tailor the investigations, the evidence, and the arguments either to provide the evidence the jury seeks or to explain to them why that evidence is not forthcoming in a particular case. If, on the other hand, juror expectations arise simply from watching a television show, as the *CSI* effect label suggests, then lawyers can ask simply ask jurors whether they watch those shows and whether they understand the differences between fiction and reality as applied to criminal proceedings. Indeed, the latter approach is significantly easier and, probably predictably, is the approach most often used.

Prosecutors argue that heightened jury expectations, regardless of their source, have improperly increased their burden of proof.[20] Prosecutors who do so violate the admonition of Judge Margaret Hinkle that "an effective advocate cannot ignore or talk down to jurors, whatever the composition of the jury," and that, especially in the area of forensic science evidence, they should "[n]ever underestimate jurors' intelligence, wisdom and common sense."[21] The constitutional commitment to a jury system is a judgment that justice in individual cases *should* reflect the values of popular culture. The jury system dictates that those trends, regardless of their source, will be reflected in individual cases.

Jurors think that DNA and other modern scientific techniques are extremely accurate — and they are right. DNA evidence is viewed by jurors as being qualitatively different from other traditional forms of evidence with a "special aura of credibility."[22] One recent study found that jurors rated DNA evidence as 95% accurate.[23] One reason why *CSI* is so popular, and perhaps so threatening to prosecutors, is that "although *CSI* depicts unrealistic crimes in a melodramatic fashion, this crime drama does so in a manner that suggests that its science is valid, that the audience understands science and can use it to solve crimes."[24] As Edward Imwinkelried put it, "Common sense suggests that a rational trier of fact would treat testimony about a random-match probability of one in 7.87 trillion as highly probative, if not dispositive."[25] The trends by jurors to expect and demand scientific evidence, exemplified by the tech effect, will undoubtedly continue. It is the government and the judicial system that must respond and adapt to those trends.

"Negative" Evidence

Regardless of the empirical evidence to the contrary, prosecutors for the most part continue to strongly believe that the "CSI effect" exists and can hurt their chances of obtaining a conviction.[26] As Prof. Imwinkelried put it:

> Even if only a few jurors are likely to be led astray by the effect, the prosecutor cannot ignore the effect. If even a single juror succumbs, the denouement may be a hung jury, wasting valuable time and government resources. From the perspective of the policymaker, the effect may indeed be a fiction or myth; but for the prosecutor in the trenches, the danger posed by the effect remains a troublesome reality.[27]

Prosecutors, and indeed police, have changed how they investigate, prepare and try criminal cases on the supposition that the CSI effect exists.[28]

One prosecutor response to the increasing tech effect demand for scientific evidence by jurors is to introduce evidence about tests that were not done or tests that did not incriminate the defendant. As one "CSI effect" believer put it, "Essentially, prosecutors are now not only faced with presenting and explaining the evidence that exists, they now also have to explain why certain evidence does not exist or is not applicable to the situation."[29] This "negative evidence" technique is designed to anticipate questions that jurors may have about the thoroughness of the government investigation so they will not speculate that had such testing been done it may have had exculpatory results. For example, in *United States v. McNeil*[30] the defendant was charged with using a firearm in furtherance of drug trafficking. A prosecution fingerprint expert was offered to testify his examination of the gun that was found in the defendant's shared residence did not reveal his or any other fingerprints. The defendant moved to exclude further proffered testimony from the expert "to explain why no latent print appeared on the firearm, and cite to other cases in which she has experience or is aware of in that effort." The Court stated that "[i]n the end, the question in dispute is why no fingerprints appeared in this case and held "[t]o the extent that the expert has knowledge of the frequency of firearms without latent prints, the expert could testify to that knowledge."

A broader example of this technique was presented in the Delaware case of *State v. Cooke*[31] in which the defendant was charged with murder, rape, burglary, and arson.[32] The prosecutor attempted to introduce several test results which were either inconclusive or exculpatory, and the defense filed a motion in *limine* to exclude that evidence as irrelevant.[33] The government's offer of proof read like a recitation of many modern forensic science testing procedures, including DNA prediction analysis, video enhancement, trace (hair) analysis, toolmark analysis, hair comparison, fingerprint analysis, voice identification analysis, footwear analysis, fabric impression analysis, and handwriting comparison.[34] The prosecution claimed that the "C.S.I. Effect" can encourage improper speculation by jurors and that it needed to show all of the tests that were done, even if they had negative results. In his extensive opinion, Judge Herlihy reviewed several studies and opinions regarding the so-called *CSI* effect, and the debate over whether it exists.[35] In the end, he did not conclude that there was any effect attributable to *CSI*, but observed that jurors appear to have expectations for scientific evidence and that those expectations are influencing trials that would justify the prosecution's desire to present such "negative" evidence.

Increased juror demands for scientific evidence may in fact justify the introduction of evidence that might otherwise be considered more prejudicial than probative. In *United States v. Fields*[36], a death penalty case, the defendant argued that admitting nineteen photos of the body at the crime scene and thirteen autopsy photos was an abuse of discretion by the trial judge.[37] Although the United States Court of Appeals for the Fifth Circuit found many of the pictures shocking and gruesome, including photos of the victim's decomposing body, it found them nevertheless to be highly probative based on the defense's position that there was no reliable DNA evidence and little crime scene evidence regarding the body itself.[38] The court held that "[i]n this age of the supposed 'CSI effect,' explaining to the jury why the Government had little in the way of physical or scientific evidence was arguably critical to the Government's case" and found no error in the admission of the photographs.[39]

Voir Dire, Argument and Jury Instructions

A second method of coping with the tech effect expectations of jurors is to address those expectations directly with the jurors at the trial. Attorneys have begun to do so using voir dire and opening and closing statements, and requesting jury instructions that pose the issue. Voir dire about *CSI* watching habits has been a typical prosecutorial approach.

Prosecutors' questions about whether potential jurors watch the program are certainly proper, and comments about the program or attempts to distinguish the investigations depicted on the program from reality have generally been upheld. For example, in *People v. Marquez* the court approved a prosecutor's voir dire, which asserted: "All of you have watched one kind of show, whether it's 'Law and Order,' 'CSI,' any of those shows. How many of you do that? How many of you have a certain expectation that both Mr. Mack and I, and the judge will perform in a similar manner as in those shows? Those are shows and that's not real life, and this is real life." [40] *People v. Smith* held that the prosecutor's remarks during voir dire that "real life is not akin to CSI television shows and that he was not trying to 'pull the wool' over the juror's eyes" were "merely" attempts to ensure that the jury not hold the prosecution to a higher burden of proof than was required. [41] Yet another example, *State v. Latham*, held that there was no prejudice in prosecutor's statements during voir dire that:

> [C]ertain types of forensic evidence were not technologically possible. . . . CSI is a bunch of you know what. . . .It doesn't happen that way. . . . The guy on CSI who's now a heart throb and everything else, this William Peterson, that might be— make for a good TV show, but that's not reality, okay. . . . That would be great if we could do that. That would be fabulous. But you can't. Okay. In all the years I been doing this, I've never had—that's just not something that— technologically is not there yet. [42]

Failing to object to a long prosecutor voir dire statement about *CSI* was held not to be a sign of ineffective counsel by the Ohio Court of Appeals of Ohio in *State v. Taylor*, in which the prosecutor had stated:

This is kind of an interesting story. I tell it in every one of my Voir Dires. I had a rape case a few years back when I was a fairly new Prosecutor. They found a pubic hair on the victim's underwear. Now, the victim knew the perpetrator, the alleged perpetrator, so I said, let's test it and see if it is his pubic hair. So, I call the Attorney General's Office, who does our genetic testing, and they tell me that is not good science. No, no. I just saw it on CSI. Of course it is good science. Just to double-check I called the county Coroner's Office, and they tell me the same thing. So, a lot of those TV shows are fictional, or the science is no good. It is fictional for purposes of solving their fictional crimes.[43]

In *United States v. Harrington*,[44] the trial judge took it upon herself to state to the jury venire during voir dire that "*CSI* evidence" was not required to convict the defendant.[45] The judge in that case conducted her own voir dire about *CSI* and has said that jurors who indicate that they will require a showing of *CSI*-type evidence in order to convict are appropriate candidates to be dismissed for cause.[46] On appeal, the defendant asserted that the judge's voir dire, especially the use of the word "convict" lessened the state's burden of proof in the eyes of the jurors. The Court of Appeals for the Eleventh Circuit found that the trial judge district court's use of the word "convict" was "a matter of phrasing and did not change the burden of proof and that the judge "did not err by questioning jurors about whether they would be able to separate television shows from the facts of the case and stating that there may not be 'CSI' evidence presented to them."[47]

However, the Maryland Court of Appeals recently considered the same issue in a more thoughtful fashion in *Charles v. State*[48] . In that murder case the trial judge stated in voir dire:

I'm going to assume that many of you, from having done a few of these, watch way too much TV, including the so-called realistic crime shows like CSI and Law and Order. I trust that you understand that these crime shows are fiction and fantasy and are done for dramatic effect and for this dramatic effect they purport to rely upon, "scientific evidence," to convict guilty persons. While this is certainly acceptable as entertainment you must not allow this entertainment experience to interfere with your duties as a juror. Therefore, if you are currently of the opinion or belief that you cannot convict a defendant without "scientific evidence," regardless of the other evidence in the case and regardless of the instructions that I will give you as to the law, please rise. (emphasis in original)[49]

The Maryland court reviewed the literature and empirical studies about the so-called *CSI* effect in the context of the judge's language, stating, "Specifically, we consider whether the use of the term 'convict' in the heart of the inquiry, rendered the question untenable . . . "[50] The court concluded that ". . . the voir dire question at issue here suggested that the jury's only option was to convict, regardless of whether scientific evidence was adduced"[51] and held that "the judge abused his discretion by suggesting to the panel that 'convict[ing]' Drake and Charles was the only option in the present case; this suggestive question poisoned the venire, thereby depriving Drake and Charles of a fair and impartial jury."[52]

Many of the reported cases involving *CSI* voir dire have arisen in the context of a *Batson* challenge,[53] where the prosecutor must prove that it was the juror's answers to *CSI* questions, rather than race, that motivated a peremptory challenge. In *United States v. Hendrix*,[54] the prosecution claimed that it had excused the only two black jurors on race neutral grounds: as to one of the black jurors, the prosecutor explained that the exclusion was because he was "one of those CSI guys," and the prosecutor had "great concern about the jurors who watch a lot of CSI."[55] The United States Court of Appeals for the Seventh Circuit held that, coupled with other factors, the *CSI* explanation was not pretextual and defeated the *Batson* challenge.[56] In *State v. Carson*,[57] a juror's response to the defense during defense voir dire about *CSI* was offered as the basis for the prosecution's peremptory challenge of a minority juror, and the court found that to be a race neutral reason.[58] Other cases have similarly found answers to *CSI* voir dire to be a race neutral basis for excusing minority jurors.[59]

Opening statements and closing arguments about the "CSI effect" have caused more difficulty for prosecutors. In *Boatswain v. State*,[60] the prosecutor's closing argument included the following:

The one issue left in this case is: Was it him? The defense would say, well—and you know they will—there's [sic] no fingerprints of him [sic]. They didn't print the money. They didn't find his prints on the note. In today's day and age, unfortunately, the police and the State isn't [sic] put to the same test that they wrote 200 years ago in the Constitution [in] which they said the proof must be beyond a reasonable doubt. Unfortunately, the test, of course, of criminal defendants now is, can they meet the TV expectation that they hope folks like you want. Can they meet CSI?

[Objection overruled]

[I]f they don't have fingerprints, he can't be guilty. On TV, they would have found fingerprints. But this isn't TV, this is real life.[61]

Although the Supreme Court of Delaware did not find that the argument required reversal, it did find clear error in allowing such an argument because statements that trivialize the actual constitutional standard of the burden of proof are improper.

In the subsequent case of *Mathis v. State*,[62] the Supreme Court of Delaware distinguished *Boatswain* in a situation where it found that the prosecutor's opening statement did not disparage the burden of proof.[63] Later, in *Morgan v. State*,[64] the Supreme Court of Delaware reaffirmed *Boatswain* and found that it was improper for the prosecutor to argue that "[t]his is not CSI Las Vegas or CSI New York where police do all sorts of different tests all the time. It's fact specific. In this case it wouldn't have worked. So why do it?"[65] The court held that the argument was improper because there was no evidentiary basis for the statement that the tests were unavailable or would have been to no avail.[66] Other courts have followed the *Boatswain* reasoning and found *CSI* statements or arguments to be improper.[67] In *People v. Compean*, the court found it to be error, although corrected by a jury instruction, when a prosecutor stated:

Nobody is going to fingerprint a little baggie like you see there. This is not 'CSI.' These are the economic realities and times of Contra Costa County. . . . All of ya'll lives [sic] in this county, I think you know the economic realities of it.[68]

On the other hand, some courts have approved arguments or statements that urge the jury to consider the *CSI* effect in a way that reinforces rather than disparages the burden of proof. For example, in *State v. Pittman*,[69] the prosecutor's opening statement included the following comments:

> Do not hold the State of New Jersey to a standard that is not given to you by the Court. Do not hold the State of New Jersey to what I call the Hollywood standard. This is not TV. This is not CSI New York. This is not CSI New Brunswick, okay. What you see on TV is not real. This is what happens. Not what you see on Law & Order. Not what you see on Court TV. Not what you see on the Grammys that come from a Hollywood producer with writers and producers that, to sell commercials. It is not real. Do not hold the State of New Jersey to the Hollywood standard. Hold it to the standard of what reality is. You're going to hear reality in this courtroom. That is how it's done. It is what happens on the streets. . . . .
> Do not hold the State of New Jersey to that Hollywood standard. Hold it to the standard of reality and what the Court gives you. Keep that in mind when you are hearing the testimony.[70]

The Appellate Division of the New Jersey Superior Court found no error and held that the prosecutor was just "trying to dispel any illusion jurors may have had that a trial in the real world is like a trial in the world of fiction."[71]

Objections that comments about *CSI* are based on facts outside the record have been rejected on the basis that "the prosecutor was merely referring to the jurors' common knowledge that, unlike in the real world, investigations on television typically wrap up in less than an hour."[72] Similar *CSI* arguments have been allowed by trial judges and approved on appeal.[73] On the other hand, the Supreme Court of Montana brought up *CSI* in an interesting context dealing with a motion to suppress a search of a drug dealer, saying in *State v. Goetz*:

> Truly, it is a different world today, not only in terms of technological advances, but also in the expectation of the use of technology. I would submit, as the questioning italicized

above likewise indicates, that our citizens, especially young people in today's society who have been raised in the age of *Law and Order* and *CSI*, would think it unusual that a drug dealer would have a *reasonable* expectation that his conversations during a drug sale to a non-confidant were not being consensually monitored. The drug dealer may have a *subjective* expectation, but it is not an expectation that our society would deem reasonable.[74]

Prosecutors and even defense attorneys have also elicited testimony referring to *CSI*, or the *CSI* effect, that has been the subject of appeals. For example, in *State v. McKinney*,[75] the prosecutor questioned witnesses about whether the defendant watched *CSI* and the defendant objected that the questioning was improper character evidence.[76] On appeal, the Ohio court ruled that it was "not willing to hold that watching network crime series such as *CSI* or in previous decades *Perry Mason*, *Dragnet*, and others constitutes evidence of bad character."[77] Other courts have also allowed testimony referring to *CSI*.[78]

To address the tech effect, some courts have given jury instructions about how the jury should consider issues concerning the lack of scientific evidence. In *United States v. Saldarriaga*,[79] the defense had questioned government witnesses in a drug delivery trial about the failure of the government to record, photograph, or videotape the undercover transaction or to test the bag containing the drugs for fingerprints.[80] Apparently *sua sponte*, the trial judge gave the following instructions to the jury:

> The law is clear that the government has no obligation to use any particular techniques. The government's techniques [are] not on trial here. The government has no obligation to use all the possible techniques that are available to it. The government's function is to give enough evidence to satisfy you beyond a reasonable doubt that the charges are true, and the fact that there are a thousand other things they could have done is wholly irrelevant.
> However, if suggesting things that they could have done leads you to think, well, maybe I have a reasonable doubt because I

didn't have any evidence on that subject, if that happens, why, then, of course, that is a reasonable doubt like anything else.

. . . If evidence is such that without the picture you would have a reasonable doubt as to whether the government established the defendant['] s identity as the person who did these things, then you have a reasonable doubt and it doesn't make any difference whether the government could have or could not have. Maybe the government could establish beyond peradventure that it would be impossible to have that picture, it doesn't make any difference. If you have a reasonable doubt because you didn't get the picture, then you [have] a reasonable doubt.

It is wholly immaterial whether the government could have done it or couldn't have done it or how many people the government had available that would do it.[81]

The United States Court of Appeals for the Second Circuit, *per curiam*, held:

[T]he jury correctly was instructed that the government has no duty to employ in the course of a single investigation all of the many weapons at its disposal, and that the failure to utilize some particular technique or techniques does not tend to show that a defendant is not guilty of the crime with which he has been charged.[82]

A similar instruction about the failure to conduct fingerprint tests was approved by the United States Court of Appeals for the Fourth Circuit earlier in *United States v. Mason*.[83]

Some proponents of the strong prosecutor view of the *CSI* effect suggest that judges should give specifically tailored instructions about both before and after the evidence is presented. Professor Lawson has suggested adding an element to the usual preliminary instructions about what constitutes evidence:

In the age of the CSI Infection, an additional fifth bullet could be added to the standard instruction already entitled "What is not Evidence." This would highlight that information learned outside the courtroom from fictional television, movies, and books about criminal investigations cannot be considered in the jurors' decision-making process. This fifth point would address the difficulties faced by lay jurors attempting to differentiate between fact and fiction. The blurring between fact and fiction is becoming grayer and increasingly difficult for lay jurors to separate. Although many television shows are based on plots ripped from the headlines, they are not legally accurate depictions of the cases, but rather, sensationalized versions. Television shows are not bound by the Constitution or rules of evidence. The general facts depicted can be similar to reality, but the manner by which those facts are discovered, and the reliability of the investigative methods used in obtaining them, as well as their admissibility in court, are stretched and manipulated by producers for entertainment purposes and better ratings. Due to the widespread popularity of this type of entertainment, jurors must be cautioned. [84]

She generally suggests a post-evidentiary jury instruction that:

. . . is one focused on the sources of CSI Infection that originate outside of the courtroom--television, media, films, books, and the like. An instruction not to use outside standards, like those used in forensic crime television shows, when making judgments about guilt or innocence inside the courtroom more appropriately balances the mutual interests of the litigants. The secondary goal is to remind jurors to apply only the legal standard as instructed by the judge, i.e., the burden of proof beyond a reasonable doubt, not some fictional standard of proof. [85]

In *Evans v. State*,[86] the defense attacked the government's heroin delivery case because no video record had been made of the alleged undercover drug purchase.[87] In its instructions to the jury, the court addressed the claimed testing deficiency:

During this trial, you have heard testimony of witnesses and may hear argument of counsel that the State did not utilize a specific investigative technique or scientific test. You may consider these facts in deciding whether the State has met its

> burden of proof. You should consider all of the evidence or lack of evidence in deciding whether a defendant is guilty. However, I instruct you that there is no legal requirement that the State utilize any specific investigative technique or scientific test to prove its case. Your responsibility as jurors is to determine whether the State has proven, based on the evidence, the defendants' guilt beyond a reasonable doubt.[88]

The appeals court noted that such arguments are commonly used by the defense to raise a reasonable doubt.[89] Relying on *Saldarriaga*, the court found that the instruction did not undermine the prosecution's duty to prove guilt beyond a reasonable doubt and affirmed the conviction.[90] However, the court offered some advice as to a better way of giving such an instruction:

> [W]e stress that the salutary effect of the instruction is found in the advisement that the absence of such evidence should be factored into the juror's determination of whether the State has shouldered its burden if, *and only if*, the absence of such evidence, itself, creates reasonable doubt. The absence of evidence, available to the State, may not, *ipso facto*, constitute reasonable doubt. The risk is greatest that such an instruction will run afoul of the prohibition against relieving the State of its burden where the instruction is predominant in the overall instructions and its relation to the reasonable doubt standard unclear. Consequently, the preferable practice is for the court's instruction to be promulgated in conjunction with the explication of the State's burden to prove the defendant guilty beyond a reasonable doubt.[91]

The advice in *Evans* is worth heeding. If the trial judge gives an instruction regarding the lack of scientific evidence, whether requested or *sua sponte*, it should be cast in terms of reasonable doubt to make sure that the jury understands that while a lack of scientific evidence *alone* does not mean there is reasonable doubt, they must never nevertheless determine whether the government has proven, without such scientific evidence, the defendant's guilt beyond a reasonable doubt.

[1] For a listing of a few of the multitude of media reports of the *CSI* effect see Donald E. Shelton, Young S. Kim & Gregg Barak, *A Study of Juror Expectations and Demands Concerning Scientific Evidence: Does the "CSI Effect" Exist?*, 9 Vand. J. Ent. & Tech. L. 331, 363-64 (2006).

[2] Lawson, Tamara F., *Before the Verdict and Beyond the Verdict: The CSI Infection Within Modern Criminal Jury Trials*, 41 Loy. U. Chi. L.J. 119 (2009).

[3] "To a prosecutor surprised, or just disappointed, by an acquittal, the CSI Effect presents a ready, appealing explanation." Cole, Simon A. and Rachel Dioso-Villa, *CSI and Its Effects: Media, Juries, and the Burden of Proof*, 41 New Eng. L. Rev. 435 (2007), at 463.

[4] Cole and Dioso-Villa explain: "Both sides may be seen as trying to influence the jury pool by getting the media to propagate the story that their side is being increasingly disadvantaged by the CSI Effect. In other words, litigators seek to benefit from media stories that claim that the other side has been unfairly benefited by television programming." *Id.* at 464.

[5] Shelton, Donald E., *Juror Expectations for Scientific Evidence in Criminal Cases: Perceptions and Reality About the "CSI Effect" Myth* , 27 T. M. Cooley L. Rev. 1 (2010); Shelton, Donald E., Young S. Kim & Gregg Barak, *A Study of Juror Expectations and Demands Concerning Scientific Evidence: Does the "CSI Effect" Exist?*, 9 Vand. J. Ent. & Tech. L. 331 (2006); and Shelton, Donald E., Young S. Kim & Gregg Barak, *An Indirect-Effects Model of Mediated Adjudication: The CSI Myth, the Tech Effect, and Metropolitan Jurors' Expectations for Scientific Evidence*, 12 Vand. J. Ent. & Tech. L. 1 (2009). For a further analysis of the 2006 study data, see Kim, Young S., Gregg Barak, and Donald E. Shelton, *Examining the "CSI-effect" in the Cases of Circumstantial Evidence and Eyewitness Testimony: Multivariate and Path Analyses*, 37 J. Crim. Justice 452 (2009).

[6] *Id.*

[7] *Id.*

[8] "We conclude that there is little support for the gravest of the CSI Effects, which is that jurors who watch *CSI* are wrongfully acquitting in cases lacking forensic evidence or that they are wrongfully convicting based on an unrealistic belief in the infallibility of forensic science." Cole, Simon A. and Rachel Dioso-Villa, *CSI and Its Effects: Media, Juries, and the Burden of Proof*, 41 New Eng. L. Rev. 435(2007),at 436.

[9] See Cole, Simon A. and Rachel Dioso-Villa, *Investigating the "CSI Effect"*

Effect: Media and Litigation Crisis in Criminal Law, 61 Stan. L. Rev. 1335 (2009).

[10] Gerbner, George et al., *Growing Up With Television: Cultivation Processes*, *in* Media Effects: Advances In Theory And Research 43, 43-44 Bryant, Jennings & Dolf Zillmann eds., 2d ed. 2002); Gerbner, George and Larry Gross, *Living with Television: The Violence Profile*, 26 J. Comm. 173 (1976).

[11] Gerbner, George and Larry Gross, *Living with Television: The Violence Profile*, 26 J. Comm. 173(1976), at 191.

[12] *Id.*

[13] *Id.,* at 193.

[14] See Stark, Steven D., *Perry Mason Meets Sonny Crockett: The History of Lawyers and the Police as Television Heroes*, 42 U. Miami L. Rev. 229, 229-35 (1988); Keslowitz, Steven, Note, *The Simpsons, 24, and the Law: How Homer Simpson and Jack Bauer Influence Congressional Lawmaking and Judicial Reasoning*, 29 Cardozo L. Rev. 2787, 2787-98 (2007).

[15] See Dimmick, John, Yan Chen, & Zhan Li, *Competition Between the Internet and Traditional News Media: The Gratification-Opportunities Niche Dimension*, 17 J. Media Econ. 19, 27 (2004); Press Release, The Pew Research Ctr., *Social Networking and Online Videos Take Off: Internet's Broader Role in Campaign 2008* (Jan. 11, 2008), available online at http://people-press.org/reports/pdf/384.pdf (last visited December 14, 2011) (indicating that the number of people who get political information from the internet, as opposed to television, almost doubled between 2004 and 2008).

[16] Papke, David Ray, *The Impact of Popular Culture on American Perceptions of the Courts*, 82 Ind. L. J. 1225, 1226-28 (2007).

[17] Shelton, Donald E. Young S. Kim & Gregg Barak, *A Study of Juror Expectations and Demands Concerning Scientific Evidence: Does the "CSI Effect" Exist?*, 9 Vand. J. Ent. & Tech. L. 331 (2006), at 368.

[18] Shelton, Donald E., *Juror Expectations for Scientific Evidence in Criminal Cases: Perceptions and Reality About the "CSI Effect" Myth* , 27 T. M. Cooley L. Rev. 1 (2010).

[19] For an interesting discussion of the literature concerning the existence of any CSI effect, and a rather ambiguous conclusion about the role that judicial actors must play in response to it, see Georgette, Luke F., *The Hung Jury: Scholarly Consensus on the Value of the CSI Effect in the Future of American Justice*, 3 Intersect Stan. J. Sci. Tech & Society 1 (2010).

[20] Cole and Dioso-Villa suggest that what prosecutors really mean is that jurors may be rejecting the adversarial system in favor of more scientific truth finding. "Writ larger, this perhaps speaks to law's more fundamental anxiety about science encroaching on the law's role as a truth-making institution. Perhaps this, then, is the real CSI Effect." Cole, Simon A. and Rachel Dioso-Villa, *CSI and Its Effects: Media, Juries, and the Burden of Proof*, 41 New Eng. L. Rev. 435 (2007), at 469.

[21] Hinkle, Margaret R., *Criminal Practice in Suffolk Superior Court*, Boston Bar J., Nov./Dec. 2007, at 6,7.

[22] Lieberman, Joel D., Courtney A. Carrell, Terance D. Miethe, and Daniel A. Krauss, *Gold Versus Platinum: Do Jurors Recognize the Superiority and Limitations of DNA Evidence Compared to Other Types of Forensic Evidence?*, 14 Psychology, Pub. Pol'y & L. 27 (2008), at 32. Shelton, et al., also found that 22% of jurors expect to see DNA evidence in all criminal cases, with that number expanding to 46% in murder cases and 73% in rape cases. Shelton, Donald E., Young S. Kim & Gregg Barak, *A Study of Juror Expectations and Demands Concerning Scientific Evidence: Does the "CSI Effect" Exist?*, 9 Vand. J. Ent. & Tech. L. 331(2006).

[23] Lieberman Joel D., Courtney A. Carrell, Terance D. Miethe, and Daniel A. Krauss, *Gold Versus Platinum: Do Jurors Recognize the Superiority and Limitations of DNA Evidence Compared to Other Types of Forensic Evidence?*, 14 Psychology, Pub. Pol'y & L. 27 (2008), at 52.

[24] Deutsch, Sarah Keturah and Gray Cavender, *CSI and Forensic Realism*, 15 J. Crim. Just. & Popular Culture 34, 34 (2008), available online at http://www.albany.edu/scj/jcjpc/vol15is1/Deutsch_Cavender.pdf (last visited December 14, 2011).

[25] Imwinkelried, Edward J., *The Relative Priority That Should Be Assigned to Trial Stage DNA Issues*, in *DNA And The Criminal Justice System: The Technology Of Justice*, ed. David Lazer, (2004), at 97.

[26] See Stevens, Dennis J., *CSI Effect, Prosecutors, and Wrongful Convictions*, 45 No. 4 Crim. Law Bulletin ART 2 (2009).

[27] Imwinkelried, Edward J., *Dealing With Supposed Jury Preconceptions About the Significance of the Lack of Evidence: The Difference Between the Perspective of the Policymaker and That of the Advocate*, 27 T.M. Cooley L. Rev. 37 (2010).

[28] See Gabel, Jessica D., *Forensiphilia: Is Public Fascination with Forensic Science a Love Affair or Fatal Attraction*, 36 New Eng. J. on Crim. & Civ.

Confinement 233 (2010).

[29] Durnal, Evan W., *Crime Scene Investigation (as seen on TV)*,199 For. Sci. Int'l 1 (2010).

[30] *United States v. McNeil*, 2010 WL 56096 (M.D. Pa. 2010).

[31] *State v. Cooke*, 914 A.2d 1078, 1082 (Del. Super. Ct. 2007).

[32] *Id,.* at 1080.

[33] *Id.,* at 1080-81.

[34] *Id.,* at 1083.

[35] *Id.,* at 1087-88.

[36] *United States. v. Fields*, 483 F.3d 313 (5th Cir. 2007).

[37] *Id.,* at 323, 354.

[38] *Id.,* at 355.

[39] *Id.* (citing Tom R. Tyler, *Viewing* CSI *and the Threshold of Guilt: Managing Truth and Justice in Reality and Fiction,* 115 Yale L. J. 1050, 1050 (2006)).

[40] *People v. Marquez*, No. B184697, 2006 WL 2665509, at *4-*5 & n.5 (Cal. Ct. App. Sept. 18, 2006).

[41] *People v. Smith*, No. 271036, 2007 WL 4248571, at *5 (Mich. Ct. App. Dec. 4, 2007).

[42] *State v. Latham*, No. 92,521, 2005 WL 1619235, at *2 (Kan. Ct. App. Nov. 1, 2005).

[43] *State v. Taylor*, No. 06CA009000, 2008 WL 834437, at *3-*4 (Ohio Ct. App. March 31, 2008).

[44] *United States v. Harrington,* 204 F. App'x 784 (11th Cir. 2006)

[45] *Id.,* at 788.

[46] Interview with Judge Marcia Cooke reported in Lawson, Tamara F., *Before the Verdict and Beyond the Verdict: The CSI Infection Within Modern Criminal Jury Trials,* 41 Loy. U. Chi. L.J. 119 (2009) at 146-147.

[47] *United States v. Harrington,* 204 F. App'x 784 (11th Cir. 2006) at 789.

[48] *Charles v. State,* 997 A.2d 154 (Md. Ct. App. 2010).

[49] *Id,.* at 156-157.

[50] *Id,.* at 160.

[51] *Id,.* at 161.

[52] *Id,.* at 162.

[53] *Batson v. Kentucky,* 476 U.S. 79 (1986) (holding that exclusion of jurors based on race violates the Equal Protection Clause of the United States Constitution).

[54] *United States v. Hendrix,* 509 F.3d 362 (7th Cir. 2007).

[55] *Id,.* at 367 (internal quotation marks omitted).

[56] *Id,.* at 372.

[57] *State v. Carson*, No. C-040042, 2005 WL 497290 (Ohio Ct. App. March 4, 2005).

[58] *Id.,* at *6.

[59] *See, e.g.*, *Wells v. Ricks*, No. 07 Civ. 6982(CM)(AJP), 2008 WL 506294, at *28-*30, *33 (S.D.N.Y. Feb. 26, 2008) (reading detective novels or watching *CSI* is a race neutral basis for excluding a juror); *People v. Reyes*, No. E040509, 2007 WL 4427856, at *9-*11 (Cal. Ct. App. Dec. 19, 2007) (responding to prosecutor's suggestion that the case "would not be like the CSI television show," juror indicated that she thought "it would be harder to evaluate the case just on testimony"; this was found to be a race neutral ground for excluding Hispanics); *People v. Henderson*, No. A102395, 2004 WL 2526448, at *4-*5 (Cal. Ct. App. Nov. 9, 2004) (holding juror's statement that *CSI* " shows how they get evidence that they do and things like that " was a race neutral ground for exclusion (internal quotation marks omitted)).

[60] *Boatswain v. State*, No. 408, 2004, 2005 WL 1000565 (Del. April 27, 2005).

[61] *Id.,* at *1-*2 (alterations in original).

[62] *Mathis v. State*, No. 25, 2006, 2006 WL 2434741, at *4 (Del. 2006) (delivering closing argument, the prosecutor told the jury: "Now, keep in mind when you're listening to the testimony from the witness stand this is not CSI Miami, it's not Law and Order. Nobody involved in this case, no one in this room is an actor. These are real people."

[63] *Id.,* (citing *Boatswain*, 2005 WL 1000565, at *2-*3).

[64] *Morgan v. State*, 922 A.2d 395 (Del. 2007).

[65] *Id.,* at 401 (citing *Mathis v. State*, No. 25, 2006, 2006 WL 2434741, at *4 (Del. Aug. 21, 2006); *Boatswain v. State*, No. 408, 2004, 2005 WL 1000565 (Del. April 27, 2005); *Wainwright v. State*, 504 A.2d 1096, 1100 (Del. 1986).

[66] *Id.,* at 402-03. The court held that, unlike *Boatswain*, there had not been a timely objection, and therefore did not require reversal on that ground. *Id.*; see also *State v. Snowden*, Nos. 04-07-2546, 03-09-3175, 2007 WL 1119339, at *4 (N.J. Super. Ct. App. Div. April 17, 2007) (per curiam) (finding a lack of evidentiary basis for prosecution arguments).

[67] *See, e.g.*, *State v. Hill*, No. A05-570, 2006 WL 1320075, at *3-*5 (Minn. Ct. App. May 16, 2006) (finding harmless error); *State v. Minor*, No. C-060043, 2007 WL 196504, at *3 (Ohio Ct. App. Jan. 26, 2007).

[68] *People v. Compean*, No. A111367, 2007 WL 1567603, at *8 (Cal. Ct. App. May 31, 2007).

[69] *State v. Pittman*, No. 04-03-00373, 2007 WL 4482159 (N.J. Super. Ct. App. Div. Dec. 26, 2007).

[70] *Id.*, at *3.

[71] *Id.*, at *7.

[72] *State v. Strong*, 142 S.W.3d 702, 724-25 (Mo. 2004) (en banc) (citing *State v. Christeson*, 50 S.W.3d 251, 268-69 (Mo. 2001) (*en banc*)). The holding apparently presumes that jurors have a common knowledge about the length of criminal investigation and/or that CSI has assumed such popularity that it can now be considered "popular knowledge." *Id.*; *State v. Snowden*, Nos. 04-07-2546, 03-09-3175, 2007 WL 1119339, at *4 (N.J. Super. Ct. App. Div. April 17, 2007).

[73] *State v. Snowden*, Nos. 04-07-2546, 03-09-3175, 2007 WL 1119339, at *4 (N.J. Super. Ct. App. Div. April 17, 2007), holding that the prosecutor was legitimately responding to a defense argument that mistakes had been made in the investigation); see also *United States v. Duronio*, No. 02-0933 (JAG), 2006 WL 3591259, at *3 (D.N.J. Dec. 11, 2006) (holding the statement that the defense attorney's "favorite television program" must be CSI was not an ad hominem attack on counsel, but was a permissible response to the defense argument that fingerprints were not found on a computer); *State v. Ash*, No. A07-0761, 2008 WL 2965555, at *7 (Minn. Ct. App. Oct. 21, 2008) (citing *State v. Walsh*, 495 N.W.2d 602, 607 (Minn. 1993) (holding that the prosecutor's closing statement, asking the jury not to hold the State to a burden like CSI was not improper).

[74] *State v. Goetz*, 191 P.3d 489, 517 (Mont. 2008).

[75] *State v. McKinney*, No. 2007-T-0004, 2008 WL 2582860 (Ohio Ct. App. June 27, 2008).

[76] *Id.* at *25.

[77] *Id.* A similar objection as to character and relevance was rejected in *People v. Brooks*, No. F051251, 2008 WL 2897093, at *15 (Cal. Ct. App. July 29, 2008).

[78] See, e.g., *Cox v. State*, 966 So.2d 337, 353-54 (Fla. 2007) (citing *Holland v. State*, 916 So. 2d 750, 758 (Fla. 2005); *Gordon v. State*, 863 So.2d 1215, 1223 (Fla. 2003)) (holding that it was not ineffective representation for failing to object to expert testimony that DNA evidence could be wiped from a murder weapon was "preposterous" because "anybody else with walking-

around sense would think the same thing . . . in this day and age of watching
CSI".

[79] *United States v. Saldarriaga*, 204 F.3d 50 (2d Cir. 2000).

[80] *Id.,* at 51 (quoting the district court's charge).

[81] *Id.,* at 51-52.

[82] *Id.,* at 53.

[83] *United States v. Mason*, 954 F.2d 219, 222 (4th Cir. 1992).

[84] Lawson, Tamara F., *Before the Verdict and Beyond the Verdict: The CSI Infection Within Modern Criminal Jury Trials*, 41 Loy. U. Chi. L.J. 119 (2009) at 154-155.

[85] *Id.,* at 164.

[86] *Evans v. State*, 922 A.2d 620 (Md. Ct. Spec. App. 2007).

[87] *Id.,* at 628-29 (quoting the trial court's instruction).

[88] *Id.,* at 628.

[89] *Id.,* at 627.

[90] *Id.,* at 631-33.

[91] *Id.,* at 633.

Chapter 16
Summary and Conclusions

The Last Twenty Years - An Era of Doubt

The status of forensic science evidence began to change in the 1990s. As Professor Michel J. Saks put it recently:

> Whatever tests of admissibility of expert testimony might formally have existed in various jurisdictions at various periods over the past century or so, they were applied infrequently to government proffers of forensic science. . . . The casual acceptance by courts over the past century of whatever the government proffered in the name of scientific expert testimony is beginning to catch up with the law."[1]

It is important to understand that the questioning of the rather routine admission of forensic science evidence in criminal prosecutions began during an era when science and technology, including information technology, was experiencing a surge of development. It was, and still is, an amazing technological age of discovery and information exchange. A 2006 Rand research study stated:

> Based on our technical foresights . . . , we see no indication that the accelerated pace of technology development is abating, and neither is the trend toward multidisciplinarity nor the increasingly integrated nature of technology applications. . . . Underlying all of this is the continuing trend toward globally integrated publications media, Internet connectivity, and scientific conferences, as well as the development and

crossfertilization of ever more sensitive and selective instrumentation.[2]

The development and miniaturization of computers and the application of computer technology to almost every human endeavor has been a primary force in scientific and technological developments, and of our awareness of those developments.[3]

Perhaps no other development exemplifies this age as poignantly as the discovery of the ability to understand the complexity of DNA that is at the source of our being, and then to begin to effectively "map" the entire human genome. DNA mapping also illustrates another feature of modern technology that is relevant to developments in forensic science. This modern technology made it possible to gather and systematically analyze enormous amounts of empirical data. Specifically as it affects forensic science, this hyperextension of the abilities of quantitative analysis presents a much more scientific model in some areas where we had been content to rely on anecdotal or experiential, or perhaps more generously called "qualitative analysis," conclusions.

Against this technological backdrop, some specific changes in the legal, scientific and cultural landscape have cast some significant doubts on our continued use of several types of previously admitted forensic science evidence in criminal cases. Professor Saks recently posited three such events:

> First, the Supreme Court's decision in *Daubert v. Merrill Dow Pharmaceuticals* changed the inquiry for admissibility to essentially the question scientists ask: What empirical evidence supports the validity of the expert's claims? . . .
> Second, the advent of DNA typing provided a general model of how forensic identification could be accomplished: basing it on a sound theoretical foundation, borrowed from normal science, developing an acceptable probabilistic model, and building a database of empirical data on which to base case-by-case probabilistic conclusions.
> Third, the use of DNA typing to exonerate innocent individuals who had been erroneously convicted led to analysis of the underlying cases in search of understanding

what went wrong in those trials. Forensic science emerged as a surprisingly large part of the problem.[4]

Those events are certainly three of the developments that have helped create the current view that existing forensic science may not be always properly being admitted in criminal cases. In the context of the larger changes in science and technology, two other specific forces should be added - the recent report of the National Research Council (NRC)[5] and the impact that technology changes are having on the expectations and demands of jurors.

Daubert's Change in the Legal Standard for Admissibility

As to *Daubert*, it is ironic, and perhaps significant, that the issue of the admissibility of forensic science evidence was decided by the Supreme Court in a civil rather than criminal case. Indeed, the three cases involved in the *Daubert* trilogy were all civil cases in which the plaintiff was offering scientific evidence that the corporate defendant wanted to be excluded. One can only speculate as to whether the Court would have reached the same conclusions had the issue been presented in the context of a prosecutor attempting to use an expert to prove the guilt of an accused, rather than in the context of a civil plaintiff trying to use an expert to prove liability for damages against a large corporation. The speculation is especially intense in the *Kumho* case in which the Court applied *Daubert* to "technical" as well as "scientific" testimony, because much of the prosecution evidence proffered in criminal cases is often regarded as more technical than scientific at its foundation.

Whatever the motivation, *Daubert* significantly changed the legal landscape for the admission of forensic science evidence in criminal cases, as well as civil, in two important ways. First, the *Daubert* trilogy changed the basic question of admissibility from simply "general acceptance" to a requirement that the proponent of the evidence establish the scientific validity of the evidence being offered, by demonstrating that its foundations are empirically sound and that its application to the particular case is appropriate. In addition to general acceptance, the new criteria required proof of testability, error rate, and peer review. Second, the Court firmly established the trial judge as the "gatekeeper" of forensic science evidence, who must make the scientific reliability and applicability assessment of the proffered evidence before it is allowed to be presented to the jury. On the criminal side, while the bulk of criminal cases are in state court and several of those states still adhere to some version of the *Frye* test, the *Daubert* criteria have resulted in new challenges to prosecution use of forensic evidence that have forced trial judges in *Daubert* courts to at least re-examine the basis for their admissibility. Even in some state versions of *Frye*, courts have begun to address the fundamental questions posed by a *Daubert* form of legal analysis.

The Emergence of DNA as a New Model for Forensic Scientific Evidence

The impact of DNA testing and typing developments on forensic evidence in criminal cases has been dramatic. The prosecution use of DNA in criminal cases has become the new "gold standard" of criminal identification techniques. This is due not to the claimed expertise of a technical examiner based on anecdotal or experiential comparisons, as was the case of the former "gold standard" of fingerprint comparison, but rather on the basis of a firm scientific foundation established outside of the context of criminal litigation. This feature of DNA, when compared to other forms of prosecution proffered scientific evidence, is significant.

After the Supreme Court remanded the *Daubert* case, the Ninth Circuit did not send the matter back to the trial court for the hearing that *Daubert* requires. Instead, they again found without any additional facts, that the plaintiff's evidence was still inadmissible notwithstanding the Supreme Court's opinion. Tom accomplish that result, the Court of Appeals added a significant amplification to the *Daubert* requirement for peer review. Writing for a panel of the Ninth Circuit, Judge Kozinski stated:

> One very significant fact to be considered is whether the experts are proposing to testify about matters growing naturally and directly out of research they have conducted independent of the litigation, or whether they have developed their opinions expressly for purposes of testifying. That an expert testifies for money does not necessarily cast doubt on the reliability of his testimony, as few experts appear in court

merely as an eleemosynary gesture. But in determining whether proposed expert testimony amounts to good science, we may not ignore the fact that a scientist's normal workplace is the lab or the field, not the courtroom or the lawyer's office. That an expert testifies based on research he has conducted independent of the litigation provides important, objective proof that the research comports with the dictates of good science. . . . For one thing, experts whose findings flow from existing research are less likely to have been biased toward a particular conclusion by the promise of remuneration; when an expert prepares reports and findings before being hired as a witness, that record will limit the degree to which he can tailor his testimony to serve a party's interests. Then, too, independent research carries its own indicia of reliability, as it is conducted, so to speak, in the usual course of business and must normally satisfy a variety of standards to attract funding and institutional support. Finally, there is usually a limited number of scientists actively conducting research on the very subject that is germane to a particular case, which provides a natural constraint on parties' ability to shop for experts who will come to the desired conclusion. That the testimony proffered by an expert is based directly on legitimate, preexisting research unrelated to the litigation provides the most persuasive basis for concluding that the opinions he expresses were "derived by the scientific method."

. . .

If the proffered expert testimony is not based on independent research, the party proffering it must come forward with other objective, verifiable evidence that the testimony is based on "scientifically valid principles." One means of showing this is by proof that the research and analysis supporting the proffered conclusions have been subjected to normal scientific scrutiny through peer review and publication.[6]

Thus, according to Kozinski, experts "who have developed their opinions expressly for purposes of testifying" are more "likely to have been biased toward a particular conclusion by the promise of remuneration" and therefore their opinions are so suspect that additional verification is required. Based on that rationale, summary judgment was again affirmed for the pharmaceutical company. The Supreme Court refused to review that ruling.

In the criminal forensic science field, however, most of the testimony has no origin or basis outside of the context of criminal investigation and litigation. The testimony was developed expressly for purposes of testifying in the prosecution of alleged criminal activity in court. Kozinski seems to have been aware of the obvious problems that his added criterion would pose for prosecutors in criminal cases. He added a footnote:

> There are, of course, exceptions. Fingerprint analysis, voice recognition, DNA fingerprinting and a variety of other scientific endeavors closely tied to law enforcement may indeed have the courtroom as a principal theatre of operations. *See, e.g., United States v. Chischilly*, 30 F.3d 1144, 1153 (9th Cir. 1994) (admitting expert testimony concerning a DNA match as proof the defendant committed sexual abuse and murder). As to such disciplines, the fact that the expert has developed an expertise principally for purposes of litigation will obviously not be a substantial consideration.[7]

Most disturbing is Kozinski's sweeping suggestion that expert testimony in criminal cases is somehow "obviously" so different that the potential bias of the expert is not the "substantial consideration" he thought appropriate in civil cases. If there was any difference to be acknowledged, expert testimony that could deprive a person of life or liberty should be more, not less, rigorous than testimony used to protect the interests of civil defendants. The danger that expert testimony developed principally to aid one side in litigation will be biased and unreliable is an important factor in criminal cases. Precisely because most scientific evidence in criminal cases arises out of scientific activities closely tied to law enforcement, the danger of biased testimony is very high.

His reliance on the admission of DNA analysis is clearly inappropriate. DNA, the model for scientific evidence admissibility that Judge Kozinski and others presumably prefer, was developed entirely outside the courtroom context and rests upon a foundation of empirical data that forms a database for identification testimony that is probabilistic to an almost astronomical degree of certainty. Only in the cloisters of the law would one think that DNA has "the courtroom as a principal theater of operations."

The Impact of DNA Exonerations

Beyond its new status as the scientific model for admissible evidence, DNA typing and testing has had another dramatic effect on the re-examination of other forensic science evidence that was certainly never intended by prosecutors when they embraced the use of DNA in criminal proceedings. DNA typing in closed cases has led to the exoneration of persons who were erroneously convicted, often by the use of other supposedly reliable forms of forensic science evidence. A recent study was conducted of 137 of the persons who have been exonerated by later DNA testing. That study specifically found:

> In conducting a review of these 137 exonerees' trial transcripts, this study found invalid forensic science testimony was not just common but prevalent. This study found that 82 cases—60% of the 137 in the study set—involved invalid forensic science testimony.
>
> . . .
>
> The testimony at these 137 exonerees' criminal trials chiefly involved serological analysis (100 cases) and microscopic hair comparison (65), because most of these cases involved sexual assaults for which such evidence was commonly available at the time. Indeed, in many cases, where both hair and semen were recovered from the crime scene, both disciplines were utilized. Some cases also involved testimony concerning: fingerprint comparison (13 cases), DNA analysis (11), forensic geology (soil comparison) (6), forensic odontology (bite mark comparison) (6), shoe print comparison (4), fiber comparison (2), voice comparison (1), and fingernail comparison (1).
>
> In the two main categories of evidence present in the study set, serology and hair comparison testimony, this study found the following: Of the 100 cases involving serology in which transcripts were located, 57 cases, or 57%, had invalid forensic science testimony. Of the 65 cases involving

microscopic hair comparison in which transcripts were located, 25 cases, or 38%, had invalid forensic science testimony.[8]

These exonerations, and the apparent association of their underlying convictions with many forms of routinely admitted prosecution forensic science evidence, are clearly factors in causing the public, defense lawyers and the courts to doubt or at least re-examine the scientific validity of such evidence. As one observer optimistically put it :

> The issues raised by DNA exonerations have led to an overhaul of the criminal justice system. Some states now require that evidence be preserved; others require mandatory videotaping of interrogations. Several states, including Illinois, New Jersey and New York, abolished the death penalty largely because of concerns about executing an innocent person. North Carolina, meanwhile, has created an independent commission to review innocence claims. And some prosecutors' offices, including those in New York and Dallas, have created conviction-integrity units. [9]

On the other hand, many prosecutors simply refuse to accept any notion that DNA evidence actually exonerates persons against whom they have "won" a conviction. They seek to explain away newly discovered DNA evidence in any manner that is consistent with the defendant's guilt. For example, where a postconviction DNA test reveals sperm of someone else in a sexual assault murder case, prosecutors will then claim that the victim must have had intercourse with a different unknown person before the defendant killed her.[10] In the highly publicized case of *People v. Rivera* [11] the Illinois Court of Appeals recently overturned a murder conviction after a retrial where the prosecution claimed that the sperm found in the victim, which was admittedly not that of the defendant, must have been from prior intercourse. The prosecution claim was based solely on "anecdotal testimony from the victim's sister recounting a masturbation experience and an alleged sexual molestation three years prior by a neighborhood friend's brother."[12] The appeals court found that the "State's theories distort to an absurd degree the real and undisputed testimony that the sperm was deposited shortly before the victim died."[13] But, as one prosecutor revealingly explained, "The taxpayers don't pay us for intellectual curiosity. They pay us to get convictions."[14]

The Impact of the NAS Report

The DNA exonerations, at least in part, led to what should now be another factor in the current questioning of criminal scientific evidence - the results of the National Research Council study commissioned by Congress. The Congressional charge to the committee was to:

1) assess the present and future resource needs of the forensic science community, to include State and local crime labs, medical examiners, and coroners;

2) make recommendations for maximizing the use of forensic technologies and techniques to solve crimes, investigate deaths, and protect the public;

3) identify potential scientific advances that may assist law enforcement in using forensic technologies and techniques to protect the public;

4) make recommendations for programs that will increase the number of qualified forensic scientists and medical examiners available to work in public crime laboratories;

5) disseminate best practices and guidelines concerning the collection and analysis of forensic evidence to help ensure quality and consistency in the use of forensic technologies and techniques to solve crimes, investigate deaths, and protect the public;

6) examine the role of the forensic community in the homeland security mission;

7) [examine] interoperability of Automated Fingerprint Information Systems [AFIS]; and

8) examine additional issues pertaining to forensic science as determined by the Committee.[15]

The Council conducted a lengthy two-year study of the use of forensic science in criminal cases and made specific findings both generally and as to several specific areas of commonly admitted evidence. Those findings were relayed to Congress in 2009 in a report of over 300 pages.

The summary included this caustic analysis of the use of forensic science in criminal cases:

> The bottom line is simple: In a number of forensic science disciplines, forensic science professionals have yet to establish either the validity of their approach or the accuracy of their conclusions, and the courts have been utterly ineffective in addressing this problem. For a variety of reasons—including the rules governing the admissibility of forensic evidence, the applicable standards governing appellate review of trial court decisions, the limitations of the adversary process, and the common lack of scientific expertise among judges and lawyers who must try to comprehend and evaluate forensic evidence— the legal system is ill-equipped to correct the problems of the forensic science community.[16]

The specific analyses of each of the separate areas of forensic evidence were, for the most part, damning. The Council committee researched the alleged scientific basis for each specialty, the training requirements for persons holding themselves out as experts in that field, and the nature of the substantive testimony proffered in court by those persons. With the exception of nuclear DNA typing and testing, in most areas of forensic science the NAS Report found a distinct failure to provide the type of criteria mandated by a *Daubert* analysis.

The Council made thirteen recommendations for improving the system,[17] beginning with the creation of a new National Institute of Forensic Science to oversee improvements in the system. The recommendations also included the following:

> Research is needed to address issues of accuracy, reliability, and validity in the forensic science disciplines. The National Institute of Forensic Science (NIFS) should competitively fund peer-reviewed research in the following areas:
>
> (a) Studies establishing the scientific bases demonstrating the validity of forensic methods.

(b) The development and establishment of quantifiable measures of the reliability and accuracy of forensic analyses. Studies of the reliability and accuracy of forensic techniques should reflect actual practice on realistic case scenarios, averaged across a representative sample of forensic scientists and laboratories. Studies also should establish the limits of reliability and accuracy that analytic methods can be expected to achieve as the conditions of forensic evidence vary. The research by which measures of reliability and accuracy are determined should be peer reviewed and published in respected scientific journals.

(c) The development of quantifiable measures of uncertainty in the conclusions of forensic analyses.

(d) Automated techniques capable of enhancing forensic technologies.[18]

Congress has not yet acted on the recommendations, but the findings in the NAS Report have quickly reverberated throughout the forensic science community and parts of the legal community. The response of the forensic science community has been mixed. Formally, the scientific organizations have supported the general recommendations of the NAS Report, while continuing to believe that future scientific research will validate most of the bases for forensic science disciplines. The American Academy of Forensic Sciences (AAFS) made an official "Position Statement" in response to the Report:

The American Academy of Forensic Sciences supports the recommendations of the National Academy of Sciences report *Strengthening Forensic Science in the United States: A Path Forward* 1 (NAS Report). From among the various views and recommendations espoused, we particularly emphasize, endorse and promote the following principles:

1. All forensic science disciplines must have a strong scientific foundation.

2. All forensic science laboratories should be accredited.
3. All forensic scientists should be certified.
4. Forensic science terminology should be standardized.
5. Forensic scientists should be assiduously held to Codes of Ethics.
6. Existing forensic science professional entities should participate in governmental oversight of the field.
7. Attorneys and judges who work with forensic scientists and forensic science evidence should have a strong awareness and knowledge of the scientific method and forensic science disciplines.[19]

The organization added that it would undertake its own validation studies, beginning with latent fingerprint identification and handwriting comparison analysis.[20] This prominent organization is apparently taking the challenge of the NAS Report seriously, even titling its 2010 convention "Putting Our Forensic House in Order: Examining Validation and Expelling Incompetence." Notwithstanding this positive formal response, the organization president acknowledged that some of the practitioners in various disciplines have taken a more hostile or evasive tack:

> . . . [I]t certainly is inappropriate to attack the person or entity that questions whether the needed validation has been done. I have been dismayed to see and hear attacks on the NAS Report, not because what it says is untrue but rather because it "gives aid to the enemy" (by which is meant the defense bar) or because it puts "forensic science" in a bad light, in short because it "gives scandal."
>
> . . . After *Daubert* came down, requiring scientific evidence to be shown to be reliable before it could be introduced in court, a shameful period followed in which various practitioners, in spite of having long claimed to engage in scientific investigation, began to deny that they were scientists. These word games played by some experts, sometimes in response to advice from their professional organizations, were undertaken in the mistaken belief that somehow they would remove these experts' testimony from

having to be shown to be reliable, that by denying science in their work they could continue to justify their testimony on no more than "my years and years of experience in the field." The Supreme Court of the United States put reasonably short shrift to this maneuver in *Kumho Tire*, ruling that the reliability requirement applied to all expert testimony in federal court. In the wake of the NAS Report, and in advance of the legislative Juggernaut feared by some to be coming down the track, history is repeating itself. There are attempts to define forensic science so narrowly that (1) no injustices have ever occurred as the result of flawed forensic science testimony and (2) expected certification and other requirements for forensic practitioners will not apply to huge sectors of practitioners. Attempts to downgrade to "investigative science" or "police science" work that clearly constitutes forensic science under the Academy's definition must be combated by our broad-based and diverse scientific organization.[21]

Some parts of the practitioner communities have been more subtle in their defensive posture, including their repeated contention that such things as "error rates" cannot be properly applied to their discipline.[22] Regardless of the positions taken, the forensic science community has taken notice of the contents of the NAS report and is at least beginning to alter, or at least re-evaluate, the basic premises of some of its disciplines.

In the meantime, practitioners are being told to expect new challenges in court. Barry A. Fisher testified before Congress and later advised his AAFS testifiers that they should expect courtroom challenges and perhaps consider modifying their proffered testimony:

> While Congress and the Administration consider their responses to the NAS report, forensic scientists may be confronted with fresh attacks by the defense bar on the reliability of pattern evidence . . . Challenges on the question of adequate research to support statements of single source uniqueness can most certainly be anticipated. . . . It may be that absolute statements of uniqueness are not possible to support statistically. Non-the-less, strong statements can still be made to convey to juries the idea that there is a close

relationship between the known sample and the questioned sample. Expressing that kind of opinion will be a challenge to articulate.[23]

In spite of the expected challenges, the legal community has been, perhaps predictably, slower and more muted in its response to the NAS Report. Appellate decisions take time to materialize and there is no way to measure whether *Daubert* motions have increased in the short time since the NAS Report. There are few reported trial court rulings on the issue. And at least one or two of them indicate that the courts may not give the NAS Report a great deal of weight in making an admissibility threshold determination. As discussed infra, the judge in *United States v. Rose*[24] had the benefit of the NAS findings regarding fingerprint testimony but also noted the fingerprint examiners opposition to those findings. The judge relied on a statement by the NAS committee chair, Judge Harry T. Edwards, to support his conclusion that "nothing in the Report was intended to answer the 'question whether forensic evidence in a particular case is admissible under applicable law'."[25] That citation seems to be an example of selective excerpting from Judge Edwards' more complete remarks in which he indicates that he fully expects that the findings of the Report will be considered by trial judges in making admissibility determinations:

> It will be no surprise if the report is cited authoritatively for its findings about the current status of the scientific foundation of particular areas of forensic science. And it is certainly possible that the courts will take the findings of the committee regarding the scientific foundation of particular types of forensic science evidence into account when considering the admissibility of such evidence in a particular case. However, each case in the criminal justice system must be decided on the record before the court pursuant to the applicable law, controlling precedent, and governing rules of evidence. The question whether forensic evidence in a particular case is admissible under applicable law is not coterminous with the question whether there are studies confirming the scientific validity and reliability of a forensic science discipline.[26]

In other cases, a federal magistrate considered the NAS Report at great length in a hearing involving the admissibility of toolmark firearms comparison testimony and eventually recommended that the proffered government testimony be severely limited.[27] On the other hand, a federal district court judge has recently upheld a magistrate's refusal to admit the NAS report at a hearing regarding the reliability of drug sniffing dogs, finding that the balance of the evidence was overwhelming and that "the Court finds little value in" the Report.[28]

The Impact of New Technology Awareness by Jurors

A final factor needs to be added to understand the doubt that is emerging about the reliability of certain forensic evidence in criminal cases. As is apparent from recent studies, jurors know a great deal about modern scientific developments, and about how they intersect with the criminal justice system.[29] They know about DNA and its tremendous identification powers to both convict and exonerate. In fact, many jurors expect the prosecution to present DNA evidence in virtually every case, even in property offenses or relatively minor assault cases.[30] As a result, jurors have come to demand scientific evidence from the government in many types of cases as a prerequisite to conviction.[31] And the scientific evidence they demand from the prosecution may need to have the same degree of both reliability and certainty that jurors know that DNA can provide. When an expert witness is forced to limit identification or other comparisons to a statement that the crime scene evidence is "consistent with" as opposed to "matches" the evidence from the defendant, jurors may well find that testimony to be so pale in comparison with what they know about DNA's capabilities that it will simply not be enough to satisfy their demands. The jury becomes a factor in the suspicions about non-DNA forensic science evidence when they begin to conclude that proof beyond a reasonable doubt means that it is reasonable to demand that the prosecutor present scientific evidence - and scientific evidence that is reliable and convincing.

The pressure to either produce very convincing scientific evidence or to attempt to exclude jurors who have such demands is already showing on prosecutors in their courtroom conduct. It seems rational that it is also influencing the investigative and charging decisions that prosecutors are making. Judges are also responding with instructions, sometimes *sua sponte.*[32]

The Current State of Forensic Science Evidence in Criminal Cases

Some judges have taken the revelations of the NAS Report seriously. Most notable are the efforts of recently retired federal Judge Nancy Gertner in Massachusetts. Judge Gertner adopted a standard pretrial order addressing, in concrete terms, the NAS Report and applying its concerns to existing cases. In her *Procedural Order: Trace Evidence,* she orders counsel to identify forensic science issues, addresses possible funding of expert defense witnesses, and to prepare for a *Daubert/Kumho* hearing. The order concludes with the following:

> In the past, the admissibility of this kind of evidence was effectively presumed, largely because of its pedigree -- the fact that it had been admitted for decades. As such, counsel rarely challenged it, and if it were challenged, it was rarely excluded or limited. . . . The NAS report suggests a different calculus -- that admissibility of such evidence ought not to be presumed; that it has to be carefully examined in each case, and tested in the light of the NAS concerns, the concerns of *Daubert/Kumho* case law, and Rule 702 of the Federal Rules of Evidence. This order is entered to accomplish that end.[33]

Unfortunately, Judge Gertner seems to be the exception rather than the rule.

Whatever doubts have arisen about the continued validity of forensic science evidence in the last twenty years, most criminal courts seem to have continued business as usual and routinely admit almost all expert testimony offered by prosecutors. Even though there are serious questions about the scientific validity of many non-DNA forms of forensic science evidence, criminal court judges, both at the trial and appellate level, continue to admit virtually all prosecution proffered expert testimony. Only when the government itself decides that a particular type of supposedly scientific evidence is not reliable, as in the case of bullet lead analysis, do the courts stop routinely admitting it.

Some state courts have labored to avoid the demands of a *Daubert* analysis when faced with prosecution proffers of evidence in criminal cases. As we have seen, some seize upon the language of *Daubert* indicating that its criteria are not "all inclusive" and simply disregard such basic requirements as an established error rate that would seem to be of primary importance in criminal cases.[34] Many others have decided that, while their rule of evidence is exactly like the federal rule, they just reject *Kumho*'s application of *Daubert* criteria to "technical" testimony and then consider many forms of government evidence to be "technical" so as to avoid any critical analysis.[35] Perhaps most strikingly, many courts, both state and federal, have chosen to misinterpret the "generally accepted" leg of *Daubert* analysis to mean generally accepted in the courts rather than the relevant scientific community. They then rely on the legal principal of *stare decisis* to, in effect, find that since a particular form of forensic evidence has been admitted in the past it should continue to be admitted without any new analysis.[36] And even when trial judges have admitted clearly unreliable testimony, appellate courts are prone to find that it was "harmless error" and sustain convictions. The use of "harmless error" rationalizations has turned out to be a significant factor in many cases where the defendant was later exonerated by postconviction DNA testing.[37]

Studies by scholars have substantiated this form of pro-prosecution pattern in the admissibility of scientific evidence in criminal cases. Risinger's 2000 study found that while the rate of challenges to scientific evidence increased markedly after *Daubert*, most of that increase was in civil cases in which the defendant was attempting to preclude expert testimony proffered by the civil plaintiff.[38] And they were significantly more successful after *Daubert*.[39] The opposite was true in criminal cases.[40] The Risinger study found that criminal defense *Daubert* challenges to government evidence were successful less than 10% of the time in federal trial courts and 25% of the time in state trial courts.[41] An experienced attorney for the Innocence Project concluded that "despite the frequency with which scientific and expert testimony is proffered in criminal cases, there is a dearth of *Daubert* challenges and hearings. When the issue *is* raised in criminal proceedings, the outcome is vastly different than what occurs in civil cases."[42] In a study of appellate decisions before and after *Daubert*, Groscup, et al, concluded that "the basic rates of admission at the trial and the appellate court levels did not change significantly after *Daubert* in criminal cases on appeal" and that:

One explanation for the lack of any changes in the observed rates of admission before versus after *Daubert* is that admissibility depends on the party offering the testimony. The party for whom the key expert testified was significantly related to admission at both the trial court, . . . and the appellate court levels, . . . At both adjudicative levels, experts proffered by the prosecution were more likely to be admitted than experts proffered by defendants. At the trial court level, prosecution experts were admitted 95.8% . . . of the time, and defendant–appellant experts were admitted only 7.8% . . . of the total number of times they were offered. This pattern was slightly less pronounced at the appellate level, with prosecution experts admitted 85.1%. . . of the time and defense experts admitted 18.8% . . . of the total number of times they were offered.[43]

The trend does not seem to be changing in spite of *Daubert* and even more importantly in spite of the findings in the NAS Report. Many trial courts at both the State and federal level continue to routinely admit any prosecution evidence that has been traditionally admitted without regard to the scientific developments in the field and in many cases without allowing the defense to even obtain a hearing on the reliability of the evidence against them. Appellate courts seem anxious to bless, or at least allow, trial judges to continue the admission of what the prosecution claims to be scientific evidence without regard to whether it has a scientific, rather than historical, basis.

Judicial Bias and Forensic Evidence in Criminal Cases

What accounts for the current relative lack of defense challenges to government expert testimony in criminal cases and the overwhelming court rejection of those challenges that are made? As to the lack of challenges, some have suggested that it is "poorly funded, unskilled counsel" and "inadequate pool of experts" available to the defense, especially when compared to resources available to civil plaintiffs.[44] As to the overwhelming judicial rejection of criminal defense challenges that are made, there are several possibilities.

One possibility is that the science being proffered by the government in criminal cases is simply of higher quality than that being offered by civil plaintiffs. The findings in the NAS Report indicating that many non-DNA forms of expert testimony used by prosecutors is of questionable validity should dispel that notion. Moreover, judicial decisions for the most part do not indicate that the judges, trial or appellate, weighed the scientific validity of the proffered evidence in any meaningful way.[45] Rather, most of the decisions simply rationalized admissibility based on the prior admission of such evidence by other judges.

More likely is the suggestion that there is a systemic pro-prosecution bias on the part of judges and that such a bias is reflected in admissibility decisions, regardless of what the standard of admissibility is under *Frye* or *Daubert*.[46] As Groscup, *et al*, found, "the *Daubert* decision did not impact on the admission rates of expert testimony at either the trial or the appellate court levels."[47] To put the bias question another way, "as a general proposition, judges disfavor civil plaintiffs and criminal defendants and, are more likely to rule against them than against their opposites even when presenting equivalent evidence or arguments."[48]

Systemic pro-prosecution bias is a function of fairly obvious psychological concepts. Dean Chris Guthrie described judicial bias as a reflection of an "attitudinal blinder," relying on significant empirical studies of judicial attitudes and actions:

> Whether elected or appointed, judges come to the bench with political views. This is not to say that they have pre-committed to positions in particular cases, but it strains credulity to claim, as, for example, Justice Alito claimed during his Supreme Court confirmation hearings, that a judge "can't have any preferred outcome in any particular case." Rather, judges do have opinions, and these opinions or attitudes can predispose them to rule in ways that are consistent with those opinions or attitudes.
>
> To establish the presence of attitudinal blinders among judges, political scientists have developed, and provided empirical evidence to support, the so-called attitudinal theory or model. Most of this work has focused on the Supreme Court, but political scientists and legal scholars have also explored whether judicial attitudes influence judges on the courts of appeals and on the trial bench. The evidence suggests that

attitudinal blinders are an issue not only at the highest court in the land but also in these lower courts.[49]

These "attitudinal blinders" are especially prevalent in criminal cases and especially in the state courts where most criminal cases are tried. As Professor Rodney Uphoff put it, "In the end, state court judges are, for the most part, rational actors whose attitudinal biases reflect their self-interest and their backgrounds. Most are answerable to a tough-on-crime electorate and are often reluctant, therefore, to make risky political decisions upholding the constitutional rights of criminal defendants."[50] Specifically, Uphoff comments on how this attitudinal bias manifests itself in criminal cases:

> Most judges, especially those with prosecutorial experience, presume that most defendants are, in fact, guilty, even though some are, in fact, innocent. This presumption of guilt, pro-prosecution perspective not only affects the manner in which many judges rule on motions, evaluate witnesses, and exercise their discretion, but it also adversely affects the willingness of many judges to police law enforcement agents and prosecutors. Judges tolerate sloppy police work because they do not want to be viewed as micro-managing the police. Judicial reluctance to let the guilty go free has meant a decreased use of the exclusionary rule. Similarly, courts are hesitant to dismiss cases because of Brady violations or take other steps to reign in prosecutorial misconduct. Finally, even when courts find error, too many errors are deemed harmless. The expanded use of harmless error not only allows questionable verdicts to stand, it does little to discourage misconduct and sloppy practices in the administration of justice."[51]

As the result of what appears to be a distinct pro-prosecution bias in trial and appellate judges, the current legal state of forensic science evidence in criminal cases is somewhat schizophrenic. While many scientists and scholars, and even a congressionally mandated national study, seriously question whether there is validity to non-DNA forensic evidence, trial judges simply continue to admit such evidence and appellate judges continue to affirm those decisions.

[1] Michael J. Saks, *The Past and Future of Forensic Science and the Courts*, 93 Judicature 94 (2009) at 94.

[2] Richard Silberglitt, Philip S. Antón, David R. Howell, and Anny Wong, *The Global Technology Revolution 2020: In-Depth Analyses: Bio/Nano/Materials/Information Trends, Drivers, Barriers, and Social Implications*, (2006) at xxvi, available online at http://www.rand.org/pubs/technical_reports/2006/RAND_TR303.sum.pdf (last visited December 14, 2011).

[3] See the further discussion of the impact of these developments on popular culture and the court system in Donald E. Shelton, Young S. Kim and Gregg Barak, *A Study of Juror Expectations and Demands for Scientific Evidence: Does the "CSI Effect" Exist?*, 9 Vanderbilt J. Ent. & Tech. L. 334 (2006), at 362-365.

[4] Michael J. Saks, *The Past and Future of Forensic Science and the Courts*, 93 Judicature 94 (2009) at 95.

[5] Professor Saks also suggested that the NAS Report must be a separate factor as well. "The NRC Report might be come to be viewed as yet another event pushing the non-science forensic sciences toward the construction of sound scientific moorings." *Id.*, at 95

[6] *Daubert v. Merrell Dow Pharm., Inc.*, 43 F.3d 1311 (1995), at 1317-1318. And see the discussion of this position in the context of criminal cases in Peter J. Neufeld, *The (Near) Irrelevance of Daubert to Criminal Justice and Some Suggestions for Reform*, 95 Am. J. Pub. Health 107 (2005), available online at http://www.defendingscience.org/upload/NeufeldDAUBERT.pdf

[7] *Id.*, at 1322, fn6.

[8] Brandon L. Garrett and Peter J. Neufeld, *Invalid Forensic Science Testimony and Wrongful Convictions*, 95 Va. L. Rev. 1 (2009), at 14-15.

[9] Martin, Andrew, *The Prosecution's Case Against DNA*, The New York Times Magazine (November 27, 2011), available online at http://www.nytimes.com/2011/11/27/magazine/dna-evidence-lake-county.html?ref=magazine (last visited November 27, 2011).

[10] "The unnamed-lover-theory has been floated so many times that defense lawyers have a derisive term for it: 'the unindicted co-ejaculator'". *Id* at 46-47.

[11] *People v. Rivera*, 2011 Ill. App. 2d No. 091060 (Dec. 9, 2011), available online at http://www.state.il.us/court/Opinions/AppellateCourt/2011/2ndDistrict/December/2091060.pdf (last visited December 14, 2011).

[12] *Id,* at 15.

[13] *Id.*, at 16.

[14] Mills, Steve and Lisa Black, *Learning Victim's Name Not Enough for New Trial*, Chicago Tribune (October 10, 2010), available online at http://articles.chicagotribune.com/2010-10-11/news/ct-met-confession-conviction-new-vers20101011_1_murder-conviction-mary-kate-sunderlin-dna-evidence (last visited November 27, 2011).

[15] *Science, State, Justice, Commerce, and Related Agencies Appropriations Act of 2006*, P.L. No. 109-108, 119 Stat. 2290 (2005); S. Rep. No. 109-88, at 46 (2005); National Research Council of the National Academies, *Strengthening Forensic Science in the United States: A Path Forward* (2009), at 1-2.

[16] National Research Council of the National Academies, *Strengthening Forensic Science in the United States: A Path Forward* (2009), at 53.

[17] National Research Council of the National Academies, *Strengthening Forensic Science in the United States: A Path Forward* (2009), at 19-33. The recommendations are set forth in the Appendix.

[18] *Id.*, at 22-23; see Appendix.

[19] American Academy of Forensic Sciences, *AAFS Position Statement in Response to the NAS Report*, 39 AAFS Academy News 4 (November 2009), available online at
http://www.aafs.org/sites/default/files/pdf/AAFS_Position_Statement_for_Press_Distribution_090409.pdf (last visited December 14, 2011).

[20] Bohan, Thomas L., *President's Message*, 39 AAFS Academy News 1 (November 2009).

[21] Bohan, Thomas L., *President's Message*, 39 AAFS Academy News 1 (November 2009), at 35.

[22] See, e.g. Peterson, Peter E., et al, *Latent Prints: A Perspective on the State of the Science*, 11 Forensic Sci. Comm, No. 4 (October 2009), available online at http://www.fbi.gov/hq/lab/fsc/current/review/2009_10_review01.htm (last visited December 14, 2011).

[23] Fisher, Barry A. , *Legislative Corner*, 39 AAFS Academy News 3 (November 2009).

[24] *United States v. Rose*, No. CCB-08-0149 (D. Md., December 8, 2009), available online at
http://www.mdd.uscourts.gov/Opinions/Opinions/Brian%20Rose%20Mem-FINAL.pdf (last visited December 14, 2011.

[25] *Id.*, citing Hon. Harry T. Edwards, *Statement before U.S. Senate Judiciary Committee* (Mar. 18, 2009).

[26] Edwards, Hon. Harry T., *Statement before U.S. Senate Judiciary Committee* (Mar. 18, 2009) at p. 10, available online at http://judiciary.senate.gov/pdf/09-03-18EdwardsTestimony.pdf (last visited December 14, 2011).

[27] *Unites States v. Mouzone*, Criminal No. WDQ-08-086, United States District Court (D. Maryland, October 29, 2009).

[28] *United States. v. Prokupek*, Case No. 8:08CR183United States District Court (D. Nebraska, August 14, 2009).

[29] Shelton, Donald E., Young S. Kim & Gregg Barak, *An Indirect-Effects Model of Mediated Adjudication: The CSI Myth, the Tech Effect, and Metropolitan Jurors' Expectations for Scientific Evidence*, 12 Vand. J. Ent. & Tech. L. 1 (2009).

[30] *Id.*; Shelton, Donald E., and Young S. Kim and Gregg Barak, *A Study of Juror Expectations and Demands for Scientific Evidence: Does the "CSI Effect" Exist?*, 9 Vanderbilt J. Ent. & Tech. L. 334 (2006).

[31] *Id.*

[32] *Id.*

[33] Gertner, Hon. Nancy, *Pretrial Oder Trace Evidence*, U.S Dist Ct. Md. (March 2010), available online at http://www.google.com/url?sa=t&rct=j&q=&esrc=s&frm=1&source=web&cd=1&ved=0CEYQFjAA&url=http%3A%2F%2Fwww.mad.uscourts.gov%2Fboston%2Fpdf%2FProcOrderTraceEvidenceUPDATE.pdf&ei=zaDbTr3PHOWZ2QWRxYGnDg&usg=AFQjCNIIEx_al9Xow3DfKRfyniOu3yn2IzA (last visited December 4, 2011). See also Gertner, Nancy, *Commentary on the Need for a Research Culture in the Forensic Sciences*, 58 UCLA L. Rev. 789 (2011).

[34] See Jabbar, Munia, *Overcoming Daubert's Shortcomings in Criminal Trials: Making Error Rate the Primary Factor in Daubert's Validity Inquiry*, 85 N.Y.U. L. Rev. 2034 (2010).

[35] See Bernstein, David E, and Jeffrey D. Jackson, *The Daubert Trilogy in the States*, 44 Jurimetrics 351 (2003-2004).

[36] Perhaps the most glaring example is in Maryland where in *Markham v. State*, 984 A.2d 262 (Md. App. 2009) the appellate court relied on a 1978 ruling in *Reed v. State*, 283 Md. 374, 391 A.2d 364 (1978) that not only is fingerprint

testimony still admissible without any hearing as to its reliability, the court may actually take judicial notice of it reliability and admissibility.

[37] Garrett, Brandon L., *Convicting the Innocent*, Harvard Univ. Press: Cambridge, Mass. (2011) at 200-205.

[38] D. Michael Risinger, *Navigating Expert Reliability: Are Criminal Standards of Certainty Being Left on the Dock?*, 64 Alb. L. Rev. 99 (2000).

[39] Dixon, Lloyd and Brian Gill, *Changes In The Standards For Admitting Expert Evidence In Federal Civil Cases Since The Daubert Decision*, Rand Corp. (2001); Krafka, Carol, et al, *Judge and Attorney Experiences, Practices, and Concerns Regarding Expert Testimony in Federal Civil Trials*, 8 Psychol., Pub. Pol'y and Law 309 (2002), excerpt available online at http://files.ali-aba.org/thumbs/datastorage/skoobesruoc/pdf/CJ081-CH05_thumb.pdf (last visited December 14, 2011).

[40] *Modern Scientific Evidence: The Law and Science of Expert Testimony*, (eds. David L. Faigman, Michael J. Saks, Joseph Sanders, and Edward K. Cheng), 2009-2010 edition, at §1:35.

[41] Risinger, D. Michael, *Navigating Expert Reliability: Are Criminal Standards of Certainty Being Left on the Dock?*, 64 Alb. L. Rev. 99 (2000).

[42] Neufeld, Peter J., *The (Near) Irrelevance of* Daubert *to Criminal Justice and Some Suggestions for Reform*, 95 Am. J. Pub. Health 107 (2005), available online at http://www.defendingscience.org/upload/NeufeldDAUBERT.pdf (last visited December 14, 2011).

[43] Groscup, Jennifer L., et al., *The Effects of* Daubert *on the Admissibility of Expert Testimony in State and Federal Criminal Cases*, 8 Psychol. Pub. Pol'y & L. 339 (2002), at 345-346.

[44] Neufeld, Peter J., *The (Near) Irrelevance of Daubert to Criminal Justice and Some Suggestions for Reform*, 95 Am. J. Pub. Health 107 (2005), at 110, available online at http://www.defendingscience.org/upload/NeufeldDAUBERT.pdf (last visited December 14, 2011).

[45] See *Modern Scientific Evidence: The Law and Science of Expert Testimony*, (eds. David L. Faigman, Michael J. Saks, Joseph Sanders, and Edward K. Cheng), 2009-2010 edition, at §1:35.

[46] See Shelton, Donald E., *Forensic Science Evidence and Judicial Bias in Criminal Cases*, 49 Judges' J. 18 (2010).

[47] Groscup, Jennifer L., et al., *The Effects of* Daubert *on the Admissibility of Expert Testimony in State and Federal Criminal Cases*, 8 Psychol. Pub. Pol'y & L. 339 (2002), at 364.

[48] *Modern Scientific Evidence: The Law and Science of Expert Testimony*, (eds. David L. Faigman, Michael J. Saks, Joseph Sanders, and Edward K. Cheng), 2009-2010 edition, at §1:35, p. 112.

[49] Guthrie, Chris, *Misjudging*, 7 Nev. L. J. 420 (2007) at 438-440, citing *The Hearing of Samuel A. Alito, Jr.'s Nomination to the Supreme Court*, Hearing Before the S. Judiciary Comm., 109th Cong. 56 (2006).

[50] Uphoff, Rodney J., *On Misjudging and its Implications for Criminal Defendants, Their Lawyers and the Criminal Justice System*, 7 Nev. L. J. 521 (2007), at 532; and see Fredric N. Tulsky, *How Judges Favor the Prosecution*, Mercury News.com (February 12, 2007), available online at http://www.mercurynews.com/search/ci_5128172?IADID=Search-www.mercurynews.com-www.mercurynews.com (last visited December 14, 2011) (claiming that "in a fourth of all jury cases, a review finds, members of the bench apply their tremendous powers in ways that hurt defendants").

[51] *Id.*

Chapter 17

Thoughts about the Future of Criminal Forensic Science

How, and even whether, significant improvements are made in the quality of either criminal forensic science or the rulings of trial and appellate courts on its admissibility is not a single-faceted issue. The problem is not single faceted. As Professor Saks has said:

> To view the problems identified by the NRC Committee as problems owned exclusively by the forensic science community would be a mistake. There is no lack of blame to go around. In addition to the forensic science community, we find an academic community that has taken little interest in building the scientific foundations of forensic science; lawyers on both sides of the courtroom who have not informed themselves adequately about the state of the art and science; an absence of any institutional forensic science resources for the defense, preventing the adversary process from working to keep prosecution witnesses honest; a federal government that has offered few resources for building the basic science needed in many areas of forensic science; state governments that never fully accepted their responsibility for ensuring that the many things the NRC found lacking were done and done well; and courts whose judges lacked the information they needed, or the courage or desire to apply the law as stringently to government proffers in criminal cases as they did to private parties' proffers in civil cases."[1]

Responses may come from all, or none, of these sources.

Implementation of the recommendations contained in the NAS Report by legislation could create a new federal organization that could mandate the research and testing to validate or finally discredit many forms of non-DNA forensic evidence. Meaningful legislative action by Congress, however, seems unlikely. Within just a few months of presentation of the NAS Report to Congress, commentators predicted that major proposals in the Report appeared to be "all but dead" in Congress.[2] In January 0f 2011, Senator Patrick Leahy introduced the *Criminal Justice and Forensic Science Reform Act of 2011*, which would create many of the structural improvements recommended by the Report.[3] Given the reality that they currently can get almost any type of evidence they want admitted, prosecutors have quite predictably lined up against the proposals.[4] In Congress, as in the courts, prosecutors generally get what they want, and what they clearly want is the status quo. Various federal agencies have also opposed the bill in apparent parochial fights over funding and agency control.[5] With the level of opposition, the current economic condition of the nation, and the pressures to spend federal monies on the prevention and prosecution of terrorism, the prospect for any action in Congress that might benefit accused defendants, and cost a considerable sum doing so, is very dim. No action has been taken and the bill remains in committee.

Given the spotlight created by the NAS report, the scientific and academic communities may make progress on their own. Practitioners in forensic science may be led by true scientist leaders, like some members of the American Academy of Forensic Sciences, to conduct meaningful research into the alleged bases for their claimed expertise. Some beginning steps have been taken in that direction. A recent analysis published in the Academy Journal concluded:

> While statistics regarding the admission versus exclusion of forensic evidence may not be accurate because of problems relating to selection of cases, availability of judgments, and bias, it is clear that there is a sizable proportion of forensic identification evidence that is failing to meet evidentiary standards in U.S. courts. It is also apparent that in such cases, the reliability of forensic identification science evidence, encompassing the concerns regarding the discipline's underlying theory, the expert's testimony, and their

methodology, accounts for the majority of judges' concerns regarding its admission. The forensic identification sciences need to address these concerns if they wish to enjoy continued acceptance of their evidence by the judicial system in the future. [6]

Hopefully, purely academic scientists may undertake independent research, perhaps even without the lure of federal grant money, to establish or dispel claimed scientific foundations for non-DNA forensic evidence. On the other hand, there is a strong temptation, as Dr. Bohan of the AAFS has stated,[7] for practitioners to try to avoid such studies, or even disregard their potential results, by claiming to base their testimony on "experience and judgment" rather than quantitative or empirical analysis. That tack has continued to be successful, especially in State courts, so it has some attraction, in spite of the holding in *Kumho*.[8]

The best prospect for improving or eliminating questionable forms of non-DNA forensic criminal evidence may lie in the courtroom, but probably not with trial or appellate judges. The systemic pro-prosecution bias of trial judges is one of the reasons for the current state of affairs and is not likely to change. As for appellate judges, Professor Uphoff puts it well:

Given electoral politics and the pro-prosecution perspective of a significant numbers of appellate judges, it is hard to be particularly optimistic about criminal justice reform. Certainly some judges do change dramatically during their tenure on the bench. Nonetheless, unless and until more judges recognize the effects of their attitudinal blinders and acknowledge the significant flaws in our criminal justice system, it is unlikely that we shall see many appellate courts taking a more active role in policing the system.[9]

There is always hope that trial and appellate judges, hopefully in the same case, will begin to recognize and overcome any such bias and rule fairly and intelligently on forensic evidence admissibility motions. It will take courage to do so. Those who do will remember the admonition of Justice William Brennan about judges who are tempted to make decisions based on the natural tendency to want to help put away a dangerous criminal:

> Yet the judge's job is not to yield to the visceral temptation to help prosecute the criminal, but to preserve the values and guarantees of our system of criminal justice, whatever the implications in an individual case.[10]

Collective breaths will not be held awaiting that day.

Perhaps the most promising impetus for change lies in another part of the courtroom - the jury box. Defense counsel may not win pretrial motions seeking to exclude prosecution experts from testifying but they may have a better chance of limiting the testimony and prohibiting exaggerated conclusions from being presented to the jury.[11] Using the NAS Report, attorneys who are unable to convince judges to exclude prosecution testimony at a *Daubert* hearing may nevertheless be able to limit the testimony of a particular expert to such terms as "consistent with" rather than declaring a "match" to the defendant.

Given the reluctance, to put it mildly, of judges to prohibit prosecutors from presenting questionable scientific evidence to the jury, defense lawyers who lose motions *in limine* could take up judges on their often used cliché that such issues are to be weighed by the jury. Defense counsel can present all of the now well-documented frailties of the particular claimed expertise to the jury. For indigent defendants, counsel can request, and constitutionally insist on, public funds to retain expert witnesses to attack the foundation of the government expert's testimony and in effect, re-litigate the *Daubert* or *Frye* hearing before the jury. As was demonstrated in the *Casey Anthony* case,[12] jurors can impressed with defense expert testimony about the lack of a scientific basis for the prosecution's evidence.

Even without such an expert, at least the findings of the NAS report should be admissible themselves as a learned treatise under the Federal Rules of Evidence or its state counterpart.[13] Jurors are becoming very technologically savvy, regardless of their formal education. Jurors may well be skeptical of prosecution experts who are impeached with evidence that their so-called science has been characterized by a government study as faulty, or "of questionable validity." Jurors are well aware that DNA can identify perpetrators with certainty. As the NAS report states, "With the exception of nuclear

DNA analysis, however, no forensic method has been rigorously shown to have the capacity to consistently, and with a high degree of certainty, demonstrate a connection between evidence and a specific individual or source."[14] The point is that this era of doubt about the validity of non-DNA forensic science may not yet have persuaded judges to refuse to admit such evidence, but it has provided evidence which may be effectively used to impeach some prosecution experts. In the end, what may cause legal reform in this area is acquittals. Jurors, not judges, may be the source of the strongest message to the government about the vulnerability of some evidence prosecutors try to use to gain convictions. When prosecutors begin to lose cases which they have built around such non-DNA "experts", they will stop using them until their validity can be scientifically proven.

---

[1] Saks, Michael J., *The Past and Future of Forensic Science and the Courts*, 93 Judicature 94 (2009) at 97.

[2] Shapiro, Ari, *Foolproof Forensics? The Jury Is Still Out, National Public Radio*, August 24, 2009, available online at http://www.npr.org/templates/story/story.php?storyId=112111657 (last visited December 14, 2011).

[3] S. 132, *Criminal Justice and Forensic Science Reform Act of 2011*, available online at http://www.govtrack.us/congress/bill.xpd?bill=s112-132 (last visited December 4, 2011). For an analysis of the legislation as introduced, see Driver, Amy, *Senator Patrick Leahy Introduces the Criminal Justice and Forensic Science Reform Act*, (January 27, 2011), available online at http://www.bulletpath.com/2011/leahy-introduces-cjfsra/ (last visited December 4, 2011).

[4] Shapiro, Ari, *Foolproof Forensics? The Jury Is Still Out, National Public Radio*, August 24, 2009, available online at http://www.npr.org/templates/story/story.php?storyId=112111657 (last visited December 14, 2011), quoting Scott Burns, Executive Director of the National District Attorneys Association. The official policy of the prosecutors' organization is that the "NDAA has several significant concerns with the bill". National District Attorneys Association, *Policy Issues*, available online at http://www.ndaa.org/ga_policy.html (last visited December 4, 2011).

[5] See Driver, Amy, *The Awesome Anger of Congress*, (October 30, 2011), available online at http://www.bulletpath.com/2011/the-awesome-anger-of-congress/ (last visited December 4, 2011); and see the remarks of former ATF Director Kenneth Melson. Melson, Kenneth E., *Firearms Identification: A Shot in the Dark?*, Proceedings of the American Academy of Forensic Science, Annual Scientific Meeting (2011), transcript available online at http://www.bulletpath.com/wp-content/uploads/2011/07/Melson-at-AAFS-Transcript.pdf (last visited December 4, 2011*)*.

[6] Page, Mark, Jane Taylor, and Matt Blenkin, *Forensic Identification Science Evidence Since Daubert: Part I—A Quantitative Analysis of the Exclusion of Forensic Identification Science Evidence*, 56 J. Forensic Sci. 1180 (2011).

[7] Bohan, Thomas L., *President's Message*, 39 AAFS Academy News 1 (November 2009).

[8] See Bernstein, David E, and Jeffrey D. Jackson, *The Daubert Trilogy in the States*, 44 Jurimetrics 351 (2003-2004).

[9] Uphoff, Rodney J., *On Misjudging and its Implications for Criminal Defendants, Their Lawyers and the Criminal Justice System*, 7 Nev. L. J. 521 (2007), at 547.

[10] Brennan, William J. Jr., *Reason, Passion and "The Progress of the Law"*, 10 Cardozo L. Rev. 3 (1988).

[11] See Giannelli, Paul C., *The NRC Report and Its Implications For Criminal Litigation*, 50 Jurimetrics 53 (2009), available online at http://ssrn.com/abstract=1568910 (last visited December 6, 2011).

[12] *State v. Anthony*, Ninth Judicial Circuit of Florida, Case No. 48-2008-CF-015606-O (2011), motions and orders available online at http://www.ninthcircuit.org/news/High-Profile-Cases/Anthony/orders&motions.shtml (last visited December 6, 2011).

[13] Federal Rule of Evidence 803 (18), *Learned Treatises*; Giannelli, Paul C., *The NRC Report and Its Implications For Criminal Litigation*, 50 Jurimetrics 53 (2009), available online at http://ssrn.com/abstract=1568910 (last visited December 6, 2011).

[14] National Research Council of the National Academies, *Strengthening Forensic Science in the United States: A Path Forward* (2009), at p. 7.

Recommendations of the National Research Council of the National Academy of Sciences (2009)

Recommendation 1:

To promote the development of forensic science into a mature field of multidisciplinary research and practice, founded on the systematic collection and analysis of relevant data, Congress should establish and appropriate funds for an independent federal entity, the National Institute of Forensic Science (NIFS). NIFS should have a full-time administrator and an advisory board with expertise in research and education, the forensic science disciplines, physical and life sciences, forensic pathology, engineering, information technology, measurements and standards, testing and evaluation, law, national security, and public policy. NIFS should focus on:

(a) establishing and enforcing best practices for forensic science professionals and laboratories;
(b) establishing standards for the mandatory accreditation of forensic science laboratories and the mandatory certification of forensic scientists and medical examiners/forensic pathologists—and identifying the entity/entities that will develop and implement accreditation and certification;
(c) promoting scholarly, competitive peer-reviewed research and technical development in the forensic science disciplines and forensic medicine;

(d) developing a strategy to improve forensic science research and educational programs, including forensic pathology;

(e) establishing a strategy, based on accurate data on the forensic science community, for the efficient allocation of available funds to give strong support to forensic methodologies and practices in addition to DNA analysis;

(f) funding state and local forensic science agencies, independent research projects, and educational programs as recommended in this report, with conditions that aim to advance the credibility and reliability of the forensic science disciplines;

(g) overseeing education standards and the accreditation of forensic science programs in colleges and universities;

(h) developing programs to improve understanding of the forensic science disciplines and their limitations within legal systems; and

(i) assessing the development and introduction of new technologies in forensic investigations, including a comparison of new technologies with former ones.

Recommendation 2:

The National Institute of Forensic Science (NIFS), after reviewing established standards such as ISO 17025, and in consultation with its advisory board, should establish standard terminology to be used in reporting on and testifying about the results of forensic science investigations. Similarly, it should establish model laboratory reports for different forensic science disciplines and specify the minimum information that should be included. As part of the accreditation and certification processes, laboratories and forensic scientists should be required to utilize model laboratory reports when summarizing the results of their analyses.

Recommendation 3:

Research is needed to address issues of accuracy, reliability, and validity in the forensic science disciplines. The National Institute of Forensic Science (NIFS) should competitively fund peer-reviewed research in the following areas:

(a) Studies establishing the scientific bases demonstrating the validity of forensic methods.
(b) The development and establishment of quantifiable measures of the reliability and accuracy of forensic analyses. Studies of the reliability and accuracy of forensic techniques should reflect actual practice on realistic case scenarios, averaged across a representative sample of forensic scientists and laboratories. Studies also should establish the limits of reliability and accuracy that analytic methods can be expected to achieve as the conditions of forensic evidence vary. The research by which measures of reliability and accuracy are determined should be peer reviewed and published in respected scientific journals.
(c) The development of quantifiable measures of uncertainty in the conclusions of forensic analyses.
(d) Automated techniques capable of enhancing forensic technologies.

Recommendation 4:

To improve the scientific bases of forensic science examinations and to maximize independence from or autonomy within the law enforcement community, Congress should authorize and appropriate incentive funds to the National Institute of Forensic Science (NIFS) for allocation to state and local jurisdictions for the purpose of removing all public forensic laboratories and facilities from the administrative control of law enforcement agencies or prosecutors' offices.

Recommendation 5:

The National Institute of Forensic Science (NIFS) should encourage research programs on human observer bias and sources of human error in forensic examinations. Such programs might include studies to determine the effects of contextual bias in forensic practice (e.g., studies to determine whether and to what extent the results of forensic analyses are influenced by knowledge regarding the background of the suspect and the investigator's theory of the case). In addition, research on sources of human error should be closely linked with research conducted to quantify and characterize the amount of error. Based on the results of these studies, and in consultation with its advisory board, NIFS should develop standard cooperating procedures (that will lay the foundation for model protocols) to minimize, to the greatest extent reasonably possible, potential bias and sources of human error in forensic practice. These standard operating procedures should apply to all forensic analyses that may be used in litigation.

Recommendation 6:

To facilitate the work of the National Institute of Forensic Science (NIFS), Congress should authorize and appropriate funds to NIFS to work with the National Institute of Standards and Technology (NIST), in conjunction with government laboratories, universities, and private laboratories, and in consultation with Scientific Working Groups, to develop tools for advancing measurement, validation, reliability, information sharing, and proficiency testing in forensic science and to establish protocols for forensic examinations, methods, and practices. Standards should reflect best practices and serve as accreditation tools for laboratories and as guides for the education, training, and certification of professionals. Upon completion of its work, NIST and its partners should report findings and recommendations to NIFS for further dissemination and implementation.

Recommendation 7:

Laboratory accreditation and individual certification of forensic science professionals should be mandatory, and all forensic science professionals should have access to a certification process. In determining appropriate standards for accreditation and certification, the National Institute of Forensic Science (NIFS) should take into account established and recognized international standards, such as those published by the International Organization for Standardization (ISO). No person (public or private) should be allowed to practice in a forensic science discipline or testify as a forensic science professional without certification. Certification requirements should include, at a minimum, written examinations, supervised practice, proficiency testing, continuing education, recertification procedures, adherence to a code of ethics, and effective disciplinary procedures. All laboratories and facilities (public or private) should be accredited, and all forensic science professionals should be certified, when eligible, within a time period established by NIFS.

Recommendation 8:

Forensic laboratories should establish routine quality assurance and quality control procedures to ensure the accuracy of forensic analyses and the work of forensic practitioners. Quality control procedures should be designed to identify mistakes, fraud, and bias; confirm the continued validity and reliability of standard operating procedures and protocols; ensure that best practices are being followed; and correct procedures and protocols that are found to need improvement.

Recommendation 9:

The National Institute of Forensic Science (NIFS), in consultation with its advisory board, should establish a national code of ethics for all forensic science disciplines and encourage individual societies to incorporate this national code as part of their professional code of ethics. Additionally, NIFS should explore mechanisms of enforcement for those forensic scientists who commit serious ethical violations. Such a code could be enforced through a certification process for forensic scientists.

Recommendation 10:

To attract students in the physical and life sciences to pursue graduate studies in multidisciplinary fields critical to forensic science practice, Congress should authorize and appropriate funds to the National Institute of Forensic Science (NIFS) to work with appropriate organizations and educational institutions to improve and develop graduate education programs designed to cut across organizational, programmatic, and disciplinary boundaries. To make these programs appealing to potential students, they must include attractive scholarship and fellowship offerings. Emphasis should be placed on developing and improving research methods and methodologies applicable to forensic science practice and on funding research programs to attract research universities and students in fields relevant to forensic science. NIFS should also support law school administrators and judicial education organizations in establishing continuing legal education programs for law students, practitioners, and judges.

Recommendation 11:

To improve medicolegal death investigation:

(a) Congress should authorize and appropriate incentive funds to the National Institute of Forensic Science (NIFS) for allocation to states and jurisdictions to establish medical examiner systems, with the goal of replacing and eventually eliminating existing coroner systems. Funds are needed to build regional medical examiner offices, secure necessary equipment, improve administration, and ensure the education, training, and staffing of medical examiner offices. Funding could also be used to help current medical examiner systems modernize their facilities to meet current Centers for Disease Control and Prevention-recommended autopsy safety requirements.

(b) Congress should appropriate resources to the National Institutes of Health (NIH) and NIFS, jointly, to support research, education, and training in forensic pathology. NIH, with NIFS participation, or NIFS in collaboration with content experts, should establish a study section to establish goals, to review and evaluate proposals in these areas, and to allocate funding for collaborative research to be conducted by medical examiner offices and medical universities. In addition, funding, in the form of medical student loan forgiveness and/or fellowship support, should be made available to pathology residents who choose forensic pathology as their specialty.

(c) NIFS, in collaboration with NIH, the National Association of Medical Examiners, the American Board of Medicolegal Death Investigators, and other appropriate professional organizations, should establish a Scientific Working Group (SWG) for forensic pathology and medicolegal death investigation. The SWG should develop and promote standards for best practices, administration, staffing, education, training, and continuing education for competent death scene investigation and postmortem examinations. Best practices should include the utilization of new technologies such as laboratory testing for the molecular basis of diseases and the implementation of specialized imaging techniques.

(d) All medical examiner offices should be accredited pursuant to NIFS-endorsed standards within a timeframe to be established by NIFS.

(e) All federal funding should be restricted to accredited offices that meet NIFS-endorsed standards or that demonstrate significant and measurable progress in achieving accreditation within prescribed deadlines.

(f) All medicolegal autopsies should be performed or supervised by a board certified forensic pathologist. This requirement should take effect within a timeframe to be established by NIFS, following consultation with governing state institutions.

Recommendation 12:

Congress should authorize and appropriate funds for the National Institute of Forensic Science (NIFS) to launch a new broad-based effort to achieve nationwide fingerprint data interoperability. To that end, NIFS should convene a task force comprising relevant experts from the National Institute of Standards and Technology and the major law enforcement agencies (including representatives from the local, state, federal, and, perhaps, international levels) and industry, as appropriate, to develop:

(a) standards for representing and communicating image and minutiae data among Automated Fingerprint Identification Systems. Common data standards would facilitate the sharing of fingerprint data among law enforcement agencies at the local, state, federal, and even international levels, which could result in more solved crimes, fewer wrongful identifications, and greater efficiency with respect to fingerprint searches; and

(b) baseline standards—to be used with computer algorithms— to map, record, and recognize features in fingerprint images, and a research agenda for the continued improvement, refinement, and characterization of the accuracy of these algorithms (including quantification of error rates)

Recommendation 13:

Congress should provide funding to the National Institute of Forensic Science (NIFS) to prepare, in conjunction with the Centers for Disease Control and Prevention and the Federal Bureau of Investigation, forensic scientists and crime scene investigators for their potential roles in managing and analyzing evidence from events that affect homeland security, so that maximum evidentiary value is preserved from these unusual circumstances and the safety of these personnel is guarded. This preparation also should include planning and preparedness (to include exercises) for the interoperability of local forensic personnel with federal counterterrorism organizations.

Bibliography and Table of Cases

Cases

Ake v. Oklahoma, 470 U.S. 68 (1985)

Allstate In. Co. v. Hugh Cole Builder, Inc. 137 F.Supp.2d 1283 (M.D. Ala. 2001)

American Family Ins. Group v. JVC Americas Corp., 2001 WL 1618454 (D. Minn. 2001)

Andrews v. State, 533 So.2d 841(Fla. Dist. Ct. App. 1988)

Arcoren v. United States, 929 F.2d 1235 (8th Cir. 1991)

Arizona v. Youngblood, 488 U.S. 51 (1988)

Ayers v. State, 334 Ark. 258 , 975 S.W.2d 88 (1998)

Bahura v. S.E.W. Investors, 754 A.2d 928 (D.C. 2000)

Baker Valley Lumber, Inc. v. Ingersoll-Rand Company, 813 A.2d 409 (N.H. 2002)

Banks v. State, 725 So.2d 711 (Miss. 1997)

Barber v. State, 952 So.2d 393 (Ala.Crim.App.2005)

Batson v. Kentucky, 476 U.S. 79, (1986)

Benn v. United States, 978 A.2d 1257 (D.C. Ct. App. 2009)

Berry v. City of Detroit, 25 F.3d 1342 (6th Cir. 1994)

Boatswain v. State, No. 408, 2005 WL 1000565 (Del. April 27, 2005)

Bookins v. State, 922 A.2d 389 (Del. Supr. 2007)

Booth v. Black & Decker, Inc., 166 F.Supp.2d 215 (E.D. Pa. 2001)

Brady v. Maryland, 373 U.S. 83 (1963)

Briones v. State, 2009 WL 2356626 (Tex.App.-Hous. (14 Dist.)

Brooks v. State, 748 So. 2d 736 (Miss. 1999)

Brott v. State, 97 N.W. 593 (Neb.1903)

Bryson v. Gonzales, 534 F.3d 1282 (10th Cir. 2008)

Bullcoming v. New Mexico, ___ U.S. ___, 131 S.Ct. 2705 (2011)

Bunting v. Jamieson, 984 P.2d 467 (Wyo. 1999)

Carmichael v. Samyang Tire, Inc., 131 F.3d 1433 (11th Cir. 1997), *cert. granted sub nom. Kumho Tire Co. v. Carmichael*, 526 U.S. 137 (1999)

Chapman v. State, 18 P.3d 1164 (Wyo. 2001)

Charles v. State, 997 A.2d 154 (Md. Ct App. 2010)

Clemons v. State, 392 Md. 339, 896 A.2d 1059 (2006)

Comer v. American Elec. Power, 63 F. Supp.2d 927 (N.D. Ind. 1999)

Commonwealth v. Bizanowicz, 945 N.E.2d 356 (Mass. 2011)

Commonwealth. v. Federico, 425 Mass 844, 683 N.E. 2d 1035 (1997)

Commonwealth v. Brison, 618 A.2d 420 (Pa. Super. Ct. 1992)

Commonwealth v. DiBenedetto, 941 N.E.2d 580 (Mass. 2011)

Commonwealth v. Dixon, 458 Mass. 446 (Mass. 2010)

Commonwealth v. Dunkle, 602 A.2d 830 (Pa. 1992)

Commonwealth v. Goodman, 54 Mass. App. Ct. 385, 765 N.E.2d 792 (2002)

Commonwealth v. Heang, 942 N.E.2d 927 (Mass. 2011)

Commonwealth v. Lanigan, 641 N.E.2d 1342 (Mass. 1994)

Commonwealth v. Matei, 892 N.E.2d 826 (Mass.App.Ct. 2008)

Commonwealth v. Meeks, Nos. 2002-10961, 2003-10575, 2006 WL 2819423, (Mass. Sup. Ct. Sept. 28, 2006)

Commonwealth v. Melendez-Diaz, No. 05-P-1213, 2007 WL 2189152 (Mass. App. Ct. July 31, 2007), *cert. granted*, 128 S. Ct. 1647 (2008)

Commonwealth. v. Patterson, 840 N.E.2d 12 (Mass. 2005)

Commonwealth v. Powell, 940 N.E.2d 521 (Mass. App. Ct. 2011)

Commonwealth v. Simmons, 662 A.2d 621 (Pa. 1995)

Commonwealth v. Verde, 827 N.E.2d 701 (Mass. 2005)

Cox v. State, 966 So. 2d 337 (Fla. 2007)

Crawford v. Washington, 541 U.S. 36 (2004)

Cuadros-Fernandez v. State, 316 S.W.3d 645 (Tex. Ct. App. 2009)

Dabbs v. Vergari, 570 N.Y.S.2d 765 (Sup. Ct. 1990)

Dagner v. Anderson, 651 S.E.2d 640 (Va. 2007)

Daubert v. Merrell Dow Pharm., Inc., 509 U.S. 579 (1993)

Daubert v. Merrell Dow Pharm., Inc., 43 F.3d 1311 (1995)

Davis v. Washington, 547 U.S. 813 (2006)

Debruler v. Commonwealth, 231 S.W.3d 752 (Ky. 2007)

Dist. Attorney's Office v. Osborne, 557 U.S. ___, 129 S. Ct. 2308 (2009)

Dowling v. United States, 493 U.S. 342 (1990)

E.I. du Pont Nemours and Co., Inc. v. Robinson, 923 S.W.2d 549 (Tex. 1995)

Echavarria v. State, 839 P.2d 589 (Nev. 1992)

Ege v. Yukins, 380 F. Supp. 2d 852 (E.D. Mich. 2005)

Evans v. Commonwealth, 230 Ky. 411, 19 S.W.2d 1091 (1929)
Evans v. State, 922 A.2d 620 (Md. Ct. Spec. App. 2007)
Farm Bureau Mut. Ins. Co. of Arkansas, Inc. v. Foote, 14 S.W.3d 512, 519 (Ark. 2000)
Figueroa v. State, 2009 WL 2183460 (Tex.App.-San Antonio)
Fletcher v. Lane, 446 F. Supp. 729 (S.D. Ill. 1978)
Fowler v. State, 958 S.W.2d 853 (Tex. App. 1997)
Frye v. United States, 293 F. 1013 (D.C. Cir 1923)
Gen. Elec. Co. v. Joiner, 522 U.S. 136 (1997)
Gilbert v. DaimlerChrysler Corp., 470 Mich.749, 685 N.W.2d 391(2004)
Goddard v. State, 144 S.W.3d 848 (Mo. Ct. App. 2004)
Gordon v. State, 863 So.2d 1215 (Fla. 2003)
Grady v. Frito-Lay, Inc., 839 A.2d 1038 (Pa. 2003)
Hadden v. State, 690 So.2d 573 (Fla. 1997)
Hallmark v. Eldridge, 189 P.3d 646 (Nev. 2008)
Haupt v. Heaps, 775 P.2d 388 (Utah App., 2005)
Harrington v. Richter, ___ U.S. ___, 131 S. Ct. 770 (2011) rev'g *Richter v. Hickman*, 578 F.3d 944 (9th Cir. 2009)
Harrison v. State, 635 So.2d 894 (Miss. 1994)
Hawaii v. Maelega, 907 P.2d 758 (1995)
Higgs v. State, 222 P.3d 648 (Nev. 2010)
Holland v. State, 916 So.2d 750, 758 (Fla. 2005)
Holmes v. State, 135 S.W.3d 178 (Tex. Ct. App 2004)
Houston v. Commonwealth, 2011 WL 3962511 (Ky.App. 2011)
Hynes v. Energy West, Inc. 211 F.3d 1193 (10th Cir. 2000)
In re Commitment of Simons, 821 N.E.2d 1184 (Ill. 2004)
In re Investigation of W. Va. State Police Crime Lab., Serology Div. (Zain I), 438 S.E.2d 501, (W. Va. 1993)
In re Investigation of W. Va. State Police Crime Lab., Serology Div. (Zain II), 445 S.E.2d 165 (W. Va. 1994)
In Re Mackenzie C., 877 A.2d 674 (R.I. 2005)
In re Renewed Investigation of State Police Crime Lab., Serology Division, 633 S.E.2d 762 (W. Va. 2006)
In re Petition to Amend Rules of Evidence and Rule 17.4 (f), Arizona Rules of Criminal Procedure, Ariz. Sup. Ct. No R-10-35 (Sept. 7, 2001), available online at http://www.azcourts.gov/Portals/21/MinutesCurrent/R100035.pdf (last visited November 10, 2011)
Jacobs v. Government of Virgin Islands, 53 Fed. Appx. 651 (3d Cir. 2002)

John v. Im, 559 S.E.2d 694 (Va. 2002)

Jones v. Murray, 962 F.2d 302 (4th Cir. 1992)

Jones v. United States, ___ A.3d ___, 2011 WL 3847414 (D.C. App 2011)

Kelly v. State, 824 S.W.2d 568 (Tex. Crim. App. 1992)

Knotts v. Black & Decker, Inc., 204 F.Supp.2d 1029 (N.D. Ohio 2002)

Kovach v. Alpharma, Inc., 890 N.E.2d 55 (Ind. Ct. App. 2008)

Kumho Tire Co. v. Carmichael, 526 U.S. 137 (1999)

Leaf v. Goodyear Tire & Rubber Co., 591 N.W.2d 10 (Iowa 1999)

Markham v. State, 984 A.2d 262 (Md. App. 2009)

Marron v. Stromstad, 123 P.3d 992 (Alaska 2005)

Mathis v. State, No. 25, 2006, 2006 WL 2434741, at *4 (Del. 2006)

McCloud v. Commonwealth, 286 S.W.3d 780 (Ky. 2009)

McIntyre v. State, 530 N.Y.S.2d 898 (N.Y. App. Div. 1988)

McDaniel v. CSX Transp., Inc., 955 S.W.2d 257 (Tenn. 1997)

Mebane v. State, 902 P.2d 494 (Kan. Ct. App. 1995)

Melandez-Diaz v. Massachusetts, 557 U.S. 1256 (2009)

Michigan Millers Mut. Ins. Corp. v. Benfield, 140 F.3d 915 (11th Cir. 1998)

Miller v. State, ___A.3d ___, 2011 WL 4363938 (Md. 2011)

Miss. Transp. Comm'n v. McLemore, 863 So.2d 31 (Miss. 2003)

Mitchell v. Commonwealth, 908 S.W.2d 100 (Ky. 1995)

Moran v. Kia Motors, Inc., 622 S.E.2d 439 (Ga. App. 2005)

Morgan v. State, 922 A.2d 395 (Del. 2007)

Murphy v. State, 941 N.E.2d 568 (Ind. App. 2011)

Neal v. State, 2011 WL 766546 (Alaska App.)

Nelson v. State, 628 A.2d 69 (Del. 1993)

Nenno v. State, 970 S.W.2d 549, 560-61 (Tex.Crim.App.1998), *overruled on
    other grounds, State v. Terrazas*, 4 S.W.3d 720, 727 (Tex.Crim.App.1999)

Newkirk v. Commonwealth, 937 S.W.2d 690 (Ky. 1996)

985 Associates, Ltd. v. Daewoo Electronics America, Inc., 945 A.2d 381 (Vt.
    2008)

Osborne v. Dist. Attorney's Office, 521 F.3d 1118 (9th Cir. 2008), *cert. granted*,
    129 S. Ct. 488 (2008)

Parrish v. State, 514 S.E.2d 458 (Ga. Ct. App. 1999)

People v. Abney, 31 Misc.3d 1231(A), 2011 WL 2026894 (N.Y.Sup. 2011)

People v. Bailey, 2009 WL 3323252 (Mich.App.)

People v. Beckley, 434 Mich. 691, 456 N.W.2d 391 (1990)

People v. Bledsoe, 681 P.2d 291 (Cal. 1984) (en banc)

People v. Bowker, 249 Cal. Rptr. 886 (Ct. App. 1988)

People v. Brooks, No. F051251, 2008 WL 2897093, at *15 (Cal. Ct. App. July 29, 2008)

People v. Brown, 94 P.3d 574 (Cal. 2004)

People v. Burkett, No. 254996, 2005 WL 2401634, at *4-5 (Mich. Ct. App. Sept. 29, 2005)

People v. Callace, 573 N.Y.S.2d 137 (Gen. Term. 1991)

People v. Christel, 449 Mich. 578, 537 N.W.2d 194 (1995)

People v. Compean, No. A111367, 2007 WL 1567603, at *8 (Cal. Ct. App. May 31, 2007)

People v. Craig, 86 Cal.App.3d 905 (1978)

People v. Cruz, 643 N.E.2d 636 (Ill. 1994)

People v. Donastorg, 83 Fed. R. Serv. 434 (V.I. Super 2010)

People v. Fasy, 829 P.2d 1314 (Colo. 1992) (en banc)

People v. Genrich, 928 P.2d 799 (Colo. Ct. App. 1996)

People v. Henderson, No. A102395, 2004 WL 2526448, at *4-*5 (Cal. Ct. App. Nov. 9, 2004)

People v. Howard, 712 N.E.2d 380 (Ill. Ct. App. 1999)

People v. Humphrey, 2011 WL 1671560 (Cal.App. 3 Dist.)

People v. Jennings, 252 Ill. 534, 96 N.E. 1077 (1911)

People v. Kelly, 549 P.2d 1240 (Cal. 1976)

People v. Kowalski, 2010 WL 3389741 (Mich.App. 2011)

People v. Lee, 750 N.E.2d 63 (N.Y. 2001)

People v. LeGrand, 867 N.E.2d 374 (N.Y. 2007)

People v. Linscott, 566 N.E.2d 1355, 1358-60 (Ill. 1991)

People v. Marquez, No. B184697, 2006 WL 2665509, at *4-*5 & n.5 (Cal. Ct. App. Sept. 18, 2006)

People v. Martinez, 855 N.Y.S.2d 522 (App. Div. 2008)

People v. Melcher, 2011 WL 4432935 (Cal.App. 1 Dist. 2011)

People v. Milone, 356 N.E.2d 1350, 1355 (Ill. App. Ct. 1976)

People v. Montoya, 63 Cal. Rptr. 73 (Ct. App. 1967)

People v. Moore, 662 N.E.2d 1215 (Ill. 1996)

People v. Nelson, 43 Cal. 4th 1242, 1247 (2008)

People v. Peterson, 450 Mich. 349, 537 N.W.2d 857 (1995)

People v. Radcliffe, 764 N.Y.S.2d 773 (Sup. Ct. 2003)

People v. Rector, 248 P.3d 1196 (2011)

People v. Reyes, No. E040509, 2007 WL 4427856 (Cal. Ct. App. Dec. 19, 2007)

People v. Rivera, 2011 Ill. App. 2d No. 091060 (Dec. 9, 2011), available online at

http://www.state.il.us/court/Opinions/AppellateCourt/2011/2ndDistrict/De
cember/2091060.pdf (last visited December 14, 2011)

People v. Robinson, 67 Cal. Rptr. 3d 392 (Ct. App. 2007) (depublished),
   petition for review granted, 177 P.3d 230, 230 (Cal. 2008)

People v. Robinson, 222 P.3d 55 (Cal. 2010)

People v. Robles, No. D048357, 2007 WL 1140380, at *3 (Cal. Ct. App. 2007)

People v. Sandoval-Ceron, 2010 WL 3021861 (Mich.App.)

People v. Seaman, 657 N.Y.S.2d 242 (1997)

People v. Shreck, 22 P.3d 68 (Colo. 2001) (en banc)

People v. Smith, 443 N.Y.S.2d 551 (Sup. Ct. 1981)

People v. Smith, No. 271036, 2007 WL 4248571, at *5 (Mich. Ct. App. Dec. 4,
   2007)

People v. Spicola, 947 N.E.2d 620 (N.Y. 2011)

People v. Stull, 338 N.W.2d 403 (Mich. Ct. App. 1983)

People v. Taylor, 75 N.Y.S. 2d 277, 552 N.E. 2d 131 (1990)

People v. Thompson, 699 N.Y.S.2d 770 (App. Div. 1999)

People v. Todmann, 2010 WL 684009 (V.I. 2010)

People v. Wilkes, 280 P.2d 88 (Cal. App 1955)

People v. Williams, 939 N.E.2d 268 (2010), cert. granted *sub nom Williams v.*
   Illinois, __ U.S. __, 131 S. Ct. 3090 (2011)

Pierce v. State, 777 S.W.2d 399 (Tex. Crim. App. 1989) (en banc)

Pride v. BIC Corp., 218 F.3d 566 (6th Cir. 2000)

Ragland v. Comm., 191 S.W.3d 569 (Ky. 2006)

Ramirez v. State, 542 So.2d 352 (Fla. 1989)

Reed v. State, 283 Md. 374, 391 A.2d 364 (1978)

Revis v. State, ___ So.2d ___ (2011), 2011 WL 109641 (Ala.Crim.App.)

Richter v. Hickman, 578 F.3d 944 (9th Cir. 2009), rev'd *Harrington v. Richter,*
   ___ U.S. ___, 131 S. Ct. 770 (2011).

Rivera v. State, 2005 WL 16193 (Tex. Ct. App 2005)

Roberts v. United States., 916 A.2d 922 (D.C. 2007)

Robbins v. Commonwealth, 336 S.W.3d 60 (Ky. 2011)

Roe v. Marcotte, 193 F.3d 72 (2d Cir. 1999)

Royal Ins. Co. of America v. Joseph Daniel Const., Inc., 208 F.Supp.2d 423
   (S.D. N.Y. 2002)

Ryan v. State, 988 P.2d 46 (Wyo. 1999)

Schafersman v. Agland Coop., 631 N.W.2d 862 (Neb. 2001)

Sewell v. State, 592 N.E.2d 705 (Ind. Ct. App. 1992)

Shaffer v. Saffle, 148 F.3d 1180 (10th Cir. 1998)

Smither v. Commonwealth, 2011 WL 1642333 (Ky. 2011).

Souza v. United States, 304 F.2d 274 (9th Cir. 1962)

State Board of Registration for the Healing Arts v. McDonaugh, 123 S.W.3d 146 (Mo. 2003)

State v. Adams, 713 S.E.2d 251, 2011 WL 1938270 (N.C.App. 2011)

State v. Alberico, 116 N.M. 156, 861 P. 2d 192 (1993)

State v. Anthony, Ninth Judicial Circuit of Florida, Case No. 48-2008-CF-015606-O (2011), motions and orders available online at http://www.ninthcircuit.org/news/High-Profile-Cases/Anthony/orders&motions.shtml (last visited December 6, 2011)

State v. Ash, No. A07-0761, 2008 WL 2965555, at *7 (Minn. Ct. App. Oct. 21, 2008)

State v. Bander, 208 P.3d 1242 (Wash. App. 2009)

State v. Behn, 868 A.2d 329, (N.J. Super. Ct. App. 2005)

State v. Belt, 179 P.3d 443 (Kan. 2008)

State v. Bickart, 963 A.2d 183 (Me. 2009)

State v. Boushack, Nos. 94-1389-CR, 94-1392-CR, 94-1390-CR, 94-1393-CR, 94-1391-CR, 1995 WL 117028 (Wis. Ct. App. 1995)

State v. Boles, 933 P.2d 1197 (Ariz. 1997)

State v. Bowman, 89 P.3d 986 (Mont. 2004)

State v. Brown, 291 S.W.2d 615 (Mo. 1956)

State v. Campbell, 2002 WL 398029 (Ohio Ct. App. 1st Dist. 2002)

State v. Canaan, 265 Kan. 835, 964 P.2d 681 (1998)

State v. Carson, No. C-040042, 2005 WL 497290 (Ohio Ct. App. March 4, 2005)

State v. Chapple, 660 P.2d 1208 (Ariz. 1983) (en banc)

State v. Christeson, 50 S.W.3d 251 (Mo. 2001) (en banc)

State v. Chul Yun Kim, 318 N.C. 614, 350 S.E.2d 347 (1986)

State v. Chun, 943 A.2d 114 (N.J. 2008)

State v. Clark, 156 Wash. 543, 287 P. 18 (1930)

State v. Clopten, 223 P.3d 1103 at 1112 (Utah 2009)

State v. Coley, 32 S.W.3d 831 (Tenn. 2000)

State v. Cooke, 914 A.2d 1078 (Del. Super. Ct. 2007)

State v. Coon, 974 P.2d 386 (Alaska 1999)

State v. Copeland, 922 P.2d 1304 (Wash. 1996)

State v. Council, 515 S.E.2d 508, (S.C. 1999)

State v. Craven, 790 N.W.2d 225 (Neb. App. 2010)

State v. Dabney, 663 N.W.2d 366 (Wis. Ct. App. 2003)

State v. Danley, 138 Ohio Misc.2d 1 (Ct. Com. Pleas 2006)

State v. Davis, 698 N.W.2d 823 (Wis. Ct. App. 2005)

State v. Davolt, 207 Ariz. 191, 84 P.3d 456, 475 (2004)

State v. Dominguez, 2011 WL 3207766 (Tex.App. 2010)

State v. Drummond, 111OhioSt.3d (2006)

State v. Eickmeier, 187 Neb. 491, 191 N.W.2d 815 (1971)

State v. Ellis, 799 N.W.2d 267 (Neb. 2011)

State v. Escobido-Ortiz, 126 P.3d 402 (Haw. Ct. App. 2005)

State v. Fasick, 149 Wash. 92, 270 P. 123 (1928), *aff'd* 149 Wash. 92, 174 P. 712 (1929)

State v. Foret, 628 So.2d 1116 (La. 1993)

State v. Fuentes, 228 P.3d 1181 (N.M. Ct. App. 2011)

State v. Goetz, 191 P. 3d 489, 517 (Mont. 2008)

State v. Goldsby, 650 P.2d 952 (Or. Ct. App. 1982)

State v. Goode, 461 S.E. 2d 631 (N.C. 1995)

State v. Green, 2009 WL 3353595 (Ohio App. 2 Dist. 2009)

State v. Grube, 126 Idaho 377, 883 P.2d 1069 (1994)

State v. Hall, 406 N.W.2d 503 (Minn. 1987)

State v. Hall, 412 S.E.2d 883 (N.C. 1992)

State v. Harvey, 699 A.2d 596 (N.J. 1997)

State v. Hauptmann, 180 A. 809 (N.J. 1935)

State v. Heath, 957 P.2d 449, 464 (Kan. 1998)

State v. Henderson, 27 A.3d 872 (N.J. 2011)

State v. Hernandez, 707 N.W.2d 449 (N.D. 2005)

State v. Higgins, 898 So.2d 1219 (La. 2005)

State v. Hill, 463 N.W.2d 674 (S.D. 1990)

State v. Hill, No. A05-570, 2006 WL 1320075, at *3 (Minn. Ct. App. May 16, 2006)

State v. Hofer, 512 N.W.2d 482, 484 (S.D. 1994)

State v. Humberto, 2011 WL 2518976 (Ohio App. 10 Dist.)

State v. J.Q., 617 A.2d 1196 (N.J. 1993)

State v. Jensen, 432 N.W.2d 913 (Wis. 1988)

State v. Johnson, 2010 WL 5464926 (La.App. 1 Cir. 2010)

State v. Keightley, 147 S.W.3d 179 (Mo. Ct. App. 2004).

State v. Kim, 645 P.2d 1330 (Haw. 1982)

State v. King, 713 S.E.2d 772 (N.C. 2011)

State v. Kinney, 171 Vt. 239, 762 A.2d 833 (2000)

State v. Krone, 897 P.2d 621 (Ariz. 1995) (en banc)

State v. Lang, 129 Ohio St.3d 512 (2011).

State v. Latham, No. 92,521, 2005 WL 1619235, at *2 (Kan. Ct. App. Nov. 1, 2005)

State v. Leep, 569 S.E.2d 133 (W.Va. 2002)

State v. Lyons, 924 P.2d 802 (Or. 1996)

State v. MacDonald, 718 A.2d 195 (Me. 1998)

State v. Maner, 2011 WL 3671909 (Conn. Super. 2011)

State v. Manson, 984 A.2d 1099 (Conn. App. 2009)

State v. Maynard, 954 S.W.2d 624 (Mo. Ct. App. 1997)

State v. McKinney 74 S.W.3d 291 (Tenn. 2002), *cert. denied*, 537 U.S. 926 (2002)

State v. McKinney, No. 2007-T-0004, 2008 WL 2582860 (Ohio Ct. App. June 27, 2008)

State v. Middleton, 657 P.2d 1215 (Or. 1983)

State v. Minor, No. C-060043, 2007 WL 196504, at *3 (Ohio Ct. App. Jan. 26, 2007)

State v. Moore, 885 P.2d 457 (Mont. 1994)

State v. Moran, 728 P.2d 248 (Ariz. 1986)

State v. Mosely, 13 So.3d 705 (La.App. 5 Cir. 2009)

State v. Newell, 710 N.W.2d 6, 28 (Iowa 2006)

State v. Noel, 157 N.J. 141, 723 A.2d 602 (1999)

State v. Olsen, 212 Or. 191, 317 P.2d 938 (1957)

State v. Onunwor, 2010 WL 4684717 (Ohio App. 8 Dist. 2010)

State v. Oral H., 125 Conn.App. 276, 7 A.3d 444 (2010)

State v. Pappas, 776 A.2d 1091 (Conn. 2001)

State v. Parkinson, 909 P.2d 647 (Idaho 1996)

State v. Perry, 218 P.3d 95 (Ore. 2009)

State v. Pittman, No. 04-03-0037/3, 2007 WL 4482159 (N.J. Super. Ct. App. Div. Dec. 26, 2007)

State v. Porter, 698 A.2d 739, 746 (Conn. 1997)

State v. Price, 171 P.3d 293 (Mont. 2007)

State v. Reed, 641 S.E.2d 320 (N.C. Ct. App. 2007)

State v. Rosas, 2009 WL 805404 (Ohio App. 2 Dist.)

State v. Roscoe, 700 P.2d 1312 (Ariz. 1984)

State v. Rose, Case No. K06-0545 (Md. Balt. Co. Cir. Oct. 19, 2007), available online at http://www.baltimoresun.com/media/acrobat/2007-10/33446162.pdf (last visited December 14, 2011).

State v. Segura, 2011 WL 2027912 (N.M.App.)

State v. Smith, 58 So.3d 964, 2010-830 (La.App. 3 Cir. 2011)

State v. Smith, 335 S.W.3d 706 (Tex. App. 2011)

State v. Snowden, Nos. 04-07-2546, 03-09-3175, 2007 WL 1119339, at *4 (N.J. Super. Ct. App. Div. April 17, 2007) (*per curiam*)

State v. Spigarolo, 556 A.2d 112 (Conn. 1989)

State v. Storm, 238 P.2d 1161 (Mont. 1951)

State v. Strong, 142 S.W.3d 702 (Mo. 2004) (*en banc*)

State v. Taylor, 633 S.W.2d 235 (Mo. 1984)

State v. Taylor, No. 06CA009000, 2008 WL 834437, at *3 (Ohio Ct. App. March 31, 2008)

State v. Torres, 222 P.3d 409 (Ha. 2009)

State v. Traylor, 656 N.W.2d 885 (Minn. 2003)

State v. Thomas, 586 A.2d 250 (N.J. Super. Ct. App. Div. 1991)

State v. Timmendequas, 737 A.2d 55 (N.J. 1999)

State v. Torrez, 146 N.M. 331, 210 P.3d 228 (2009)

State v. Vidrine, 9 So.3d 1095 (La.App. 2009)

State v. Wade, 465 S.W.2d 498 (Mo. 1971)

State v. Ware, 338 N.W.2d 707 (Ia. 1983)

State v. Walsh, 495 N.W.2d 602 (Minn. 1993)

State v. West, 877 A.2d 787 (Conn. 2005)

State v. Woodall, 385 S.E.2d 253 (W. Va. 1989)

State v. Wright, 2009 WL 3111047 (Del.Super. 2009)

Steward v. State, 652 N.E.2d 490 (Ind. 1995)

Taylor v. State, 889 P.2d 319 (Okla. Crim. App. 1995)

Terrell v. State, 239 A.2d 128 (Md. App. 1968)

Terry v. Caputo, 875 N.E.2d 72 (Ohio 2007)

Thompson v. State, 416 S.E.2d 755 (Ga. Ct. App. 1992)

Thurman v. Missouri Gas Energy, 107 F.Supp.2d 1046 (W.D. Mo. 2000)

Tolson v. State, 900 A.2d 639 (Del. Supr. 2006)

Townsend v. State, 734 P.2d 705 (Nev. 1987)

Travelers Property & Casualty Corp. v. General Electric Co., 150 F.Supp.2d 360 (D. Conn. 2001)

Truck Ins. Exchange v. MagneTek, Inc., 360 F.3d 1206 (10th Cir. 2004).

Tunnell v. Ford Motor Co., 320 F.Supp.2d 707 (W.D. Va. 2004)

Turner v. State, ___ N.E.2d ___(2011) WL 4479926 (Ind.)

United States v. Adams, 271 F.3d 1236 (10th Cir. 2001)

United States v. Aman, 748 F.Supp.2d 531 (E.D. Va. 2010)

United States v. Amaral, 488 F.2d 1148 (9th Cir. 1973)

United States v. Batton, 602 F.3d 1191 (10th Cir.2010)

United States v. Berry, 624 F.3d 1031 (9th Cir. 2011)

United States v. Beasley, 102 F.3d 1440 (8th Cir. 1996)

United States v. Beltran-Rios, 878 F.2d 1208 (9th Cir. 1989)

United States v. Beverly, 369 F.3d 516 (6th Cir. 2004)

United States v. Bighead, 128 F.3d 1329 (9th Cir. 1997)

United States v. Brooks, 81 Fed. R. Evid. Serv. 381 (E.D. N.Y. 2010)

United States v. Bunke, 412 Fed.Appx. 760 (6th Cir. 2011)

United States v. Cerna, 2010 WL 3448528 (N.D.Cal. 2010)

United States v. Cline, 188 F. Supp.2d 1287 (D. Kan. 2002), *aff'd* 349 F.3d 1276 (10th Cir. 2003)

United States v. Coleman, 202 F.Supp.2d 962, (E.D. Mo. 2002)

United States v. Cordoba, 104 F.3d 225 (9th Cir. 1997)

United States v. Crisp, 324 F.3d 261 (4th Cir. 2003)

United States v. Cruz-Rivera, 2002 WL 662128 (D.P.R. 2002)

United States v. Davis, 103 F.3rd 660, 46 Fed. R. Evid. Serv. 189 (8th Cir. 1996)

United States v. Davis, 602 F.Supp.2d 658 (D. Md. 2009)

United States v. Defreitas, 2011 WL 317964 (E.D.N.Y.)

United States v. Diaz, 300 F.3d 66 (1st Cir. 2002)

United States v. Doe, 703 F.2d 745 (3d Cir. 1983)

United States v. Downing, 753 F.2d 1224 (3d Cir. 1985)

United States v. Duronio, No. 02-0933 (JAG), 2006 WL 3591259, at *3 (D.N.J. Dec. 11, 2006)

United States v. Farhane, 634 F.3d 127 (2d Cir. 2011)

United States v. Feliciano, 80 Fed. R. Evid. Serv. 1813 (D. Ariz. 2009)

United States v. Fields, 483 F.3d 313 (5th Cir. 2007)

United States v. Frias, 2003 WL 296740 (S.D. N.Y 2003), *modified in part*, 2003 WL 352502 (S.D. N.Y 2003)

United States v. Fujii, 152 F. Supp.2d 939 (N.D. Ill. 2000)

United States v. Gardner, 213 F.3d 1049 (7th Cir. 2000)

United States v. Gates, 680 F.2d 1117 (6th Cir. 1982)

United States v. Gipson, 383 F.3d 689 (8th Cir. 2004)

United States v. Givens, 912 N.Y.S.2d 855 (2010)

United States v. Glynn, 578 F.Supp.2d 567 (S.D. N.Y 2008)

United States v. Green, 405 F.Supp.2d 104 (D. Mass. 2005)

United States v. Hair, 2011 WL 333236 (N.D.Okla. 2011).

United States v. Hall, 93 F. 3d 1337 (7th Cir. 1996);

United States v. Hankey, 203 F.3d 1160 (2000)

United States v. Harrington, 204 F. App'x 784 (11th Cir. 2006)

United States v. Havvard, 117 F.Supp.2d 848 (2000)

United States v. Hebshie, 754 F.Supp.2d 89 (D. Mass. 2010)

United States v. Hendrix, 509 F.3d 362 (7th Cir. 2007)

United States v. Hernandez, 299 F.3d 984 (8th Cir. 2002), *cert. denied*, 537 U.S. 1134 (2003)

United States v. Hicks, 103 F.3d 837 (9th Cir. 1996)

United States v. Hines, 55 F.Supp.2d 62, (D. Mass. 1999)

United States v. Hitt, 473 F.3d 146 (5th Cir. 2006)

United States v. Holloway, 971 F.2d 675 (11th Cir. 1992)

United States v. Jayyousi, ___ F.3d ___, 2011 WL 4346322 (C.A.11 Fla.)

United States v. John, 597 F.3d 263 (5th Cir. 2010)

United States v. Johnson, 488 F.3d 690 (6th Cir.2007)

United States v. Joseph, 2001 WL 515213 (E.D. La. 2001)

United States v. Kassir, 2009 WL 910767 (S.D.N.Y.)

United States v. Kime, 99 F.3d 870 (8th Cir. 1996)

United States v. Kimler, 335 F.3d 1132 (10th Cir. 2003)

United States v. Kincade, 345 F.3d 1095 (9th Cir. 2003), *rev'd en banc*, 379 F.3d 813 (9th Cir. 2004)

United States v. Langan, 263 F.3d 613 (6th Cir. 2001)

United States v. Larkin, 978 F.2d 964 (7th Cir. 1992)

United State v. Lim, 984 F.2d 331 (9th Cir. 1993)

United States v. Llera Plaza I,179 F.Supp.2d 492 (E.D. Pa. 2002)

United States v. Llera Plaza II, 188 F.Supp.2d 549 (E.D. Pa. 2002)

United States v. Marji, 158 F.3d 60 (2d Cir 1998)

United States v. Martin, 391 F.3d 949 (8th Cir. 2004)

United States v. Martinez-Cintron, 136 F.Supp.2d 17 (D.P.R. 2001)

United States v. Mason, 954 F.2d 219 (4th Cir. 1992)

United States v. Mathis, 264 F.3d 321 (3rd Cir. 2001), *cert. denied*, 535 U.S. 908 (2002)

United States v. McNeil, 2010 WL 56096 (M.D. Pa. 2010)

United States v. McNiece, 558 F.Supp. 612 (E.D.N.Y. 1983)

United States v. Mejia, 545 F.3d 179 (2d Cir. 2008)

United States v. Mikos, No. 02 CR 137, 2003 WL 22922197 (N.D. Ill. Dec. 9, 2003)

United States v. Mitchell, 365 F.3d 215 (3d Cir. 2004)

United States v. Mitchell, ___ F.3d ___ (3d Cir. No. 09-4718, July 25, 2011)

United States v. Monteiro, 407 F.Supp.2d 351, 354-55 (D. Mass. 2006)

United States v. Mooney, 315 F.3d 54, 60 Fed. Evid. Serv. 60 (1st Cir. 2002

United States v. Moore, 786 F.2d. 1308 (5th Cir. 1986)

United States v. Mouzone, Criminal No. WDQ-08-086, United States District Court (D. Maryland, October 29, 2009)

United States v. Myers, 2010 WL 2723196 (S.D. W.Va. 2010)

United States v. Navarro-Fletes, 49 Fed. Appx 732 (9th Cir. 2002)

United States v. Norris, 217 F.3d 262 (5th Cir. 2000)

United States v. Pool, 621 F.3d 1213 (9th Cir. 2010), rehearing en banc ordered *United States v. Pool*, ___ F.3d ___, 2011 WL 2151202, at *1 (9th Cir. June 2, 2011)

United States v. Prokupek, Case No. 08CR183, United States District Court (D. Nebraska, August 14, 2009)

United States v. Pugh, 2009 WL 2256019 (N.D.Fla. 2009)

United States v. Pugh, 80 Fed. R. Evid. Serv. 950 (S.D. Miss. 2009)

United States v. Raymond, 700 F.Supp.2d 142 (D. Me. 2010)

United States v. Reaux, 2001 WL 883221 (E.D. La. 2001)

United States v. Rincon, 28 F.3d 921 (9th Cir. 1994), *cert. denied*, 513 U.S. 1029 (1994)

United States v. Rogers, 26 Fed. App'x 171 (4th Cir. 2001)

United States v. Rose, No. CCB-08-0149 (D. Md., December 8, 2009), available online at http://www.mdd.uscourts.gov/Opinions/Opinions/Brian%20Rose%20Mem-FINAL.pdf (last visited December 14, 2011).

United States v. Saelee, 162 F.Supp.2d 1097 (D. Alaska 2001)

United States v. Saldarriaga, 204 F.3d 50 (2d Cir. 2000) (*per curiam*)

United States v. Schneider, 83 Fed. R. Evid. Serv. 820 (E.D. Pa. 2010)

United States v. Scott, 403 Fed.Appx. 392 (11th Cir. 2010)

United States v. Shay, 57 F.3d 126 (1st Cir. 1995)

United States v. Smith, 122 F.3d 1355 (11th Cir. 1997)

United States v. Smith, 736 F.2d 1103 (6th Cir. 1984)

United States v. Smith, 142 F.3d 438 (6th Cir. 1998)

United States v. Smith, 621 F.Supp.2d 1207 (M.D. Ala 2009)

United States v. Smithers, 212 F.3d 306 (6th Cir. 2000)

United States v. Starzecpyzel, 880 F.Supp. 1027, 42 Fed. R. Evid. Serv. 247 (S.D. N.Y. 1995)

United States v. Sullivan, 246 F.Supp.2d 700 (E.D. Ky. 2003)

United States v. Swanner, 237 F.Supp. 69 (E.D. Tenn. 1964)

United States v. Taylor, 663 F.Supp.2d 1170 (D. N.M. 2009).

United States v. Yee, 134 F.R.D. 161 (N.D. Ohio 1991)

VanPelt v. State, 2009 WL 4980326 (Ala.Crim.App. 2009)

Velasquez v. Woods, 329 F.3d 420 (5th Cir. 2003)

Von Dohlen v. State, 602 S.E.2d 738 (S.C. 2004), *cert. denied*, 544 U.S. 943 (2005)

Wagner v. State, 864 A.2d 1037 (Md. Ct. Spec. App. 2005)

Wainwright v. State, 504 A.2d 1096, 1100 (Del. 1986)

Weisgram v. Marley, 169 F.3d 514 (8th Cir. 1999), aff;d, 528 U.. 440 (2000)

Wells v. Ricks, No. 07 Civ. 6982(CM)(AJP), 2008 WL 506294, at *28 (S.D.N.Y. Feb. 26, 2008)

Werner v. Pittway Corp., 90 F.Supp.2d 1018 (W.D. Wis. 2000)

Williamson v. Reynolds, 904 F.Supp. 1529, (E.D. Okla. 1995), *aff'd sub nom.* Williamson v. Ward, 110 F.3d 1508, 1523 (10th Cir. 1997)

Willingham v. Dretke, 540 U.S. 986 (2003)

Willingham v. Johnson, (N.D. Tex. 2001), not reported, available, in part, online at http://www.clarkprosecutor.org/html/death/US/willingham899.htm, (last visited November 26, 2011)

Willingham v. State, 897 S.W.2d 351 (Tex. Ct. Crim. App 1995)

Wilson v. State, 370 Md. 191, 803 A.2d 1034 (2002)

Wines v. Commonwealth, 2009 WL 1830805 (Ky. 2009)

Winfrey v. State, 323 S.W.3d 875 (Tex. Crim. App. 2010)

Winters v. Campbell, 137 S.E.2d 188 (W. Va. 1964)

Wynn v. State, 56 Ga. 113, 1876 WL 2941 (1876)

Young v. State, 879 A.2d 44 (Md. 2005)

Zeigler v. Fisher-Price, Inc., 261 F.Supp.2d 1047 (N.D. Iowa 2003)

Zeigler v. Fisher-Price, Inc., 302 F.Supp.2d 999 (N.D. Ia. 2004)

Statutes and Regulations

18 U.S.C. § 3282

18 U.S.C §3600 *et seq.*

28 C.F.R. § 28.12, 73 Fed. Reg. 74932 (eff. Jan. 9, 2009)

42 U.S.C. § 14135a(a)(1)(A)

42 U.S.C. § 14135(a) (j) (2000 & Supp. V 2007)

Alabama SB 187 (June 9, 2011), available online at http://www.alabamalitigationreview.com/uploads/file/SB187-eng-1.pdf (last visited November 10, 2011), amending § 12-21-160 of the Code of Alabama 1975

Arizona Rev. Stat. Ann. § 13-4240 (2001)

Arkansas Code Ann. §§ 16-112-201 to -208 (2006)

Arkansas Code Ann. §§ 5-1-109(b)(1)(B), (i)-(j) (2006)

California Penal Code § 1405 (West Supp. 2009)

Colorado Bureau of Investigation, *DNA Familial Search Policy* (October 22, 2009), available online at http://www.denverda.org/DNA/Familial_DNA_Database_Searches.htm (last visited December 14, 2011)

Colorado Rev. Stat. Ann. §§ 18-1-411 to -416 (West 2004 & Supp. 2008)

Commerce, Justice, Science and Related Agencies Appropriations Bill, 2012, House Report 112- 169, 112th Congress (2011-2012) available online at http://thomas.loc.gov/cgi-bin/query/z?c112:H.R.2596 (last visited November 26, 2011)

Connecticut General Stat. Ann. § 54-102kk (West Supp. 2008)

Criminal Justice and Forensic Science Reform Act of 2011, S. 132, available online at http://www.govtrack.us/congress/bill.xpd?bill=s112-132 (last visited December 4, 2011)

Delaware Code Ann. tit. 11, § 3107 (2007)

Delaware. Code Ann. Title 11, § 4504 (2007)

Florida Stat. Ann. §§ 925.11, 943.3251 (West Supp. 2009)

Georgia Code Ann. § 5-5-41 (1995 & Supp. 2008)

Idaho Code Ann. §§ 19-4901 to -4902 (2004)

Illinois Comp. Stat. Ann. 725:5/116-3 (West 2002 & Supp. 2008)

Indiana Code Ann. §§ 35-38-7-1 to -19 (West 2004)

Information Bulletin from Edmund G. Brown, Jr., Attorney General, DNA Partial Match (Crime Scene DNA Profile to Offender) Policy No. 2008-BFS-01 (2008), available online at http://ag.ca.gov/cms_attachments/press/pdfs/n1548_08-bfs-01.pdf (last visited November 19, 2011)

Justice for All Act of 2004, Pub. L. 108-405, 118 Stat. 2260 (2004)

Kansas Stat. Ann. § 21-2512 (2007)

Kentucky Rev. Stat. Ann. §§ 422.285, .287 (LexisNexis 2005 & Supp. 2008)

Louisiana Code Crim. Proc. Ann. arts. 924, 926.1 (2008 & Supp. 2009)

Maine Rev. Stat. Ann. tit. 15, §§ 2136-2138 (2003 & Supp. 2008)

Massachusetts General Laws Ann. ch. 111, § 13 (West 2003)

Michigan Comp. Laws Ann. § 770.16 (West 2008)

Michigan Comp. Laws Ann. § 767.24(2) (West 2008)

Minnesota Stat. Ann. §§ 590.01-.04, .06 (2000)

Missouri Rev. Stat. §§ 547.035, 650.055 (2008)

Montana Code Ann. §§ 46-21-110, 53-1-214 (2007)

Nebraska Rev. Stat. §§ 29-4119 to -4123 (2003)

Nevada Rev. Stat. § 176.0918 (LexisNexis 2006)

New Hampshire Rev. Stat. Ann. § 592-A:7(II) (Supp. 2008)

New Jersey Stat. Ann. § 2A:84A-32A (West Supp. 2008)

New Mexico Stat. Ann. § 31-1A-2 (West Supp. 2008)

New York Crim. Proc. Law § 440.30 (McKinney 2005)

Ohio Rev. Code Ann. §§ 2953.71 to .83 (LexisNexis 2002)

Oklahoma Stat. Ann. tit. 22, §§ 1371-1371.2 (2009)

Oregon Rev. Stat. §§ 138.690-.698 (2007)

Pennsylvania Const. Stat. § 9543.1 (2006)

Rhode Island Gen. Laws §§ 10-9.1-11 to -12 (Supp. 2008)

Science, State, Justice, Commerce, and Related Agencies Appropriations Act
     of 2006, Public Law No. 109-108, 119 Stat. 2290 (2005)

Tennessee Code Ann. §§ 40-30-301 to -313 (2006)

Texas Code Crim. Proc. Ann. arts. 64.01-.05 (Vernon 2006)

The DNA Identification Act of 1994, Pub. L. 103-322, 108 Stat. 2065 (1994)

United States Constitution, amend. IV

Utah Code Ann. §§ 78B-9-301 to 304 (2008)

Vernon's Ann. Texas C.C.P. Art. 38.01 (2005).

Virginia Code Ann. § 15-2B-14 (LexisNexis 2004 & Supp. 2008)

Virginia Code Ann. § 19.2-327.1 (2008)

Washington Rev. Code Ann. § 10.73.170 (LexisNexis 2007)

Wisconsin Stat. Ann. §907.02, amended by 2011 Wis. Act 2, available online at
     https://docs.legis.wisconsin.gov/2011/related/acts/2 (last visited November
     10, 2011)

Wisconsin Stat. Ann. §§ 974.07 (West 2007)

Other References

*Admissibility of Testimony That Bullet Could or Might Have Come From
     Particular Gun*, 31 A.L.R.4th 486 (1992)

Advances in Fingerprint Technology, 2d Ed., eds. Henry C. Lee and Robert E
     Gaensslen, CRC Press: Boca Raton, Fla. (2001)

Akehurst-Moore, Scott, *An Appropriate Balance?–A Survey and Critique of
     State and Federal DNA Indictment and Tolling Statutes*, 6 J. High Tech. L.
     213 (2006)

Alschuler, Albert, *Constraint and Confession*, 74 Denver U. L. Rev. 957 (1997)

American Academy of Forensic Sciences, *AAFS Position Statement in
     Response to the NAS Report*, 39 AAFS Academy News 4 (November
     2009), available online at
     http://www.aafs.org/pdf/AAFS_Position_Statement_for_Press_Distributio
     n_090409.pdf

American Association for the Advancement of Science, *Court Appointed Scientific Experts Handbook for Judges* (2002),; available online at http://www.aaas.org/spp/case/handbookjudgesv3.pdf

American Board of Forensic Examiners, online at http://www.abfde.org/Index.html

American Board of Forensic Odontology, Inc., *Guidelines For Bite Mark Analysis*, 112 J. Am. Dental Ass'n (1986)

American Board of Forensic Odontology, Inc., *Diplomates Reference Manual* (June 28, 2009), available online at http://www.abfo.org/pdfs/ABFO%20Manual%20-%20revised%2010-28-09-B.pdf (last visited December 14, 2011)

American Federation of Firearms and Toolmark Examiners, *Theory of Identification, Range if Striae Comparison Reports and Modified Glossary Definitions - An AFTE Criteria for Identification Committee Report*, 24 J. Assoc. of Firearm and Tool Mark Examiners 336 (1992)

American Psychiatric Association, *Diagnostic and Statistical Manual of Mental Disorders*, 4th ed. American Psychiatric Pub.: Arlington, Va. (1994)

American Society for Testing Materials (ASTM), *Standard Practice for Sampling of Headspace Vapors from Fire Debris Samples*, ASTM E1388-05 (2005), available for purchase online at http://webstore.ansi.org/RecordDetail.aspx?sku=ASTM+E1388-05 (last visited December 14, 2011)

American Society for Testing Materials (ASTM), *Standard Test Method for Ignitable Liquid Residues in Extracts from Fire Debris Samples by Gas Chromatography-Mass Spectrometry*, ASTM E1618-06E1 (2006), available for purchase online at http://webstore.ansi.org/RecordDetail.aspx?sku=ASTM+E1618-11 (last visited December 14, 2011)

American Society for Testing and Materials (ASTM), *Standard Descriptions of Scope of Work Relating to Forensic Document Examiners*, ASTM E444-09 (2009)

American Society for Testing and Materials (ASTM), *Standard Guide for Minimum Training Requirements for Forensic Document Examiners*, ASTM E2388 - 05 (2005)

American Society for Testing and Materials (ASTM), *Standard Terminology for Expressing Conclusions of Forensic Document Examiners*, ASTM E1658 - 08 (2008)

Annas, George J., *Genetic Privacy*, in *DNA and the Criminal Justice System* (David Lazer ed.). MIT Press, Cambridge, Massachusetts (2004).

Ashbaugh, David R., *Quantitative-Qualitative Friction Ridge Analysis: An Introduction to Basic and Advanced Ridgeology*. CRC Press: Boca Raton, Florida (1999).

Aronson, Jay, *Genetic Witness: Science, Law,, and Controversy in the Making of DNA Profiling*, Rutgers Univ. Press: Piscataway, NJ (2007)

Askowitz, Lisa R., and Michael H. Graham, *The Reliability of Expert Psychological Testimony in Child Sexual Abuse Prosecutions,* 15 Cardozo L. Rev. 2027 (1994)

Barak. Gregg, ed., *Battleground: Criminal Justice,* Greenwood Press: Westport, Conn. (2007)

Barbour, Emily C., *DNA Databanking: Selected Fourth Amendment Issues and Analysis*, Congressional Research Service No. 7-5700 (June 6, 2011), available online at http://fulltextreports.com/2011/07/19/crs-dna-databanking-selected-fourth-amendment-issues-and-analysis/ (last visited November 17, 2011)

Beecher-Monas, Erica, *Evaluating Scientific Evidence*, Cambridge Univ. Press: Cambridge, England (2007)

Benedict, Nathan, *Fingerprints and the Daubert Standard for Admission of Scientific Evidence: Why Fingerprints Fail and a Proposed Remedy*, 46 Ariz. L. Rev. 519 (2004)

Berger, Margaret A., *Expert Testimony in Criminal Proceedings: Questions Daubert Does Not Answer*, 33 Seton Hall L. Rev. 1125 (2003)

Bernstein, David E, and Jeffrey D. Jackson, *The Daubert Trilogy in the States*, 44 Jurimetrics 351 (2003-2004)

Beyer, Craig L., *Analysis of the Fire Investigation Methods and Procedures Used in the Criminal Arson Cases Against Ernest Ray Willis and Cameron Todd Willingham* (August 17, 2009), available online at http://www.innocenceproject.org/Content/The_Texas_Forensic_Science_ Commission_and_the_Willingham_Case.php (last visited November 26, 2011)

Biasotti , Alfred A., *A Statistical Study of the Individual Characteristics of Fired Bullets,* 4 J. Forensic Sci. 34 (1959)

Bieber, Frederick R., *Science and Technology of Forensic DNA Profiling: Current Use and Future Directions*, in *DNA And The Criminal Justice System* (David Lazer ed.) , MIT Press, Cambridge, Massachusetts (2004)

Bieber, Frederick R., Charles H. Brenner, and David Lazer, *Finding Criminals Through DNA of Their Relatives*, Science: Vol. 312 no. 5778 pp. 1315-1316, (June 2, 2006) available online at http://www.sciencemag.org/content/312/5778/1315.citation (last visited November 18, 2011)

Bieber, Meredith A., Comment, *Meeting the Statute or Beating it: Using "John Doe" Indictments Based on DNA to Meet the Statute of Limitations*, 150 U. Pa. L. Rev. 1079 (2002)

Bisbing, Richard E., *The Forensic Identification and Association of Human Hair*, in *Forensic Science Handbook, 2d Ed.* (Richard Saferstein ed. Prentice Hall: Upper Saddle River, New Jersey (2001)

Black, Bert, and Patrick W. Lee, eds., *Expert Evidence: A Practitioner's Guide To Law, Science, And The FJC Manual*, West Pub.: Eagan, Minn. (1997)

Bohan, Thomas L., *Scientific Evidence and Forensic Science Since Daubert: Maine Decides to Sit out the Dance*, 56 Maine. L. Rev. 101 (2004)

Bohan, Thomas L., American Academy of Forensic Sciences, *President's Message*, 39 AAFS Academy News 1 (November 2009)

Bowers , C. Michael and Gary L. Bell eds., *Manual of Forensic Odontology*, 3d Rev. Ed., , American Society of Forensic Odontology: Lubbock, Tex. (1997)

Bowers, C. Michael, *Problem-Based Analysis in Bite Mark Misidentifications: The Role of DNA*, 159 Forensic Sci. Int'l. (Supp. 1) (2006)

Brannigern, Francis, *Fire Investigation Handbook*, National Bureau of Standards Handbook 134 (1980), available online at http://fire.nist.gov/bfrlpubs/fire80/PDF/f80004.pdf (last visited December 23, 2011)

Brennan, William J. Jr., *Reason, Passion and "The Progress of the Law"*, 10 Cardozo L. Rev. 3 (1988)

Brewer, Neil and Kipling D. Williams, *Psychology and Law: An Empirical Perspective*, Guilford Press: New York, NY (2005)

Brewer, Neil, Nathan Weber, and Carolyn Semmler, *Eyewitness Identification* in *Psychology and Law: An Empirical Perspective* (Neil Brewer and Kipling D. Williams, eds). Guilford Press: New York, New York (2005)

Breyer, Stephen, *Furthering the Conversation About Science and Society*, in *DNA And The Criminal Justice System* (David Lazer ed.), MIT Press, Cambridge, Massachusetts (2004)

Brickell, Wendy, *Is It the CSI Effect or Do We Just Distrust Juries?*, 23 A.B.A. Crim. Just. J. 10 (2008)

Brigham, John C. & Robert K. Bothwell, *The Ability of Prospective Jurors to Estimate the Accuracy of Eyewitness Identifications*, 7 Law & Human Behavior 19 (1983)

Brislawn, Christopher M., *Fingerprints Go Digital*, 42 Notices of the American Mathematical Society 1278 (1995), available online at http://www.ams.org/notices/199511/brislawn.pdf (last visited December 14, 2011).

Bryant, Jennings and Lawrence Dolf Zillmann eds., *Media Effects: Advances In Theory And Research,* 2d Ed., Erlbaum Pub.: New York, NY (2002)

Bureau of Alcohol, Tobacco, Firearms and Explosives, *Automated Firearms Ballistic Technology*, available online at http://www.nibin.gov/about/program-overview/automated-firearms-ballistics-technology.html (last visited November 24,2011)

Bureau of Alcohol, Tobacco, Firearms and Explosives, *National Integrated Ballistic Information Network*, available online at http://www.nibin.gov/ (last visited November 24, 2011)

Burgess, Ann & Linda Holmstrom, *Rape Trauma Syndrome*, 131 Am. J. Psychiatry 981 (1974)

Bush, Mary A., Raymond J. Miller, Peter G. Bush, and Robert B. J. Dorion, *Biomechanical Factors in Human Dermal Bitemarks in a Cadaver Model*, 54 J. Forensic Sci. 167 (2009)

Bykowicz Julie, & Justin Fenton, *City Crime Lab Director Fired: Database Update Reveals Employees' DNA Tainted Evidence, Throwing Lab's Reliability into Question*, Baltimore Sun (Baltimore, Md.), Aug. 21, 2008, at 1A

Byrne, James Michael and Donald J. Rebovich, eds.,*The New Technology Of Crime, Law And Social Control* , Criminal Justice Press: Monsey, NY (2007)

California Department of Justice, *NIBIN Program - Automated Firearms Evidence Imaging*, available online at www.crime-scene-investigator.net/CAnibin.pdf (last visited November 24, 2011)

Carlson, Darren K., *Americans Conclusive About DNA Evidence*, Gallup, Nov. 15, 2005, http://www.gallup.com/poll/19915/Americans-Conclusive-AboutDNA-Evidence.aspx (last visited December 14, 2011)

Chaplin, J. P., *Dictionary of Psychology*, San Val Pub.: St. Louis, Missouri (1985)

Cheng, Edward K. *Mitochondrial DNA: Emerging Legal Issues*, 13 J. L. & Pol'y 99 (2005)

Cheng, Edward K., and Albert H. Yoon, *Does Frye or Daubert Matter? A Study of Scientific Admissibility Standards* , 91 Va. L. Rev. 471 (2005)

Chu, Wei, et al, *Pilot Study of Automated Bullet Signature Identification Based on Topography Measurements and Correlations*, 55 J. Forensic Sci. 341 (March 2010)

Chojnacki, Danielle, et al, *An Empirical Basis for the Admission of Expert Testimony on False Confessions*, 40 Ariz. St. L. J. 1 (2008)

Cohen, Andrew, Note, *The Unreliability of Expert Testimony on the Typical Characteristics of Sexual Abuse Victims*, 74 Georgia L. J. 429 (1985)

Cole, Simon A., *Fingerprint Identification and the Criminal Justice System: Historical Lessons for the DNA Debate* in *DNA and the Criminal Justice System* (David Lazer ed.) , MIT Press, Cambridge, Massachusetts (2004)

Cole, Simon A., *Grandfathering Evidence: Fingerprint Admissibility Rulings from Jennings to Llera Plaza and Back Again*, 41 Amer. Crim. L. Rev. 1189 (2004)

Cole, Simon A. and Rachel Dioso-Villa, *Investigating the "CSI Effect" Effect: Media and Litigation Crisis in Criminal Law*, 61 Stan. L. Rev. 1335 (2009)

Cole, Simon A., *More Than Zero: Accounting for Error in Latent Fingerprint Identification*, 95 J. Crim. L. & Criminology 985 (2005)

Cole, Simon A., *Out of the Daubert Fire and Into the Fryeing Pan? Self-Validation, Meta-Expertise and the Admissibility of Latent Print Evidence in Frye Jurisdictions*, 9 Minn. J. L. Sci. & Tech. 453, 537 (2008)

Cole, Simon A., *The Prevalence and Potential Causes of Wrongful Conviction by Fingerprint Evidence*, 37 Golden Gate U. L. Rev. 39 (2006)

Cole, Simon A. and Rachel Dioso-Villa, *CSI and Its Effects: Media, Juries, and the Burden of Proof*, 41 New Eng. L. Rev. 435 (2007)

Conley, John M. and Jane Campbell Moriarty, *Scientific and Expert Evidence*, Aspen Pub.: New York, New York (2007)

Cormier, Karen, Lisa Calandro and Dennis Reeder, *Evolution of DNA Evidence for Crime Solving: A Judicial and Legislative History*, Forensic Magazine, June-July 2005, at 13 available at http://www.forensicmag.com/articles.asp?pid=45 (last visited December 14, 2011)

Council on Scientific Affairs, *AMA Diagnostic and Treatment Guidelines Concerning Child Abuse and Neglect*, 254 American Medical Association 796 (1985)

Cutler, Brian L., and Steven D. Penrod, *Mistaken Identification: The Eyewitness, Psychology, and the Law*, Cambridge Univ. Press. Cambridge, England (1995)

Dailey, J. C., and C. Michael Bowers, *Aging of Bitemarks: A Literature Review*, 42 J. Forensic Sci. 792 (1997)

Dao, James, *Lab's Errors in '82 Killing Force Review of Virginia DNA Cases*, N.Y. Times, May 7, 2005, at A1

Deedrick, Douglas W., and Sandra L. Koch, *Microscopy of Hair Part 1: A Practical Guide and Manual for Human Hairs*, Forensic Science Comm., Jan. 2004, http://www.fbi.gov/hq/lab/fsc/backissu/jan2004/research/2004_01_researc h01b.htm (last visted December 14, 2011)

Deitch, Adam, *An Inconvenient Tooth: Forensic Odontology is an Inadmissible Junk Science When it is Used to "Match" Teeth to Bitemarks in Skin*, 2009 Wis. L. Rev. 1205 (2009)

Delaney, Corey E., Note, *Seeking John Doe: The Provision and Propriety of DNA-Based Warrants in the Wake of Wisconsin v. Dabney*, 33 Hofstra L. Rev. 1091(2005)

Denbeaux, Mark P., and D. Michael Risinger, *Kumho Tire and Expert Reliability: How the Question You Ask Gives the Answer You Get*, 34 Seton Hall L. Rev. 15 (2003)

Deutsch, Sarah Keturah & Gray Cavender, *CSI and Forensic Realism*, 15 J. Crim Just. & Popular Culture 34 (2008), *available at* http://www.albany.edu/scj/jcjpc/vol15is1/Deutsch_Cavender.pdf. (last visited December 14, 2011)

Diehl, Jonathan W., Note, *Drafting a Fair DNA Exception to the Statute of Limitations in Sexual Assault Cases*, 39 Jurimetrics J. 431 (1999).

Dimmick, John, Yan Chen, & Zhan Li, *Competition Between the Internet and Traditional News Media: The Gratification-Opportunities Niche Dimension*, 17 J. Media Econ. 19 (2004)

DNA Research Report, *Domestic DNA Legislation*, available online at http://www.dnaresource.com/domestic.html

Dixon, Lloyd and Brian Gill, *Changes In The Standards For Admitting Expert Evidence In Federal Civil Cases Since The Daubert Decision*, Rand Inst.: Santa Monica, Cal. (2001)

Dobbin, Shirley A., and Sophia I. Gatowski, *The Social Production of Rape Trauma Syndrome as Science and as Evidence*, in *Science in Court: Issues in Law and Society* (Michael D. Freeman and Helen Reece eds.). Ashgate Publishing Ltd: London (1998)

Domitrovich, Stephanie, *The Factors Affecting the Appointment of Experts by State Trial Judges: An Exploratory Study* (May 2006) (unpublished Ph.D. dissertation, University of Nevada, Reno) presented at the annual meeting of The Law and Society Association, Berlin, Germany on July 25, 2007, available at http://www.allacademic.com/meta/p181987_index.html (last visited December 23, 2011)

Dorion, Robert B.J., ed., *Bitemark Evidence,* , CRC Press: Boca Raton, Fla. (2004)

Driver, Amy, *Senator Patrick Leahy Introduces the Criminal Justice and Forensic Science Reform Act,* (January 27, 2011), available online at http://www.bulletpath.com/2011/leahy-introduces-cjfsra/ (last visited December 4, 2011)

Driver, Amy, *The Awesome Anger of Congress,* (October 30, 2011), available online at http://www.bulletpath.com/2011/the-awesome-anger-of-congress/ (last visited December 4, 2011)

Drizin, Steve and Richard Leo, *The Problem of False Confessions in the Post-DNA World,* 82 N. Car. L. Rev. 891 (2004)

Duncan, Krista L., Note, *"Lies, Damned Lies, and Statistics"? Psychological Syndrome Evidence in the Courtroom after Daubert,* 71 Ind. L. J. 753 (1996)

Dunn, Amy, Note, *Criminal Law—Statutes of Limitation on Sexual Assault Crimes: Has the Availability of DNA Evidence Rendered Them Obsolete?,* 23 U. Ark. Little Rock L. Rev. 839 (2001)

Durnal, Evan W., *Crime Scene Investigation (as seen on TV),*199 For. Sci. Int'l 1 (2010)

Edwards, Hon. Harry T., *Statement before U.S. Senate Judiciary Committee* (Mar. 18, 2009), available online at http://judiciary.senate.gov/pdf/09-03-18EdwardsTestimony.pdf

Ellen, David, *The Scientific Examination of Documents: Methods and Techniques,* CRC Press: Boca Raton, Fla. (1989)

Epstein, Robert, *Fingerprints Meet Daubert: The Myth of Fingerprint "Science',* 75 S. Cal. L. Rev. 605 (2002)

Etzioni, Amitai, *A Communitarian Approach: A Viewpoint on the Study of the Legal, Ethical and Policy Considerations Raised by DNA Tests and Databases,* 34 J. L. Medicine & Ethics 214 (2006)

Expert Evidence to Identify Gun From Which Bullet or Cartridge Was Fired, 26 A.L.R.2d 892 (1965)

Faigman, David L., Edward K. Cheng, , Michael J. Saks, and Joseph Sanders, eds., *Modern Scientific Evidence: The Law and Science of Expert Testimony,* Thomson/West Pub.: Eagan, Minn. (2006)

Faigman, David L., Michael J. Saks, Joseph Sanders, and Edward K. Cheng, eds., *Modern Scientific Evidence: The Law and Science of Expert Testimony*, 2008-2009 Ed., , Thomson/West Pub.: Eagan, Minn. (2009)

Faigman, David L. Michael J. Saks, Joseph Sanders, and Edward K. Cheng, eds., *Modern Scientific Evidence: The Law and Science of Expert Testimony*, 2009-2010 Ed., Thomson/West Pub.: Eagan, Minn. (2010)

Faigman, David L., *The Evidentiary Status of Social Science under* Daubert: *Is It "Scientific," "Technical," or "Other" Knowledge.* 1 Psychology, Public Policyy & Law 960 (1995)

Faigman, David L., Note, *The Battered Woman Syndrome and Self-Defense: A Legal and Empirical Dissent,* 72 Virginia L. Rev. 619 (1986)

Farahany, Nita A. & William Bernet, *Behavioural Genetics in Criminal Cases: Past, Present and Future*, 2 Geonomics Society & Pol'y 72 (2006)

Faust, David, and Jay Ziskin, *The Expert Witness in Psychology and Psychiatry*, 241 Science 31 (July 1, 1988)

FBI Biometric Specifications, available online at http://www.fbibiospecs.org/biospecs.html

FBI Criminal Justice Information Services, U. S. Department of Justice, *Integrated Automated Fingerprint Information System*, available online at http://www.fbi.gov/hq/cjisd/iafis.htm (last visited December 14, 2011)

FBI Criminal Justice Information Services, U.S. Department of Justice, *Taking Legible Fingerprints*, available online at http://www.fbi.gov/hq/cjisd/takingfps.html (last visited December 14, 2011)

FBI Press Release, FBI Laboratory Announces Discontinuation of Bullet Lead Analysis, (September 10. 2005), available online at http://www.fbi.gov/news/pressrel/press-releases/fbi-laboratory-announces-discontinuation-of-bullet-lead-examinations (last visited December 23, 2011)

FBI Press Release, *National Academy of Sciences Releases FBI-Commissioned Study on Bullet Lead Analysis*, (February 10, 2004), available online at http://www.fbi.gov/news/pressrel/press-releases/national-academy-of-sciences-releases-fbi-commissioned-study-on-bullet-lead-analysis (last visited December 14, 2011).

Federal Evidence Review, *The Melendez-Diaz Resource Page*, available online at http://federalevidence.com/evidence-resources/melendez-diaz.v.massachusetts-overview (last visited November 20, 2011)

Fell, Jacqueline , Adam Longo and Kelli Cook, *Day 4: George Anthony questioned about smell in Casey's car*, Central Florida News, May 27,

2011, available online at
http://www.cfnews13.com/article/news/2011/may/252672/Day-4:-George-Anthony-questioned-about-smell-in-Caseys-car (last visited December 8, 2011)

Fell, Jacqueline , Adam Longo and Kelli Cook, *Day 11: Expert smelled death in air samples from Casey Anthony's car*, Central Florida News, June 8, 2011, available online at
http://www.cfnews13.com/article/news/2011/june/257538/ (last visited December 8, 2011)

Findley, Keith A., *Innocents at Risk: Adversary Imbalance, Forensic Science, and the Search for Truth*, 38 Seton Hall L. Rev. 893 (2008)

Fisher, Barry A. J., *Legislative Corner*, 39 AAFS Academy News 3 (November 2009)

Fisher, William C., *Defining the "Address" of Bloodstains and Other Evidence at the Crime Scene* in *Scientific and Legal Applications of Bloodstain Pattern Analysis* (Stuart H. James ed.) CRC Press: Boca Raton, Florida (1991)

Flake, Andrew B., Eric R. Harlan, and James A. King, *50 State Survey of the Applicability of Daubert*, American Bar Association Section of Litigation, available online at
http://www.abanet.org/litigation/committees/trialevidence/daubert-frye-survey.html (last visited December 14, 2011)

Foster, Kenneth R. & Peter W. Huber, *Judging Science: Scientific Knowledge and the Federal Courts*, MIT Press: Cambridge, Mass. (1999)

Freckelton, Ian *Contemporary Comment: When Plight Makes Right – The Forensic Abuse Syndrome*, 18 Criminal L. J. 29 (1994)

Freeman, Michael D. and Helen Reece, eds., *Science in Court: Issues in Law and Society*, Ashgate Pub.:London, England (1998)

Friedman, Richard D., *The Confrontation Blog*, available online at
http://confrontationright.blogspot.com/ (last visited December 14, 2011)

Gabel, Jessica D., *Forensiphilia: Is Public Fascination with Forensic Science a Love Affair or Fatal Attraction*, 36 New Eng. J. on Crim. & Civ. Confinement 233 (2010)

Galbraith, Oliver, Craig Galbraith, and Nanette Galbraith, *The "Principle of the Drunkard's Search" as a Proxy for Scientific Analysis: The Misuse of Handwriting Test Data in a Law Journal Article*, 1 Int'l J. Forensic Document Examiners 7 (1995)

Garrett, Brandon L., *Convicting the Innocent*, Harvard Univ. Press: Cambridge, Mass. (2011)

Garrett, Brandon L., *Judging Innocence,* 108 Columbia L. Rev. 55 (2008)

Garrett, Brandon L., and Peter J. Neufeld, *Invalid Forensic Science Testimony and Wrongful Convictions,* 95 Virginia L. Rev. 1 (2009.

Garrett, Brandon L, *The Substance of False Confessions,* 62 Stanford L. Rev. 1051 (2010)

Gatowski, Sophia I., Shirley A. Dobbin, James T. Richardson, and Gerald P. Ginsburg, *The Globalization of Behavioral Science Evidence About Battered Women: A Theory of Production and Diffusion,* 15 Behav. Sci. & L. 285 (1997)

Ge, Jianye, Ranajit Chakraborry, Arthur Eisenberg and Bruce Budowle, *Comparisons of Familial DNA Database Searching Strategies,* J. Forensic Sci.Vol.56, No. 6 (November 2011)

Georgette, Luke F., *The Hung Jury: Scholarly Consensus on the Value of the CSI Effect in the Future of American Justice,* 3 Intersect Stan. J. Sci. Tech & Society 1 (2010)

Gerbner, George & Larry Gross, *Living with Television: The Violence Profile,* 26 J. Comm. 173 (1976)

Gerbner, George, Larry Gross, Michael Morgan, and Nancy Signorielli, *Growing Up With Television: Cultivation Processes,* in *Media Effects: Advances In Theory And Research, 2d ed.,* Jennings Bryant and Dolf Zillmann eds., Erlbaum Assoc.: Mahwah, New Jersey (2002)

Gertner, Nancy, *Commentary on the Need for a Research Culture in the Forensic Sciences,* 58 UCLA L. Rev. 789 (2011)

Gertner, Hon. Nancy, *Pretrial Oder Trace Evidence,* U.S Dist Ct. Md. (March 2010), available online at http://www.google.com/url?sa=t&rct=j&q=&esrc=s&frm=1&source=web &cd=1&ved=0CEYQFjAA&url=http%3A%2F%2Fwww.mad.uscourts.go v%2Fboston%2Fpdf%2FProcOrderTraceEvidenceUPDATE.pdf&ei=zaD bTr3PHOWZ2QWRxYGnDg&usg=AFQjCNHEx_al9Xow3DfKRfyniOu Syn21zA (last visited December 4, 2011)

Gianelli, Paul C., *Bite Mark Analysis,* 43 Crim. L. Bull. 930 (2007)

Gianelli, Paul C., *Forensic Science,* 33 J. L. Med. & Ethics 535 (2005)

Gianelli, Paul C. and E. West, *Hair Comparison Evidence,* 37 Crim. L. Bull. 514 (2001)

Giannelli, Paul C., *The NRC Report and Its Implications For Criminal Litigation,* 50 Jurimetrics 53 (2009), available online at http://ssrn.com/abstract=1568910 (last visited December 6, 2011)

Gilmore, Carl W., *Challenging DNA in Paternity Cases: Finding Weaknesses in an Evidentiary Goliath,* 90 Illinois Bar J. 472 (2002)

Goddard, Calvin H., *Scientific Identification of Firearms and Bullets*, Northwestern University: Evanston, Ill. (1926)

Grann, David, *Trial by Fire: Did Texas Execute an Innocent Man?*, The New Yorker (Sept. 7, 2009) available online at http://www.newyorker.com/reporting/2009/09/07/090907fa_fact_grann?yr ail (last visited November 26, 2011)

Griffy, Leslie, Crime Lab in Spotlight: Senate Committee Hears Testimony Faulting DA's Internal Investigation, San Jose Mercury News, Jan. 24, 2008, at 1B

Groscup, Jennifer L., Steven D. Penrod, Christina A. Studebaker, Matthew T. Huss, and Kevin M. O'Neil, *The Effects of Daubert on the Admissibility of Expert Testimony in State and Federal Criminal Cases*, 8 Psychology, Pub. Pol'y & L. 339 (2002).

Gudjonsson, Gisli H., *The Psychology of Interrogations and Confessions*, John Wiley & Sons, Ltd.: West Sussex, England 2003

Gutheil, Thomas G., *What does DNA stand for, Daddy?' Or, What does the law do when science changes?*, American Academy of Science & Law, Vol. 25, No. 3, pp. 4-6., September 2000, available online at http://www.emory.edu/AAPL/newsletter/N253_DNA.htm.

Guthrie, Chris, *Misjudging*, 7 Nev. L. J. 420 (2007).

Haber, Lyn and Ralph N. Haber, *Scientific Validation of fingerprint evidence under Daubert*, 7 Law, Probability and Risk 87 (2008).

Hansen, Mark, *The Uncertain Science of Evidence*, A.B.A. J., July 2005, at 49

Hastings, Deborah, *Memo: Chemist May Have Altered Evidence*, Mobile Register, Apr. 21, 2004, at A5

Hawthorne, Mark R., *Fingerprints: Analysis and Understanding*, CRC Press: Boca Raton, Fla. (2008)

Hillman, Timothy, *Using Court-Appointed Experts*, 36 New Eng. L. Rev. 587 (2002)

Hinkle, Margaret R., *Criminal Practice in Suffolk Superior Court*, Boston Bar J., Nov./Dec. 2007, at 6

Hocherman, Gil, Arie Zeichner, and Tzipi Kahana, *Firearms - A Review: 2001-2004*, 14th Interpol Forensic Science Symposium Report at 47 (2004), online at http://www.interpol.int/Public/Forensic/IFSS/meeting14/ReviewPapers.pd f

Hornbeck, Mark, *Law officials: Closing of Detroit Police Crime Lab a Crisis for State Justice System*, Detroit News (Feb. 18, 2010)

Houck, Max M. and Bruce Budowle, *Correlation of Microscopic and Mitochondrial DNA Hair Comparison*, 47 J. Forensic Sci. 964 (2002)

Huber, Roy A. and A. M. Headrick, *Handwriting Identification: Facts and Fundamentals*, CRC Press: Boca Raton, Fla. (1999)

Hunter, George , *Detroit Shuts Down Error-Plagued Crime Lab*, Detroit News, Sept. 26, 2008, at 1A

Hurst, Gerald, *Cameron Todd Willingham Report of D. Gerald Hurst*, Feb. 13, 2004, available online at http://www.scribd.com/doc/37712737/Gerald-Hurst-s-Report-on-Todd-Willingham-Arson-Investigation (last visited November 26, 2011)

Huseman, Brian, Note, *Taylor v. State, Rule 706, and the DNA Database: Future Directions in DNA Evidence*, 22 Okla. City U. L. Rev. 397 (1997)

Imwinkelried, Edward J., *Dealing With Supposed Jury Preconceptions About the Significance of the Lack of Evidence: The Difference Between the Perspective of the Policymaker and That of the Advocate*, 27 T.M. Cooley L. Rev. 37 (2010)

Imwinkelried, Edward J., and D. H. Kaye, *DNA Typing: Emerging or Neglected Issues*, 76 Washington L. Rev. 413 (2001)

Imwinkelried, Edward J., *The Relative Priority That Should Be Assigned to Trial Stage DNA Issues*, in *DNA And The Criminal Justice System* (David Lazer ed.) , MIT Press, Cambridge, Massachusetts (2004)

Inbau, Fred E., *Scientific Evidence in Criminal Cases*, 24 Am. Inst. Crim. L. & Criminology 825 (1933-1934)

Innocence Project, *Innocence Project Case Profiles*, www.innocenceproject.org/know (last visited December 23, 2011)

Innocence Project, *Eyewitness Identification Reform*, available online at http://www.innocenceproject.org/ContentJI65.php (last visited December 14, 2011).

International Association for Identification, *Bloodstain Pattern Examiner Certification Requirements*, available online at http://www.theiai.org/certifications/bloodstain/requirements.php (last visited December 14, 2011).

International Association for Identification, *Friction Ridge Skin Identification Training Manual*, available online at www.theiai.org.

Jabbar, Munia, *Overcoming Daubert's Shortcomings in Criminal Trials: Making Error Rate the Primary Factor in Daubert's Validity Inquiry*, 85 N.Y.U. L. Rev. 2034 (2010)

Jackman, Tom and Rosalind S. Helderman, *Kaine Calls Session To Amend Laws On Trial Testimony*, The Washington Post, July 23, 2009

James, Stuart H., Paul E. Kish, and T. Paulette Sutton, *Principles of Bloodstain Hearing of Samuel A. Alito, Jr.'s Nomination to the Supreme Court,* Hearing Before the S. Judiciary Comm., 109th Cong. 56 (2006)

Johnston, David, *Dismal Science: When the F.B.I.'s Crime Lab Makes a Mistake, Two Journalists Contend, It's a Beaut,* N.Y. Times, Sept. 27, 1998, at BR25

Johnston, David, *Report Criticizes Scientific Testing at F.B.I. Crime Lab,* N.Y. Times, Apr. 16, 1997, at A1

Kam, Moshe, Gabriel Fielding and Robert Conn, *Effects of Monetary Incentives on Performance in Document Examination Proficiency Tests,* 43 J. For. Sci. 1000 (1997)

Kam, Moshe, Gabriel Fielding and Robert Conn, *Writer Examination by Professional Document Examiners,* 42 J. For. Sci. 778 (1997)

Kam, Moshe , J. Wettstein, and Robert Conn, *Proficiency of Professional Document Examiners in Writer Identification,* 39 J. For. Sci. 5 (1994)

Kam, Moshe, J. Wetstein, and R. Conn, *Proficiency of Professional Document Examiners in Writer Identification,* 39 J. For. Sci. 5 (1994), abstract available online at http://www.ncjrs.gov/App/Publications/abstract.aspx?ID=146638 (last visited December 14, 2011)

Kaye, D. H. & Michael E. Smith, *DNA Databases for Law Enforcement: The Coverage Question and the Case for a Population-Wide Database,* in *DNA And The Criminal Justice System* (David Lazer ed.) , MIT Press, Cambridge, Massachusetts (2004)

Kelly, John F., and Phillip K. Wearne, *Tainting Evidence: Inside the Scandals at the FBI Crime Lab.* Free Press Pub.: New York, New York (1998)

Keslowitz, Steven, Note, *The Simpsons, 24, and the Law: How Homer Simpson and Jack Bauer Influence Congressional Lawmaking and Judicial Reasoning,* 29 Cardozo L. Rev. 2787 (2007)

Khanna, Roma, and Steve McVicker, *Police Lab Tailored Tests to Theories, Report Says: Investigators Hope to Establish Whether Mistakes Were Deliberate,* Houston Chronicle, May 12, 2006, at A1.

Kiely, Terrence F. *Forensic Evidence: Science and Criminal Law* 2d Ed., CRC Press: Boca Raton, Fla. (2006)

Kieser, Jules A., *Weighing Bitemark Evidence: A Postmodern Perspective,* 1 J. Forensic Sci. 75 (2005)

Kim, Young S., Gregg Barak, and Donald E. Shelton, *Examining the "CSI-effect" in the Cases of Circumstantial Evidence and Eyewitness*

Testimony: Multivariate and Path Analyses, 37 J. Crim. Justice 452 (2009)

Kittelson, J. M., J. A. Kieser, D. M. Buckingham, and G. P. Herbison , *Weighing Evidence: Quantitative Measures of the Importance of Bitemark Evidence,* 20 J. Forensic Odonto-Stomatology 31 (2002)

Koehler, Johnathon J., *Error and Exaggeration in the Presentation of DNA Evidence at Trial,* 34 Jurimetrics J. 21 (1993)

Komar, D., *The Use of Cadaver Dogs in Locating Scattered, Scavenged Human Remains: Preliminary Field Test Results,* 44 J Forensic Sci. 405 (1999)

Koons, Robert D., and JoAnn Buscaglia, *Forensic Significance of Bullet Lead Comparisons,* 50 J. Forensic Science 1 (2005)

Krafka, Carol, Meghan A. Dunn, Molly Treadway Johnson, Joe S. Cecil and Dean Miletich, *Judge and Attorney Experiences, Practices, and Concerns Regarding Expert Testimony in Federal Civil Trials,* 8 Psychol., Pub. Pol'y and Law 309 (2002)

Kreeger, Lisa R., and Danielle M. Weiss, *Forensic DNA Fundamentals for the Prosecutor: Be Not Afraid* 3, Am. Prosecutors Research Inst. (2003), available online at http://www.ndaa.org/pdf/forensic_dna_fundamentals.pdf (last visited December 14, 2011)

Lazer, David, *DNA And The Criminal Justice System: The Technology Of Justice,* MIT Press: Cambridge, Mass. (2004)

Lasseter, A., K. Jacobi, R. Farley, and L. Hensel, *Cadaver Dog and Handler Team Capabilities in the Recovery of Buried Human Remains in the Southeastern United States,* 48 J Forensic Sci. 617 (2003)

Laux, Dale L., *Effects of Luminol on the Subsequent Analysis of Bloodstains,* 36 J. Forensic Sci. 1512 (1991)

Lawson, Tamara F., *Before the Verdict and Beyond the Verdict: The CSI Infection Within Modern Criminal Jury Trials,* 41 Loy. U. Chi. L.J. 119 (2009)

Leo´n, Fernando Puente, *Automated Comparison of Firearm Bullets,* 156 Forensic Science International 40 (2006)

Leonard, Wade H., *Brewer Seeks $18M in Damages for Wrongful 1995 Conviction,* Com. Dispatch (Columbus, Miss.), Oct. 12, 2008, at 1A

Lester, Katherine C., *The Affects of Apprendi v. New Jersey on the Use of DNA Evidence at Sentencing – Can DNA Alone Convict of Unadjudicated Prior Acts?,* 17 Wash. & Lee J. Civil Rts. & Soc. Just. 267 (2010)

Levs, Melanie Lasoff, *Bite-Mark Evidence Loses Teeth,* A.B.A. J., May 2008, at 16 available at http://www.abajournal.com/magazine/bite_mark_evidence_loses_teeth (last visited December 14, 2011)

Lieberman Joel D., Courtney A. Carrell, Terance D. Miethe, and Daniel A. Krauss, *Gold Versus Platinum: Do Jurors Recognize the Superiority and Limitations of DNA Evidence Compared to Other Types of Forensic Evidence?*, 14 Psychology, Pub. Pol'y & L. 27 (2008)

Loftus, Elizabeth F., *Eyewitness Testimony: Civil and Criminal*, LexisNexis: Albany, NY (2007)

Lorenzen, Dirk ,*The Admissibility of Expert Psychological Testimony in Cases Involving the Sexual Misuse of a Child*, 42 U. Miami L. Rev. 1033 (1988)

Lyssitzyn, Christine Beck, *Forensic Evidence in Court: A Case Study Approach*, Carolina Academic Press: Durham, N. Car. (2007)

Lystra, Tony, *Statewide Increase in Cases Delay Crime Lab Results*, The Daily News (Washington Nov. 3, 2011), available online at http://tdn.com/news/local/article_cffa5634-068a-11e1-b26f-001cc4c03286.html (last visited November 20, 2011)

Lytle, L. T., and D. G. Hedgecock, *Chemiluminescence in the Visualization of Forensic Bloodstains*, 23 J. Forensic Sci. 550 (1978)

MacKnight, Kamrin T., *The Polymerase Chain Reaction (PCR): The Second Generation of DNA Analysis Methods Takes the Stand*, 20 Santa Clara Computer & High Tech. L. J. 95 (2003)

Malcom, Brooke G., *Convictions Predicated On DNA Evidence Alone: How Reliable Evidence Became Infallible*, 38 Cumb. L. Rev. 313 (2008)

Maltoni, David, Darri Maio, Anil K Jain, and Salil Prabbakar, *Handbook of Fingerprint Recognition*, Springer Pub.: New York, NY (2009)

Martin, Andrew, *The Prosecution's Case Against DNA*, The New York Times Magazine (November 27, 2011), available online at http://www.nytimes.com/2011/11/27/magazine/dna-evidence-lake-county.html?ref=magazine (last visited November 27, 2011)

Masson, J. J., *Confidence Level Variations in Firearms Identification Through Computerized Technology*, 29 J. Assoc. of Firearm and Tool Mark Examiners 42 (1997)

Matejik, Laura, *DNA Sampling: Privacy and Police Investigation in a Suspect Society*, 61 Ark. L. Rev. 53 (2008)

McClure, Michelle, *Odontology: Bite Marks as Evidence in Criminal Trials*, 11 Santa Clara Comoputer & High Tech. L. J. 269, (1995)

McGrath, Michael, *Psychological Aspects of Victimology*, In *Forensic Victimology: Examning Violent Crime Victims in Investigative and Legal*

Contexts (Brent E. Turvey & Wayne Petherick eds.) Academic Press: Waltham, Massachusetts (2009)

McWhorter, J.C., *The Bloodhound as Witness*, 54 Am. L. Rev.109 (1920)

Meaney, Joseph R., *From Frye to Daubert: Is a Pattern Unfolding?*, 35 Jurimetrics J. 191 (1995)

Mellon, Jennifer N., Note, *Manufacturing Convictions: Why Defendants Are Entitled to the Data Underlying Forensic DNA Kits*, 51 Duke L. J. 1097 (2001)

Melson, Kenneth E., *Firearms Identification: A Shot in the Dark?*, Proceedings of the American Academy of Forensic Science, Annual Scientific Meeting (2011), transcript available online at http://www.bulletpath.com/wp-content/uploads/2011/07/Melson-at-AAFS-Transcript.pdf (last visited December 4, 2011*)*

Miller, J. and M. M. McLean, *Criteria for Identification of Toolmarks*, 30 J. Assoc. of Firearm and Tool Mark Examiners 15 (1998)

Miller, Raymond G., Peter J. Bush, Robert B. J. Dorion, and Mary A. Bush, *Uniqueness of the Dentition as Impressed in Human Skin: A Cadaver Model*, 54 J. Forensic Sci. 909 (2009)

Mills, Steve and Lisa Black, *Learning Victim's Name Not Enough for New Trial*, Chicago Tribune (Ocober 10, 2010), available online at http://articles.chicagotribune.com/2010-10-11/news/ct-met-confession-conviction-new-vers20101011_1_murder-conviction-mary-kate-sunderlin-dna-evidence (last visited November 27, 2011)

Mills, Steve, *Report Questions if Fire Was Arson*, Chicago Tribune, (Aug. 25, 2009) available online at http://www.chicagotribune.com/news/chi-090825willingham,0,7297380.story (last visited November 26, 2011)

Mills, Steve and Maurice Possley, *Man Executed on Disproved Forensics*, Chicago Tribune, (Dec. 9, 2004) available online at http://www.chicagotribune.com/news/nationworld/chi-0412090169dec09,0,1173806.story (last visited November 26, 2011)

Mills, Steve, and Maurice Possley, *Report Alleges Crime Lab Fraud: Scientist Is Accused of Providing False Testimony*, Chicago Tribune, Jan. 14, 2001, at A1

Mnookin, Jennifer *The Validity of Latent Fingerprint Identification: Confessions of a Fingerprinting Moderate*, 7 Law, Probability and Risk 111 (2008).

Moenssens, Andre A., Carol E. Henderson and Sharon G. Portwood, *Scientific Evidence in Civil and Criminal Cases*, 5th ed., Foundation Press: Eagan, Minn. (2007)

Moenssens, Andre A. Carol E. Henderson, and Sharon G. Portwood, *Scientific Evidence in Civil and Criminal Cases*, 5th Ed. 2009 Supp., Foundation Press: Eagan, Minn. (2009)

Moore, David T. *Scientific Consensus & Expert Testimony: Lessons from the Judas Priest Trial*, 17 Am. Psy. L. News 3 (1997).

Moriarty, Jane Campbell, *Psychological and Scientific Evidence in Criminal Trials*, West Pub.: Eagan, Minn. (2009)

Moriarty, Jane Campbell and Michael J. Saks, *Forensic Science: Grand Goals, Tragic Flaws, and Judicial Gatekeeping*, Judges' J., Fall 2005, p. 16 (2005)

Morris, Ron N., *Forensic Handwriting Identification: Fundamental Concepts and Principals*, Academic Press: Maryland Hts., Mo. (2000)

Muehlberger, R. J., K. W. Newman, J. Regent, and J. G. Wichmann, *A Statistical Examination of Selected Handwriting Characteristics*, 22 J. For. Sci. 206 (1977).

Murphy, Erin, *The New Forensics: Criminal Justice, False Certainty, and the Second Generation of Scientific Evidence*, 95 Cal. L. Rev. 721 (2007)

Murphy, Erin, *Relative Doubt: Familial Searches of DNA Databases*, 109 Mich. L. Rev. 291 (2010)

Myers, John E. B., J. Bays, J. Becker, L. Berliner, D. L. Corwin , and K. J. Saywitz, *Expert Testimony in Child Sexual Abuse Litigation*, 68 Nebraska L. Rev. 1 (1989)

National Association of Criminal Defense Lawyers, *Resolution of the Board of Directors Regarding John Doe DNA Warrants/Indictments* (2004), available online at http://www.nacdl.org/About.aspx?id=19672 (last visited December 14, 2011)

National Commission on the Future of DNA Evidence, U.S. Department of Justice, *Postconviction DNA Testing: Recommendations for Handling Requests* (1999), available online at www.ncjrs.gov/pdffiles1/nij/177626.pdf (last visited December 14, 2011)

National Conference of State Legislatures, *Statute of Limitations for Sexual Assaults* (2007), available online at http://www.ncsl.org/default.aspx?tabid=12723 (last visited December 14, 2011)

National District Attorneys Association, *Policy Issues*, available online at http://www.ndaa.org/ga_policy.html (last visited December 4, 2011)

National Fire Protection Association (NFPA), *Guide for Fire and Explosion Investigation* (Pub. No. 921 2008), available for purchase online at www.nfp.org (last visited December 14, 2011)

National Institute of Justice, U.S. Department Justice, *About Forensic DNA*, available online at http://www.dna.gov/basics/ (last visited November 20, 2011)

National Institute of Justice, U.S. Department of Justice, *DNA in "Minor Cases" Yields Major Benefits in Public Safety*, (Nov. 2004), available online at http://www.ncjrs.gov/pdffiles1/nij/207203.pdf (last visited December 14, 2011)

National Institute of Justice, U.S. Department of Justice, *DNA Evidence Backlogs: Forensic Casework*, 2011, available online at http://www.nij.gov/topics/forensics/lab-operations/evidence-backlogs/forensic-evidence-backlog.htm (last visited November 20, 2011)

National Institute of Justice, U.S. Department of Justice, *Convicted by Juries, Exonerated by Science: Case Studies in the Use of DNA Evidence to Establish Innocence After Trial* (1996), available online at www.ncjrs.gov/pdffiles/dnaevid.pdf (last visited December 14, 2011)

National Institute of Justice, U.S. Department of Justice, NCJ 160972, *The Validity and Use of Evidence Concerning Battering and its Effects in Criminal Trials: Report Responding to Section 40507 of the Violence Against Women Act* (1996), available online at http://www.ncjrs.gov/pdffiles/batter.pdf (last visited December 14, 2011)

National Institute of Justice, U.S. Department of Justice, *Forensic DNA Backlog Reduction Program* (2011), available online at http://www.dna.gov/funding/backlog-reduction/ (last visited November 20, 2011)

National Institute of Justice, U.S. Department of Justice, *Using DNA To Solve Cold Cases* (2002), available at http://www.ncjrs.gov/pdffiles1/nij/194197.pdf (last visited December 14, 2011)

National Institute of Standards and Technology, U.S. Department of Commerce , *American National Standard for Information Systems— Data Format for the Interchange of Fingerprint, Facial, & Other Biometric Information*, NIST Special Publication No. 500-271, ANSI/NIST-ITL 1-2007 (2007), available online at http://fingerprint.nist.gov/standard/index.html (last visited December 14, 2011)

National Research Council of the National Academies, Comm. Scientific Assessment of Bullet Lead Elemental Composition Comparison *Forensic Analysis: Weighing Bullet Lead Evidence* (2004), available at http://books.nap.edu/openbook/0309090792/html/index.html (last visited December 14, 2011)

National Research Council of the National Academies, *Strengthening Forensic Science in the United States: A Path Forward* . National Academies Press: Washington, D.C. (2009)

Neufeld, Peter J. , *The (Near) Irrelevance of* Daubert *to Criminal Justice and Some Suggestions for Reform*, 95 Amer. J. Pub. Health 107 (2005), available online at http://www.defendingscience.org/upload/NeufeldDAUBERT.pdf (last visited December 14, 2011)

Nichols, Ronald G., *Defending the Scientific Foundations of the Firearms and Tool Mark Identification Discipline: Responding to Recent Challenges,* 522 J. Forensic Sci. 586 (2007)

Office of Justice Programs, U.S. Dept. of Justice, *Census of Publicly Funded Forensic Crime Laboratories* , Bureau of Justice Statistics Bulletin, 2002, Feb. 2005, at 1 (2005), *available at* www.ojp.usdoj.gov/bjs/pub/pdf/cpffcl02.pdf (last visited December 14, 2011)

Office of the U.S. Inspector General, A *Review of the FBI's Handling of the Brandon Mayfield Case*, (March 2006), available online at http://www.justice.gov/oig/special/s0601/PDF_list.htm (last visited December 14, 2011)

Osborne, Albert S., *Questioned Documents*, 2d Ed. (1929), republished Rowman & Littlefied Pub: Lanham, Md. (1974)

Page, Mark, Jane Taylor, and Matt Blenkin, *Forensic Identification Science Evidence Since Daubert: Part I—A Quantitative Analysis of the Exclusion of Forensic Identification Science Evidence*, 56 J. Forensic Sci. 1180 (2011)

Papke, David Ray, *The Impact of Popular Culture on American Perceptions of the Courts*, 82 Ind. L.J. 1225 (2007)

Peterson, Peter E., Cherise B. Dreyfus, Melissa R. Gische, Mitchell Hollars, Maria Antonia Roberts, Robin M. Ruth, Heather M. Webster, and Greg L. Soltis, *Latent Prints: A Perspective on the State of the Science*, 11 Forensic Sci. Comm, No. 4 (October 2009); available online at http://www.fbi.gov/hq/lab/fsc/current/review/2009_10_review01.htm (last visited December 14, 2011)

Pew Research Ctr., Press Release, *Social Networking and Online Videos Take Off: Internet's Broader Role in Campaign 2008* (Jan. 11, 2008), available at http://people-press.org/reports/pdf/384.pdf

Piller, Charles , *FBI Abandons Controversial Bullet-Matching Technique*, L.A. Times, Sept. 2, 2005, at A38

Pinkerton, James, *Backlog at HPD Crime Lab is Causing Trial Delays*,
    Houston Chronicle (Sept. 28, 2010) available online at
    http://www.chron.com/news/houston-texas/article/Backlog-at-HPD-crime-
    lab-is-causing-trial-delays-1717970.php (last visited November 20, 2011)

Podlas, Kimberlianne, *"The* CSI *Effect": Exposing the Media Myth*, 16
    Fordham Intell. Prop. Media & Ent. L. J. 429 (2006)

Preston, Corey, *Faulty Foundations: How the False Analogy to Routine
    Fingerprinting Undermines the Argument for Arrestee DNA Sampling*, 19
    Wm. & Mary Bill Rts. J. 475 (2010)

Pretty, Iain, *A Web-Based Survey of Odontologist's Opinions Concerning
    Bitemark Analysis*, 48 J. Forensic Sci. 117 (2003)

Pretty, Iain and M. D. Turnbull, *Lack of Dental Uniqueness Between Two Bite
    Mark Suspects*, 46 J. Forensic Sci. 1487 (2001)

Quickenden,Terence I., and J. I. Creamer, *A Study of Common Interferences
    With the Forensic Luminol Test for Blood*, 16 Journal of Bioluminescence
    and Chemiluminescence 295 (2001)

Quickenden, Tereence I., and Paul D. Cooper, Increasing *the Specificity of the
    Forensic Luminol Test for Blood*, 16 Luminesence 251 (2001), available
    online at http://mason.gmu.edu/~pcooper6/papers/1.pdf (last visited
    December 14, 2011)

Ram, Natalie, *Fortuity and Forensic Familial Identification*, 63 Stan. L. Rev.
    751 (2011)

Randerson, James, *Bite-Mark Evidence Can Leave a False Impression*, New
    Scientist, Mar. 13, 2004, at 6, available at
    http://www.newscientist.com/article/dn4758-bitemark-evidence-can-
    leave-false-impression.html (last visited December 14, 2011)

Rawson, R. D., R. K. Ommen, and G. J. Kinard, *Statistical Evidence for the
    Individuality of the Human Dentition*, 29 J. Forensic Sci. 245 (1984)

Renaker, Teresa, *Evidentiary Legerdemain: Deciding When Daubert Should
    Apply to Social Science Evidence*, 84 Cal. L. Rev. 1657 (1996)

Reese, Helen, *Law and Science: Current Legal Issues,* Oxford Univ. Press:
    London, England (1998)

Reno, Janet, *Introduction* to National Institute of Justice, U.S. Department of
    Justice, *Eyewitness Evidence: A Guide for Law Enforcement*, at iii-iv
    (1999), available online at http://www.ncjrs.gov/pdffiles1/nij/178240.pdf
    (site last visited December 14, 2011)

Richardson, James, and Gerald Ginsberg, *"Brainwashing" Evidence in Light of
    Daubert*, in *Law and Science: Current Legal Issues* (Helen Reece ed.,)
    Oxford Univ. Press: Oxford, U.K. (1998)

Richardson, James T. , Gerald P. Ginsburg; Sophia Gatowski, and Shirley Dobbin, *The Problems of Applying Daubert to Psychological Syndrome Evidence*, 79 Judicature 1 (1995)

Risinger, D. Michael, *Handwriting Identification*, in *Modern Scientific Evidence: The Law and Science of Expert Testimony*, David L. Faigman, Edward K. Cheng, , Michael J. Saks, and Joseph Sanders, eds., Thomson/West Pub.: Eagan, Minnesota (2009-2010 edition)

Risinger, D. Michael, Mark P. Denbeaux and Michael J. Saks, *Exorcism of Ignorance as a Proxy for Rational Knowledge: The Lessons of Handwriting Identification "Expertise"*, 137 U. Pa. L. Rev. 731 (1989)

Risinger, D. Michael, Michael J. Saks, William C. Thompson and Robert Rosenthal, *The* Daubert/Kumho *Implications of Observer Effects in Forensic Science: Hidden Problems of Expectation and Suggestion*, 90 Cal. L. Rev. 1 (2002)

Risinger, D. Michael, *Navigating Expert Reliability: Are Criminal Standards of Certainty Being Left on the Dock?*, 64 Albany L. Rev. 99 (2000.

Rothwell, Bruce M. *Bitemarks in Forensic Dentistry: A Review of Legal, Scientific Issues*, 126 J Am. Dent. Assoc. 223 (1995)

Rothwell, Bruce R. and A. V. Thien, *Analysis of Distortion in Preserved Bite Mark Skin*, 46 J. Forensic Sci. 573 (2001)

Saferstein, Richard *Criminalistics: An Introduction To Forensic Science*, Prentice Hal: Upper Saddle River, NJ (2006)

Saks, Michael J., *The Past and Future of Forensic Science and the Courts*, 93 Judicature 94 (2009)

Saks, Michael J. and Holly VanderHaar, *On the "General Acceptance" of Handwriting Identification Principles*, 50 J. Forensic. Sci. 119 (2005)

Saks Michael J., and Jonathan J. Koehler, *The Coming Paradigm Shift in Forensic Identification Science*, 309 Science 892 (2005)

Saks, Michael J. *Banishing Ipse Dixit: The Impact of Kumho Tire on Forensic Identification Science*, 57 Wash. & Lee L. Rev. 879 (2000)

Saltzman, Jonathan, *State Hits Crime Lab on DNA Cache: Some Files Improperly Kept, IG Says*, Boston Globe, Feb. 4, 2009, at B1

Santos, Fernanda, *Evidence from Bite Marks, It Turns out, Is Not So Elementary*, N.Y. Times, Jan. 28, 2007, at WK 4

Schiff, Adam, *Schiff's Familial DNA Language Passes as Part of Conference Report*, Press Release (Nov. 21, 2011) available online at http://schiff.house.gov/Index.cfm?sectionid=49&parentid=6&sectiontree= 6,49&itemid=869 (last visited November 26, 2011)

Schwartz, Adina, *A Systemic Challenge to the Reliability and Admissibility of Firearms and Toolmark Identification*, 6 Colum. Sci. & Tech. L. Rev. 2 (2005)

Scientific Working Group on Bloodstain Pattern Analysis, *Guidelines for the Minimum Educational and Training Requirements for Bloodstain Pattern Analysts*, available online athttp://www.fbi.gov/about-us/lab/forensic-science-communications/fsc/jan2008/standards/2008_01_standards01.htm/ (last visited December 14, 2011)

Scientific Working Group on Materials Analysis (SWGMAT), *Forensic Human Hair Examination Guidelines*, 7(2) Forensic. Sci. Comm. (April 2005), available online at www.fbi.gov/hq/lab/fsc/backissu/april2005/standards/2005_04_standards02.htm (last visited December 14, 2011)

Scientific Working Group on Friction Ridge Analysis, Study and Technology, *Friction Ridge Examination Methodology for Latent Print Examiners*. (2002), available online at http://www.swgfast.org/Friction_Ridge_Examination_Methodology_for_Latent_Print_Examiners_1.01.pdf (last visited December 14, 2011)

Scientific Working Group on Friction Ridge Analysis, *Training to Competency for Latent Print Examiner* (2002), available online at www.SWGFAST.org

Senate Report No. 109-88, *Science, State, Justice, Commerce, and Related Agencies Appropriations Act of 2006* (2005)

Serrato, Veronica, Note, *Expert Testimony in Child Sexual Abuse Prosecutions: A Spectrum of Uses,* 68 Boston U. L. Rev. 155 (1988)

Shapiro, Ari, *Foolproof Forensics? The Jury Is Still Out,* National Public Radio, August 24, 2009, available online at http://www.npr.org/templates/story/story.php?storyId=112111657 (last visited December 14, 2011)

Shelton, Donald E., *Juror Expectations for Scientific Evidence in Criminal Cases: Perceptions and Reality About the "CSI Effect" Myth* , 27 T. M. Cooley L. Rev. 1 (2010)

Shelton, Donald E., *Twenty-First Century Forensic Science Challenges for Trial Judges in Criminal Cases: Where the "Polybutadiene" Meets the "Bitumen",* 18 Widener L. J. 309 (2009)

Shelton, Donald E., *"CSI Effect"* in *Battleground: Criminal Justice,* Gregg Barak ed., Greenwood Press: Westport, Connecticut (2007)

Shelton, Donald E., *Forensic Science Evidence and Judicial Bias in Criminal Cases*, 49 Judges' J. 18 (2010)

Shelton, Donald E., *Technology, Popular Culture and the Court System - Strange Bedfellows?*, National Center for State Courts, 2006 Future Trends in State Courts (August, 2006)

Shelton, Donald E., Young S. Kim and Gregg Barak, *A Study of Juror Expectations and Demands for Scientific Evidence: Does the "CSI Effect" Exist?*, 9 Vanderbilt J. Ent. & Tech. L. 334 (2006)

Shelton, Donald E., Young S. Kim & Gregg Barak, *An Indirect-Effects Model of Mediated Adjudication: The CSI Myth, the Tech Effect, and Metropolitan Jurors' Expectations for Scientific Evidence*, 12 Vand. J. Ent. & Tech. L. 1 (2009), available online http://law.vanderbilt.edu/publications/journal-entertainment-technology-law/archive/index.aspx (last visited December 14, 2011).

Shelton, Donald E., *The CSI Effect: Does It Exist?*, National Institute of Justice Journal, Mar. 2008, at 1, (2008), available at http://www.ojp.usdoj.gov/nij/journals/259/csi-effect.htm (last visited December 14, 2011)

Silberglitt, Richard, Philip S. Antón, David R. Howell, and Anny Wong, *The Global Technology Revolution 2020: In-Depth Analyses: Bio/Nano/Materials/Information Trends, Drivers, Barriers, and Social Implications*, (2006), available online at http://www.rand.org/pubs/technical_reports/2006/RAND_TR303.sum.pdf (last visited December 14, 2011)

Simoncelli, Tania, *Dangerous Excursions: The Case Against Expanding Forensic DNA Databases to Innocent Persons*, 34 J. L. Medicine & Ethics 390 (2006)

Sita, J., B. Found and D. Rogers, *Forensic Handwriting Examiners' Expertise for Signature Comparison*, 47 J. Forensic Sci. 1117 (2002)

Slack, Jennifer, and J. Macgregor, *Culture + Technology*, Lang Pub.: New York, NY (2005)

Sognnaes, Reider F., R. D. Rawson, B. M. Gratt, and N. B. Nguyen, *Computer Comparison of Bitemark Patterns in Identical Twins*, 105 J. Am. Dent. Assoc. 449 (1982)

Solomon, John, *FBI's Crime Lab Rocked by New DNA Allegations: Integrity of Science Testing and Bullet Analysis Questioned*, Oakland Tribune, Apr. 16, 2003, at 6

Srihari, Sargur N., Sung-Hyuk Cha, Hina Arora, Sangjik Lee, *Individuality of Handwriting: A Validation Study*, Sixth International Conference on

Document Analysis and Recognition, ICDAR'01, (2001), available online at
http://www.cedar.buffalo.edu/papers/articles/Individuality_Handwriting_2
001.pdf (last visited December 14, 2011)

Srihari, Sargur N., Sung-Hyuk Cha, Hina Arora & Sangjik Lee, *Individuality of Handwriting*, 47 J. Forensic Sci. 856 (2002)

Stafford Smith, Clive A. & Patrick D. Goodman, *Forensic Hair Comparison Analysis: Nineteenth Century Science or Twentieth Century Snake Oil?*, 27 Colum. Hum. Rts. L. Rev. 227 (1996)

Stark, Steven D., *Perry Mason Meets Sonny Crockett: The History of Lawyers and the Police as Television Heroes*, 42 U. Miami L. Rev. 229 (1988)

Statheropoulos, Miltiades, C. Spiliopoulou, A. Agapiou, *A Study of Volatile Organic Compounds Evolved from the Decaying Human Body*, 153 Forensic Sci. Int'l 147 (2005)

Steele, Dara Loren, Note, *Expert Testimony: Seeking an Appropriate Admissibility Standard for Behavioral Science in Child Sexual Abuse Prosecutions*, 48 Duke L. J. 933 (1998)

Steinhardt, Barry, *Privacy and Forensic DNA Data Banks*, in *DNA And The Criminal Justice System* (David Lazer ed.) , MIT Press, Cambridge, Massachusetts (2004)

Steinhauer, Jennifer, *'Grim Sleeper' Arrest Fans Debate on DNA Use*, N.Y. Times, July 2, 2010, available online at
http://www.nytimes.com/2010/07/09/us/09sleeper.html (last visited November 19, 2011

Stevens, Dennis J., *CSI Effect, Prosecutors, and Wrongful Convictions*, 45 No. 4 Crim. Law Bulletin ART 2 (2009)

Stone, JH Dingfelder, *Facing the Uncomfortable Truth: The Illogic of Post-Conviction Testing for Individuals Who Pleaded Guilty*, 45 U.S.F. L. Rev. 47 (2010)

Stoney, David A., *The Scientific Basis of Expert Testimony on Fingerprint Identification* in *Modern Scientific Evidence: The Law and Science of Expert Testimony*, 2009-2010 Ed., David L. Faigman, Michael J. Saks, Joseph Sanders, and Edward K. Cheng, eds., Thomson/West Pub.: Eagan, Minnesota (2010)

Strom, Kevin J. and Matthew J. Hickman, *Unanalyzed Evidence in Law-Enforcement Agencies: A National Examination of Forensic Processing in Police Departments*, 9 Crim. & Pub. Pol'y 381 (May 2010)

Strong, John W., Kenneth S. Broun, George E. Dix, Edward M. Imwinkelried, D. H. Kaye, Robert P. Mosteller, and E. F. Roberts, eds., *McCormick on Evidence*, 5th Ed., West Pub.: Eagan, Minn. (1999)

Sucherman, Micah, *People v. Robinson: Developments and Problems in the Use of "John Doe" DNA Arrest Warrants*, 99 Cal. L. Rev. 885 (2011)

Summit, Roland C., *The Child Sexual Abuse Accommodation Syndrome,*7 Child Abuse & Neglect 177 (1983).

Sun, Y., J. Paik, A. Koschan, D.L. Page, and M.A. Abidi, *Point Fingerprint: A New 3-D Object Representation Scheme*, IEEE Trans. on Systems, Man, and Cybernetics-Part B: Cybernetics, Vol. 33, No. 4, pp. 712-717, (August 2003).

Sutton, T. Paulette, *Presumptive Testing for Blood*, in *Scientific and Legal Applications of Bloodstain Pattern Analysis* (ed. Stuart H. James, CRC Press (1991).

Sweet, David J., *Human Bitemarks: Examination, Recovery, and Analysis*, in *Manual of Forensic Odontology*, C. Michael Bowers and Gary L. Bell eds., 3d rev. ed., American Society of Forensic Odontology: Lubbock, Texas (1997)

Taslitz, Andrew E., *Does the Cold Nose Know? The Unscientific Myth of the Dog Scent Lineup*, 42 Hastings L.J. 17 (1990)

Teichroeb, Ruth, *Rare Look Inside State Crime Labs Reveals Recurring Problems*, Seattle Post-Intelligencer, July 22, 2004, at A1

Texas Attorney General Opinion No. GA-0866, *Investigative Authority of the Texas Forensic Science Commission* (July 29, 2011) available online at www.fsc.state.**tx**.us/documents/11.pdf (last visited November 26, 2011)

Texas Forensic Science Commission, *Addendum to the April 15, 2011 Report of the Texas forensic Science Commission: Willingham/Willis Investigation* (Oct. 28, 2011), available online at http://www.fsc.state.tx.us/reporting.html (last visited November 26, 2011)

Texas Forensic Science Commission, *Final Report of the Texas Forensic Science Commission: Willingham/Willis Investigation* (Apr. 15, 2011), available online at http://www.fsc.state.tx.us/reporting.html (last visited November 26, 2011)

Thomas, Gordon, Honeywell Gov't Affairs, *2008 Statute of Limitations DNA Legislation* (2008), available online at http://www.dnaresource.com/documents/2008StatuteofLimitationsLegislat ion.pdf (last visited December 23, 2011)

Thompson, William C., Franco Taroni & Colin G.G. Aitken, *How the Probability of a False Positive Affects the Value of DNA Evidence*, 48 J. Forensic Science 47 (2003)

Thompson, William C., *Guide to Forensic DNA Evidence*, in *Expert Evidence: A Practitioner's Guide to Law, Science, and the FJC Manual*, (Bert Black and Patrick W. Lee., eds.) West Pub. (1997)

Thompson, William C., *Tarnish on the "Gold Standard:" Understanding Recent Problems in Forensic DNA Testing*, Champion, Jan.-Feb. 2006, at 10

Thompson, William C., *The Potential for Error in Forensic DNA Testing (and How That Complicates the Use of DNA Databases for Criminal Identification)*, Council for Responsible Genetics National Conference, *Forensic DNA Databases and Race: Issues, Abuses and Actions,* June 19-20, 2008, New York University, available online at www.gene- watch.org (last visited November 21, 2011)

Tilstone, William, *Forensic Science: An Encyclopedia of History, Methods, and Techniques*, ABC-Clio Pub.: Santa Barbara, Cal. (2006)

Triplett, Michele, and Lauren Cooney, *Etiology of ACE-V and Its Proper Use: An Exploration of the Relationship Between ACE-V and the Scientific Method of Hypothesis Testing*, 56 Journal of Forensic Identification 345 (2006)

Tulsky, Fredric N., *How Judges Favor the Prosecution*, Mercury News.com (February 12, 2007), available online at http://www.mercurynews.com/search/ci_5128172?IADID=Search-www.mercurynews.com-www.mercurynews.com (last visited December 14, 2011)

Turner, Allen, *Panel Cites 'Flawed Science' in Arson Case*, Houston Chronicle (July 24, 2010), available online at http://www.chron.com/news/houston-texas/article/Flawed-science-cited-in-arson-case-leading-to-1718240.php?plckFindCommentKey=CommentKey:9694e74b-0c4f-49d4-b368-22e307f00188 (last visited November 26, 2011)

Turvey, Brent E. and Wayne Petherick, eds., *Forensic Victimology: Examining Violent Crime Victims In Investigative And Legal Contexts*, Academic Press: Maryland Hts., Mo. (2008)

Tyler, Tom R., *Viewing CSI and the Threshold of Guilt: Managing Truth and Justice in Reality and Fiction*, 115 Yale L.J. 1050 (2006)

Ulmer, Frank B., Note, *Using DNA Profiles to Obtain "John Doe" Arrest Warrants and Indictments*, 58 Wash. & Lee L. Rev. 1585 (2001)

Uphoff, Rodney J., *On Misjudging and its Implications for Criminal Defendants, Their Lawyers and the Criminal Justice System*, 7 Nev. L. J. 521 (2007)

Van Derbeken, Jaxon, *DNA Lab Chief Quits as SFPD Considers Outsourcing*, San Francisco Chronicle (June 23, 2010), available online at http://www.sfgate.com/cgi-bin/article/article?f=/c/a/2010/06/22/BALL1E32QP.DTL (last visited November 20, 2011)

Vanderkolk, J., *ACE-V: A Model*, 54 Journal of Forensic Identification 45 (2002)

Vass, Arpad A., Rob R. Smith, Cyril V. Thompson, Michael N. Burnett, Dennis A. Wolf, Jennifer A. Synstelien, Nishan Dulgerian, and Brian A. Eckenrode, *Decompositional Odor Analysis Database*, 49 J. Forensic Sci. 1 (2004)

Vass, Arpad A., Rob R. Smith, Cyril V. Thompson, Michael N. Burnett, Nishan Dulgerian, and Brian A. Eckenrode, *Odor Analysis of Decomposing Buried Human Remains*, 52 J. Forensic Sci. 384 (2008)

Wade H. Leonard, *Brewer Seeks $18M in Damages for Wrongful 1995 Conviction*, Com. Dispatch (Columbus, Miss.), Oct. 12, 2008, at 1A, available at http://www.cdispatch.com/articles/2008/10/12/local_news/local01.txt

Walker, Lenore E. *The Battered Woman*, Harper & Rowe: New York, NY (1979)

Walker, Lenore E., *Terrifying Love: Why Battered Women Kill and How Society Responds*, Harper & Rowe: New York, New York (1989)

Walker, Lenore E., *The Battered Woman Syndrome,* Harper & Rowe: New York, NY (1984)

Walker, Lenore E., Roberta K. Thyfault & Angela Browne, *Beyond the Juror's Ken: Battered Women,* 7 Vermont L. Rev. 1 (1982)

Walker, Marlan D., Note, *Mitochondrial DNA Evidence in State v. Pappas,* 43 Jurimetrics J. 427 (2003)

Warlow, Tom A., *Firearms, the Law and Forensic Ballistics,* 2nd Ed., CRC Press: Boca Raton, Fla. (2004)

Wilkinson, Allen P. and Ronald M. Gerughty, *Bite Mark Evidence: Its Admissibility Is Hard to Swallow,* 12 W. St. U. L. Rev. 519 (1985)

Williams, G., H. McMurray, and D. Worsley, *Latent Fingerprint Detection Using a Scanning Kelvin Microprobe,* 46 Journal of Forensic Science 1005 (2001)

Willing, Richard, *Errors Prompt States to Watch over Crime Labs*, USA
     Today, Mar. 31, 2006, at 3A
Wonder, Anita, *Blood Dynamics*, Academic Press: Maryland Hts., Mo. (2001)
Worley, Christopher G., Sara S. Wiltshire, Thomasin C. Miller, George J.
     Havrilla and Vahid Majidi, *Detection of Visible and Latent Fingerprints
     Using Micro-X-ray Fluorescence Elemental Imaging*, 51 Journal of
     Forensic Sciences 57 (2005)

Index

Abuse Syndromes, *32–36*
    Battered Woman Syndrome, *33*
    Child Sexual Abuse Syndrome,
      35
    Rape Trauma Syndrome, *34*
Arson. *See* Fire, Explosion and
      Arson Evidence
Battered Woman Syndrome. *See*
      Abuse Syndromes
Bitemarks
    Admissibility, *130–33*
    Generally, *129–30*
    National Academy of Sciences
      Report, 131
Bloodstain Pattern Evidence
    Admissibility, *174*
    Collection, *169*
    Generally, 169
    National Academy of Sciences
      Report, 174
    Spattering Patterns, *171*
Bullet Lead Comparison. *See*
      Toolmarks and Firearms
Casey Anthony Case. *See* Human
      Scent Evidence
Child Sexual Abuse Syndrome.
      See Abuse Syndromes

CSI Effect. *See* Juror Expectations
      about Scientific
      Evidence
Daubert v. Merrell-Dow
    Application to Criminal Cases
      Generally, *16*
    Generally, *11–17*
    Impact, *213*
    National Academy of Sciences
      Report, 17
    Social Sciences, *25–28*
Defense Discovery and
      Assistance, *53–56*
DNA
    Admissibility, *66–71*
    As New "Gold Standard", *214*
    Databases, *49–51*
    Exonerations, *216*
    Genrally, *65–66*
    National Academy of Sciences
      Report, 66
    Postconviction testing, *71–74*
Dog Tracking. *See* Human Scent
      Evidence
Explosions. *See* Fire, Explosion
      and Arson Evidence
False Confessions, *36*
Fingerprint Evidence

Admissibility, *92–99*
Analysis, *90–92*
Generally, *83–90*
National Academy of Sciences
    Report, 91, 93, 96
Fire, Explosion and Arson
    Evidence
    Admissibility in Criminal
        Cases, *159*
    Cause and Origin Investigation,
        156
    Daubert Analysis, *156*
    Generally, *155*
    National Academy of Sciences
        Report, 158, 159
    Willingham Case, *161*
Fires. *See* Fire, Explosion and
    Arson Evidence
Hair Analysis
    DNA, *123*
    Microscopic, *121–23*
    National Academy of Sciences
        Report, 123
Handwriting Comparison
    Daubert analysis, 112–14
    Genrally, *107–10*
    National Academy of Sciences
        Report, 112
    Scientific concerns, *110–12*
History, *5–8*
Human Scent Evidence, *179–84*
    Dog Tracking, *179*
    Human Decomposition Odors,
        181
John Doe warrants, 53
Joiner, General Electric v., 15
Judicial Bias, *227*
Juror Expectations about
        Scientific Evidence, *187*

"Tech" Effect, *188*
CSI Myth, *187*
Impact, *223*
Jury Instructions, *198*
Negative Evidence, *191*
Opening Statement and Closing
    Arguments, *196*
Voir Dire, *193*
Kumho Tire v. Carmichael, 15
Kumho Tire v.Carmichael
    Social Sciences, *25*
National Academy of Sciences
    Report
    AAFS Position, 220
    Ballistics, 143, 144
    Bitemarks, 131
    Blood Pattern Analysis, 173,
        174
    Bullet Lead Analysis, 147
    Congressional Action, 236
    Daubert standard, 16
    DNA, 66
    Fingerprints, 91, 93, 96, 97
    Fire Cause and Origin, 158,
        159
    Generally, 3, 218
    Hair, 123
    Handwriting, 112
    Impact, 218–23, 236
    Pretrial Order, 224
    Recommendations, 219, 243
Profiling. *See* Social Sciences
    Evidence
Rape Trauma Syndrome. *See*
        Abuse Syndromes
Social Sciences Evidence
    Confessions. *See* False
        Confessions
    Generally, *25–38*

Profiling, 37
Syndrome Testimony. *See*
    Abuse Syndromes
State Rules of Evidence, *11*
Statutes of Limitations, *52*
Toolmarks and Firearms
    Admissibility, *143–46*

Bullet Lead Comparison, *146*
Generally, *139–43*
National Academy of Sciences
    Report, 144
Willingham Case. *See* Fire,
    Explosion and Arson
    Evidence

Milton Keynes UK
Ingram Content Group UK Ltd.
UKHW011327250823
427492UK00005B/12